Positive Behaviours, Relationships and Emotions

The Heart of Leadership in a School

Jacinta Kitt

Published by NAPD,
The National Association of Principals and Deputy Principals

11 Wentworth, Eblana Villas, Grand Canal Street Lower, Dublin 2.
T: (+353) 1 662 7025
F: (+353) 1 662 7058
E: info@napd.ie

© Jacinta Kitt 2017

ISBN 978-1-5262-0660-2

Disclaimer
The content of this book is based on professional development material used by the author over many years, copious notes made in preparation for presentations given by the author and the personal and professional experience of the author as a teacher, lecturer and organisational advisor. Every effort has been made to accurately reference, where appropriate, the sources of the material. If errors or ommissions have occurred, they are inadvertent. Any errors identified will be rectified in all further editions of the book. They will also be highlighted by the publisher, in a subsequent publication, to NAPD members. The author and publisher however, do not assume any further responsibility and hereby disclaim any liability to any party for inaccuracies or omissions.

Edited by
Derek West, NAPD

Printed by:
CRM Design and Print, Unit 6 Bridgecourt Office Park, Dublin 12.

Cover design by
Ruan van Vliet

Lay-out and typographical design by
Mark Daniel, CRM

Back cover photo by
Cáit Fahey

Dedication

This book is dedicated to my two wonderful, kind, and funny granddaughters, Elsie and Julia, and to my husband, Tom, who consistently upholds the values of caring, empathy, generosity and fairness.

About the Author

Jacinta Kitt is a passionate and inspirational speaker on *Creating and Maintaining a Positive Workplace Environment* She knows her subject intimately and presents her ideas with conviction, irreverence and boundless humour.

She teaches in Trinity College on the M.Ed. programme and in Marino Institute of Education on the B.Sc. and B.Ed. programmes. She has also worked extensively with the Irish Prison Service on *Dignity at Work* issues and recently with those who have been appointed to leadership roles in An Garda Siochána.

Jacinta is an acknowledged expert on the subject of workplace bullying. She facilitates professional development training in schools and other organisations on preventing and dealing with workplace bullying. She prepares expert witness reports in workplace bullying cases. She works with parent groups on building positive relationships in the home. Providing strategies for improving how we communicate and interact with each other in the home, school and workplace has been the focus of much of her work over the past twenty years.

She is a former primary school teacher and this is her first book.

Acknowledgements

This book would never have been completed if it were not for the help, support, and inspiration of so many people. I am especially grateful to my publisher, NAPD, and particularly to Director, Clive Byrne, for believing in me, for giving me the confidence to undertake the task, for facilitating the project in so many ways and for being unwavering in his encouragement and support; to Assistant Director, Tim Geraghty, for the warmth and generosity of his comments and company; to Michelle O'Hanlon, NAPD Administrator, for her graciousness and good humour; and, especially, to Derek West, my constant advisor through the past two years. He has been my mentor, tormentor, editor, critic and great friend. Derek has helped me to reflect on and evaluate my work in ways that only someone who understands, appreciates and loves the English language could do. Despite his reservations in relation to my irreverence and my propensity to overdo the alliterations, he has persevered and guided me through every step of the process.

I am particularly grateful to my hawk-eyed, critical friend, Dr. Bernie Collins, who is also my dear friend. She provided me with an insightful critique of the entire book and her detailed evaluation and suggestions have added greatly to the finished work.

I would like to acknowledge the numerous positive and progressive principals, deputy principals, teachers and other staff members who have influenced the contents of this book. Sincere thanks to Mary Lee, Dr. Rebecca Purcell, Dr. Mary Roche, Mary Mitchell, Ruth Kitt McAllister, Timmy Walsh, Damien Kennedy, Emer Cloak, Mary Nihill, Maria Garvey, Pat Burke-Walsh, Leonard Conaty, and Áine O'Sullivan for their kind comments and reassurance, to Sue Corbett for everything she has taught me and for her contribution to the Workplace Bullying section, to Maeve O'Callaghan for keeping me going with her herbal pills and potions, and to Donncha Ó Treasaigh for first suggesting that I undertake the task of writing the book.

Thank you to Karen Johnson for her skilful organisation of the referencing and bibliography; also to Sarah Griffin and Aileen Lee for their careful and competent proofing.

I am very grateful also to Ruan van Vliet for the cover design, which I love; to Mark Daniel of CRM, for the internal design and the printing, and for his patience, efficiency and professionalism; and to Cáit Fahey for the back-cover photo.

A very big thank you goes to my four cool, creative, compassionate and open-minded children, David, Ruth, Thomas and Robbie who are a constant source of inspiration for me. Margie, Charlie, Karen and Eibhlín add valued and diverse dimensions to the family dynamic. My husband Tom has read and re-read every word of the book and has been an amazing help in so many respects. For his constant advice, calmness, sense of humour and for his love, I am deeply grateful.

Jacinta Kitt
January 2017

Introduction

If you have been fortunate enough to catch one of Jacinta Kitt's exuberant presentations at a national conference or a school staff day, or at one of the hundreds of organisations she has addressed over a long and distinguished career [not just teachers: others who work in schools, ETBs , Universities and colleges, Gardaí, prison staff, those in the health sector, and other public and private sectors], you will have been energised by a high-voltage, non-stop onslaught of lively language and gripping ideas about how to create and maintain a positive work environment and bring emotional intelligence to bear on the work-place.

Jacinta is vernacularly adept – her language is contemporary, cheeky, informal, irreverent, peppered with references to Scud Missiles, shiny buttons, white knuckles, tight ships. She talks about cogs in wheels, elephants in the room, eggshells [walking on], fingers [in pies], sledgehammers [for cracking nuts], boats [that get rocked], knuckles [that get white], and cats [like a bag of]..

She is an anecdotalist, with a seemingly-bottomless repertoire of witty stories about bad behaviour in the work-place. She has a Stanley-knife insight into the absurdly childish behaviour of the adults you sometimes find in a school staff-room. She knows all about taking yourself too seriously, giving out, falling out, huffing and puffing and sulking.

Jacinta is an entertainer, with a gravelly, insistent voice of the *bon-viveur* that surges not only with energy and humour, but with profound insight into the follies of human nature and its capacity for amendment and improvement.

Above all, Jacinta is a great communicator, with a capacity to deliver astute perceptions through plain speaking. At the core of her work is an acknowledgement of the vital importance of Emotional and Social Intelligence, as key elements in school leadership and fundamental to the effective running of a school. Her mission is to promote positive human interaction as a means to making schools – and other organisations – work.

This book is about capturing Jacinta's vitality and wisdom in print. It has been my privilege, as Publishing Editor with NAPD, to collaborate with her over the past two years in the preparation of *Positive Behaviours, Relationships and Emotions – The Heart of Leadership in a School.*

This is not a book about 'touchy-feely stuff'; it is a distillation of Jacinta's extensive work over the years, as a teacher and facilitator, in schools and third-level colleges, with teachers and leaders (both current and potential) – the key personnel in the education system.

Each school has a particular and unique atmosphere, either positive or negative, that can be sensed as soon as one walks in. It is invariably linked to those who work in the school, how they treat each other and how well they work together.

It is impossible for a school to be effective and productive without the prevalence of appropriate interpersonal behaviours and high-quality relationships. School leaders set an example through their own positive behaviours and relationships.

The five sections in this book cover the following themes:

● **Creating and maintaining a positive/effective work environment in schools**

This section focuses on the power of positivity in a school and the value of having people on the staff who are positive in their attitudes and approaches. The quality of the relationships is the biggest determinant of the levels of positivity in a school. The essentials of trusting relationships between school leaders and their staff, collegial relationships between members of staff and democratic relationships between staff and students are outlined. The Collaborative leadership style is considered the most effective for achieving the optimal balance between the task and people elements of the role of school leaders.

● **Emotional Intelligence: a requirement for leadership**

Those skilful in dealing with emotions in themselves and others are considered as having high Emotional Intelligence. The four components of EI are self-awareness, self-management, social-awareness and relationship management. This section outlines and explores the skills and competencies associated with each of those components. It also examines the role of school leaders in managing negative emotions and maximising positive emotions in themselves and others. Emotional Intelligence in leaders is pivotal to the quality of a school's environment, the relationships in the school and the well- being of all who work and study there.

● **Managing Conflict in Schools**

This section focuses on facilitating an understanding of the various dimensions and effects of conflict in schools. Inter-personal conflicts cause the worst problems and can be prolonged and divisive. Jacinta discusses how individuals typically behave, communicate and feel when they are in conflict. She looks at the role of school leaders in managing conflict, the attitudes and skills they require to become conflict-competent. The dynamics of conflict between teachers and students, and teachers and parents are explored, with a particular focus of finding a win-win solution, the only effective means of resolving conflicts.

● **Workplace Bullying in Schools**

Workplace bullying is consistently evident in the teaching profession. Jacinta provides an overview of the main dimensions of workplace bullying, and outlines how best to deal with it. Isolation and unwarranted criticism are the two main tactics used, the nuances of which are outlined. Whereas there is no standard profile of those who are bullied, the characteristics and behaviours of those who bully show remarkable similarities: they are relentless in their attempts to make life miserable for others and they show no empathy or remorse to those they target. The experience of being bullied is captured in this section, as well as the organisational responses and the coping strategies that can help those who are bullied.

● **Effective Leadership... Getting it Right**

This section focuses on the attributes and attitudes that constitute the best opportunities for school leaders to be consistently effective and successful. Jacinta stresses the importance of establishing a shared vision and purpose among the staff members. Communication behaviours that are assertive are considered to have the best chance of getting a message across. Reciprocity is at the heart of communication and the psychological contract between school leaders and staff is the unwritten understanding of what is contributed and what is expected by both. Reflection by school leaders on how they are doing is another essential element of 'getting it right' as is having a modicum of humility.

It has been my pleasure to assist with the editing process for this book, 'sprinkling the commas and hyphens around like pepper,' as Jacinta puts it, but the chief delight has been enjoying the company of a warm-hearted, witty sage, with a barrel-load of common sense that she is dying to share with you, the reader. Jacinta is sunny and funny, but her bottom-line is earnest and serious – this is about social- and self-awareness, interpersonal skills and Emotional Intelligence as vital elements in the successful school.

Derek West
January 2017

Section A

Creating and Maintaining a Positive/Effective Work Environment in Schools

Section B

Emotional Intelligence: A Requirement for Leadership

Section C

Conflict in Schools

Section D

Workplace Bullying in Schools

Section E

School Leadership... Getting it Right

Section A

Creating and Maintaining a Positive/Effective Work Environment in Schools

A. 1. Introduction

An awareness of the environment in schools first struck me when I was working for one of the teacher training colleges, and was supervising student teachers engaged in teaching practice in various schools. Through visiting a large number of schools over a short period of time, I became aware that each and every school – irrespective of location, student numbers, socio-economic background of the students, or physical condition of the building – had a particular and unique atmosphere, something that I sensed or felt as soon as I entered the school. Although there were, of course, nuances of similarities and differences between the quality of the atmosphere in the various schools, the general sense was that a visit to a particular school proved to be either a positive experience, or a negative one.

> **A warm and welcoming principal helped to reinforce the positive impression, which could not be cemented until a visit to the staffroom was undertaken.**

The positive experience was associated with a feeling, on entering, of the school being inviting and welcoming, and a further sense of being at ease there. The negative experience, on the contrary, was associated with a slightly uneasy, anxious feeling, and a sense of the school being an unfriendly place where people should get their work done and get out as quickly as possible. Even after a short visit to a school with a negative atmosphere I would be quite stressed and I invariably had the feeling that I would not like to work there on a daily basis.

Getting a sense of a school's atmosphere is one thing, but determining what accounts for that sense is another. Unconsciously at first, and subsequently more consciously, I began to reflect on the various seemingly mundane encounters which I had had in schools, that influenced my initial feelings. Very subtle nuances in the attitudes and behaviours of those I met gave an impression of what the school's atmosphere was like. A smile on the part of the person in the reception area, who, when busy, acknowledged your presence with a brief eye contact and nonverbal indicator that he/she would be with you soon, was enough to create a feeling of being at ease.

A friendly encounter with a student on the corridor, who appeared confident and willingly escorted you to the principal's office, was also an indicator of a positive atmosphere. A tap on the principal's door by the student, and a brief, friendly interaction between student and principal to indicate the presence of a visitor, was a further positive sign. A warm and welcoming principal helped to reinforce the positive impression, which could not be cemented until a visit to the staffroom was undertaken. A buzz of banter in the staffroom was always a good sign; an informal greeting and an offer of a cup of tea were equally so.

If these examples convey an impression of a positive atmosphere, then the following convey the exact opposite: A large bolded sign at the entrance, without the inclusion of a please or thank you, insisting that all visitors must report to the office before entering the school; the lack of even a nod from the person at reception as he/she continues to conduct a long telephone conversation, while you wait to be assisted or directed; a response from a student to a request or question that indicates a disinterest in engaging, and a lack of courtesy in replying; a traffic light system outside the principal's office with a green light for 'you may enter', and a red for 'don't even think about it'; a staffroom with a hierarchy of mugs and chairs where you daren't take the wrong mug, or sit in the wrong chair, are all examples that leave a negative impression. A negative atmosphere is like a bad smell – if you do not search for and eliminate the cause of it, it lingers until you get used to it, and become inured to it. Many people live for years in homes with a negative atmosphere, and get so used to it that they no longer notice it. They can be very surprised and defensive when somene comments on it. Those who work for years in schools with a negative atmosphere often take on a 'Stepford Wives' type of demeanour, and a facade of friendliness and camaraderie that becomes the norm. This facade belies the underlying stress and tension, which can only be discerned from a glimpse of the white knuckles of the staff. Whether living or working in a negative atmosphere, it always takes its toll on people in one form or another.

A. 2. The Importance of a Positive Environment in Schools

While initial impressions of a school can be very powerful indicators of the positivity or negativity of the school environment, they are but the tip of the iceberg in terms of understanding the many elements and dimensions of school life that contribute to what constitutes an overall positive school environment. However, the sense that one initially gets is invariably to do with the people in the school and how they treat each other, get on with each other, and how well they work with each other. The quality of the behaviours and the relationships impacts not merely on the atmosphere, but also on the quality of the teaching and learning in the school. In other words, it is impossible for a school to be effective and productive without the prevalence of appropriate interpersonal behaviours and high-quality interpersonal relationships. School leaders set an example through how they behave and relate to others. They also set the tone of the behaviours and relationships which, whether positive or negative, others will emulate.

I gave a presentation about twenty years ago, around the time that I was becoming increasingly fascinated with the notion of a quality workplace environment and its potential impact on organisational effectiveness. I was in full flight, extolling the merits of creating and maintaining a positive work environment in schools, when I was interrupted by someone at the back of the lecture hall, who shouted out for all to hear, (and I quote), "You know that stuff you're talking about there?" I immediately realised that while calling the content of my presentation 'stuff', the subsequent comments were unlikely to be complimentary. He continued, "If you ask me, that's the peripheral stuff – the 'touchy feely' stuff that only a woman would be talking about." I became somewhat flummoxed in the context of the put-down and, as is often the case with put-downs, was not quick enough to provide an adequate response. However, on reflection, I knew that I should have said what I

> **"**
> Those adopting scepticism and cynicism in relation to a positive environment perhaps fail to realise the power of positivity in the workplace, and the value of having people on the staff who are positive in their attitudes and approaches.
> **"**

firmly believe – that the quality of the work environment, far from being peripheral, is absolutely central to every aspect of school life. I should have said that the work environment provides the most immediate, tangible, and relevant context for everything that is said and done in the school.

The negative comments made then would probably be considered more inappropriate now, twenty years later, particularly in terms of their sexist dimension. However, back then, the sentiments expressed in relation to the work environment were a fairly accurate reflection of a general lack of understanding of what the work environment entailed, or indeed of its significance to the work in schools. Notwithstanding the increased awareness of the work environment in schools, there remains a considerable dismissal of its relevance or importance. There is also a commensurate lack of focus by school management and school leaders on prioritising the quality of the school environment as a prerequisite for school effectiveness.

Like the detractor who, twenty years ago, made his feelings about the relevance of a positive work environment known, there are many who remain sceptical about its importance, one of whom recently suggested that, "All this talk of positive behaviours and relationships will mean a totally politically correct environment, where you will constantly have to watch your 'Ps and Qs'." Another, who interpreted the positive school environment cynically, suggested that, "The principal will be expected to stand at the door every morning welcoming each member of staff, with a hug thrown in, and a suggestion that they take it nice and easy and not be killing themselves". Those adopting scepticism and cynicism in relation to a positive environment perhaps fail to realise the power of positivity in the workplace, and the value of having people on the staff who are positive in their attitudes and approaches.

A. 2.1 The Positive Disposition of Staff in Schools

A huge body of research has been conducted on positivity in the workplace, both in the positive psychology, and positive organisational behaviour fields of study. The objective of the pioneering work undertaken by both Seligman and Csíkszentmihályi on positive psychology was to change the focus of psychology from one of healing and repairing people, to one of building and reinforcing positive qualities, and helping people to flourish in all areas of their lives including their work.

With particular reference to the value of staff who are positive in their attitudes and behaviours, Luthans et al., (2004) built on the ideas of positive psychology and organisational behaviour, to develop the concept of positive Psychological Capital (PsyCap) as a resource for workplaces. Capital refers to the resources that an individual has, and can draw from as required in the workplace. There are a number of different forms of capital, which include the more familiar Human Capital and Social Capital. Human Capital is made up of an individual's knowledge, skills, and qualifications. A person's CV would usually provide an indication of his/her level of Human Capital. A person high in Social Capital would have the ability to work co-operatively with others and contribute to collective effectiveness. Successful school leaders, in particular, are aware of the benefits of Human and Social Capital, and look to the components of both as criteria to guide their decisions in the appointment or promotion of staff.

> **"**
> **When they do get it right, and appoint someone who is a positive influence, they have a responsibility to ensure that he/she is facilitated and empowered to stay positive.**
> **"**

Psychological Capital, or PsyCap, is less well understood, and refers to an individual's positive state of mind (Luthans et al., 2007). Someone high in PsyCap has a predominantly positive disposition. Some leaders have concentrated merely on the qualifications/experience of candidates and on their accounts of how well they work with others, when making their decisions at interviews. They have often been subsequently disappointed to discover that the person they have appointed has turned out to be a negative force on the staff. When they do get it right, and appoint someone who is a positive influence, they have a responsibility to ensure that he/she is facilitated and empowered to stay positive. Pryce-Jones (2010) stated that PsyCap really matters in a job that requires motivation, creative thinking, and perseverance. These are surely among the essential hallmarks of good teaching. PsyCap becomes even more relevant to schools and teaching when we consider it in terms of its components, which are:

- Hope;
- Optimism;
- Resilience;
- Self-efficacy/confidence.

These four components are not firmly-fixed personality traits, but are relatively stable states of mind, that benefit from being appreciated and managed. All three forms of Capital – Human, Social and Psychological – are important, and contribute positively to the effectiveness of the workplace. The latter, PsyCap, as the positive state of mind of individuals, is perhaps the most important resource in itself, and in its ability to complement and make the most of the other two. All three, however, make up the human resources in an organisation.

The well worn mantra of 'our people are our best assets' is still trotted out, and included in most human resource policies and procedures. The talk is repeatedly talked but, unfortunately, not as frequently walked. Managing human resources is officially assigned to specific personnel in many large organisations. On examination of what constitutes this task, one sees that it is often technical, administrative and procedural, and less often involves the more personalised management that is required, especially in the context of maximising the positivity, (PsyCap), of staff.

In schools, the task of managing human resources is almost exclusively the responsibility of the school leader. Fortunately, in terms of positivity, the benefits of recognising and building the PsyCap of the staff more than justify the efforts that leaders have to put in. High levels of PsyCap are positively linked to work engagement, performance, and job satisfaction. The positive disposition of staff also contributes to their commitment and well-being through reduced anxiety and stress (Newman et al., 2014).

Key Points

- Each school has a unique atmosphere that can be quickly sensed to give a positive or negative impression.

- The quality of the environment in a school is determined by interpersonal behaviours and relationships.

- The positive disposition of staff, referred to as psychological capital, (PsyCap), has a significant influence of the quality of the work environment in schools.

- The components of PsyCap are: hope; optimism; resilience; and self-efficacy/confidence.

A. 2.2 Hope as a Positive Mind-set

In order to appreciate the importance and positive impact of PsyCap in schools, each of its components will be examined to ascertain how it relates to and manifests in everyday school life. Hope, as one of the constituent elements of PsyCap, is probably the most easily identified as absolutely essential in the teaching profession. Teaching has been variously described as the discipline of hope, (Kohl, 1998); the profession of hope (Perrone, 1991); and as a vocation of hopefulness (Shade, 2011). Some tired, cynical, or generally disillusioned teachers may have abandoned hope. As a result, they may have succumbed to fatalism in their attitude, and passivity in their practice. Fatalism is expressed in an unwillingness to change or improve practice, and an adherence to and contentment with the *status quo*. 'I have been doing it this way for the past thirty years, and it has served me very well, thank you very much', or, 'Leave well enough alone', are examples of the fatalism heard not too infrequently in staff rooms or at staff meetings.

Fatalism can stifle the hopes of others as they make suggestions for change and improvements. It is important not to allow the fatalism and negativity of others to silence the more positive members of staff, when they present suggestions for consideration. An assertive response to those who dismiss or denigrate a new idea can, at the very least, keep the conversation open. For example, saying something like, 'notwithstanding your reservations, I believe that my proposal is worthy of consideration and discussion', lets the detractor know that you will not be easily dissuaded from expressing your opinion. Also, asking the detractor what their reservations are in relation to a suggestion can encourage them to offer specific reasons for their rejection of the idea, rather than a general dismissal.

● Hope in Schools

Notwithstanding the damage that the fatalistic and dismissive attitude of teachers can cause in schools, in terms of the demoralisation of both staff and students, it has to be said that the vast majority of teachers and school leaders retain high levels of hope.

A school principal – a friend of mine – has been working in a school in a disadvantaged area for the past twenty years. He is adamant that unless teachers and other professionals have high hopes for the students, and can instil hope in them, there is no place for them in his school. Appointment interview questions always focus on what hopes the candidates have for students, and how they are going to realise them.

In his view, their responses should not comprise the hands-off attitude reflected in clichéd statements, such as, 'I hope that each and every one of them will reach their potential', or, 'I hope that they will be successful and happy in school'. This form of hope is commonly used in everyday interactions with phrases such as, 'I hope you have a great time', or, 'I hope you get well soon'. Whereas these are kind, empathic statements, they contain the strong inference that the messenger is not going to do anything to contribute to fulfilling the hopes. On the contrary, the answers the school principal is looking for from a prospective staff member must reflect a realistic set of aspirations and targets; an acknowledgement of potential challenges and obstacles, and an effective methodology for achieving goals. Those with high levels of hope are usually able to articulate a variety of means for achieving their goals.

> **"**
>
> **The practice of selecting student of the week, month, or year often assumes that all students are operating from a similar set of abilities and motivational circumstances. Even when they are doing so, the practice creates winners (temporarily) and losers, and has far more disadvantages than advantages.**
>
> **"**

Hope constitutes not merely the ability to identify and pursue goals but also the willpower to persevere in realising them. The type of hope that is required in teaching does not provide instant gratification. Shade (2001, p.11), put it well when he suggested that, "hope functions to energise and sustain the self as it reconstructs itself in the teeth of trying circumstances".

The principal mentioned above, also wants to know, in clear terms, how the aspiring candidate for a job in his school proposes to instil hope in the students, especially those who are coming from dysfunctional families. He certainly does not want them to treat all students as if they were on a level playing field, through pitching them against each other for praise and recognition. The practice of selecting student of the week, month, or year often assumes that all students are operating from a similar set of abilities and motivational circumstances. Even when they are doing so, the practice creates winners (temporarily) and losers, and has far more disadvantages than advantages. However, when some students are at a distinct disadvantage to begin with, this competitive practice is rendered even more damaging to student motivation and hope.

Celebrating the individual achievements of students as they occur is much more conducive to building hope. Placing the reality of their achievements in the context of future possibilities will help the latter to sustain and increase the former (Shade, 2011). Building trust and connection with students is the essence of inspiring hope in them. When a teacher facilitates and encourages students to talk about the challenges they face, rather than regarding these types of conversations as being outside their remit, it helps to put problems into a more manageable context. Alluding to challenges and adversity as something that everyone faces, irrespective of individual or family circumstances, can facilitate students in having a more hopeful approach to their problems. If teachers use examples from their own lives and experiences, or from the lives of well known people, to provide evidence of overcoming obstacles, it can resonate with students and be very empowering (Shade, 2011).

● Being Hopeful

The major advantage that the principal in the above situation had, in relation to hope, was that he practiced what he preached. He had what Shade (2001) described as practical and pragmatic hope, and had, over the years, built up a reservoir of hope. Hope had become a habit of his. From two particular perspectives, the levels of hope of the school leader are pivotal to creating a community of hope in the school. The hope that the leader articulates and demonstrates sets a tone and expectation that is contagious, and reinforced in both staff and students. School leaders who are high in hope are in a more credible position to clearly communicate the performance and relationship standards that they expect from their staff. They are also much more likely to provide the encouragement and empowerment that enhances hope in others. Without this context, neither staff nor students will sustain the levels of courage and commitment required to remain hopeful for the long haul.

> **If hope is a sense that an outcome is possible, optimism is a sense that it is probable.**

A. 2.3 Optimism as a Positive Mind-set

Hope and optimism, despite their difference in meaning, are inextricably linked, and both contribute to the levels of positivity in a school. If hope is a sense that an outcome is possible, optimism is a sense that it is probable. Those with an optimistic attitude have a positive outlook, and positive expectations. While retaining a realistic and flexible level of optimism, they generally expect good things to happen to them, and generally make the most of what does happen to them. They are also good at overcoming problems and obstacles that arise, by regarding them as manageable and/or transient. Although the aforementioned principal did not allude to optimism as a criterion in the appointment of a teacher to his school, I have no doubt that he and every other positive school leader would be delighted to be surrounded by staff with high levels of optimism.

The wonderful state of optimism, which will be further discussed in the section on conflict, manifests in school staff through, for example:

- seeing the best in their colleagues and students;
- giving decisions and ideas the benefit of the doubt;
- facing change with energy and enthusiasm.

The mind-set of optimism is a relatively stable one as, unfortunately, is the mind-set of pessimism. Whereas optimists need fellow optimists to sustain them, pessimists need to be dissuaded from their pessimism. It is important to make pessimists aware that, when they evaluate events in a positive rather than a negative light, the outcomes are more likely to be positive rather than negative. Encouraging them to shift towards a more optimistic mind-set can help them to reflect and change.

An optimistic state of mind as an element of PsyCap is a resource that needs to be valued and supported by school leaders. It is also worth their while to work on their own levels of optimism, both in terms of the impact on others, and how, more generally, they are perceived by others. One of the simplest and most effective methods for leaders to increase their optimism is to surround themselves, in as far as it is possible, with those who look on the bright side of life. Those who see the best in others can also influence, for the better, how leaders judge those around them.

Bernadette Steinmeyer posted a short piece on the internet in 2012, which I recently read. She alluded to an intervention that her son made, when he and a friend were arguing on opposing sides in a political debate. He was finding it difficult to get his point of view across, as his friend

> " ...asking the question, 'what's good about it?' in relation to a whole range of things is a sure way of getting ourselves and others to focus on the positive, and to build optimism. "

constantly alluded to what was wrong with it. He asked the friend to focus instead on 'what's good about it?' when considering his side of the argument. Steinmayer (2012) suggested that asking the question, 'what's good about it?' in relation to a whole range of things is a sure way of getting ourselves and others to focus on the positive, and to build optimism.

For example, a principal is disappointed when the majority of the staff vote to have the school social evening in an Italian restaurant, as he is, by his own admission, a 'steak and chips' man. Instead of seeing the down-side and making decisions accordingly, he asks the staff to tell him about the restaurant in terms of 'what's good about it?' Something different, a good atmosphere, low prices, good wine, not just pasta and pizza, are some of the things they might say to provide positive food for thought to the principal.

Learning to ask 'what's good about it?' in relation to numerous things, including, for example:

- a new idea;
- the cancellation of something that you were looking forward to;
- a relationship in difficulty;
- a significant birthday,

is an excellent practice for those in pursuit of a more positive and optimistic attitude.

Key Points

- Hope is essential in schools, and needs to be appreciated and facilitated by leaders.

- High levels of hope among staff members help to motivate both staff and students, and to counteract fatalism.

- Optimistic school staff contribute to positivity in a school.

- Optimism needs to be valued and supported by school leaders, in order to maximise the benefits for everyone.

- Optimists need fellow optimists in order to thrive.

A. 2.4 Resilience as a Positive Mind-set

Resilience, the ability to sustain yourself through the ups and downs of life, is a key attribute of positive psychological capital. It is essential for those who work in schools in order for them to make a positive contribution to the school environment, especially in tough times. It is generally associated with bouncing back from adversity. Resilience is also necessary for maintaining good physical and mental health and well-being.

> **" Over the past number of years, there appears to be an ongoing attrition of teachers' autonomy, through increased levels of administration; a prevalence of a competitive focus, (e.g. league tabling); decreasing support and resources. In this context, resilience is called for in spades. "**

While no-one sails through life without experiencing hard knocks, and associated consequences, those who have a mindset of resilience do not get completely bogged down in, or totally overwhelmed by them. Rather, they recover more quickly and have the ability to move on and let go. Resilience is further associated with being able to cope well, and thrive in the context of everyday and unavoidable pressures. It is absolutely necessary for building and sustaining a high-quality workplace in testing and challenging times (Gu & Day, 2007).

Over the past number of years, there appears to be an ongoing attrition of teachers' autonomy, through increased levels of administration; a prevalence of a competitive focus, (e.g. league tabling); decreasing support and resources. In this context, resilience is called for in spades. It is "a quality that enables teachers to maintain their commitment to teaching and teaching practices despite challenging conditions and recurring setbacks" (Brunetti, 2006, p. 193).

● Ego-Resilience

Block & Block (1980) alluded specifically to those with ego-resilience as having high levels of adaptability in the context of stress and change, and as being resourceful, flexible, and having a range of problem-solving strategies to draw on. Those who have such positive attributes make good colleagues, and good leaders. Whereas they acknowledge the clouds, they generally manage to see a silver lining. They are more positive than negative in their attitude and behaviour, and are not prone to taking things personally. They do not create an atmosphere where one has to tip-toe around them for fear of being misinterpreted or reacted to negatively.

On the contrary, those with what Block & Block (1980), labelled as "ego brittleness" lack flexibility, and have a difficulty recovering after a challenging experience. It is very frustrating working with a leader or a colleague who determinedly holds on to the residue of a difficult or disappointing issue, allowing it to adversely affect their behaviours, and their relationships with others. Ego-resilience and ego-brittleness are considered to be personality characteristics, and therefore less likely to alter or change significantly. However, the manifestations of ego-resilience, as outlined above, can be developed, particularly in those actively seeking to become more resilient.

● Becoming more Resilient

Arguably, the most important step in building resilience is a realisation that it involves a set of skills that can be acquired and developed. Individuals also need to have a strong belief in their ability to influence the effects of challenging situations. Dr. Martin Seligman, a social psychologist, has carried out extensive research, and has written widely on the development of resilience. He has focused particularly on the explanatory style, which refers to the learned and habitual way that people interpret the difficult and challenging things that happen to them. Resilience is helped or hindered depending on whether interpretations are positive or negative. Lifelong habits of negatively interpreting events and situations render it difficult, but not impossible, to alter and change our automatic convictions and conclusions.

Stressful situations are usually interpreted from the perspectives of personalisation, permanence and pervasiveness (Seligman, 2004). When we personalise or internalise a challenge or a problem we see ourselves as being the cause of it, and we apportion blame to ourselves.

For example, a warm and cheerful greeting by a principal to a colleague is not responded to. The principal immediately concludes that the apparent snub is related to her, and that she has done something to upset her colleague. An alternative, more positive, and frequently more accurate interpretation would involve depersonalising the issue and considering that external factors, such as the colleague's mood or preoccupation, may be the cause of the snub – or, indeed, that someone else may have caused her to be upset. Considering a range of options other than the one that names, blames, and shames ourselves lessens the potential for rumination and obsession.

When we attach permanence to our interpretation of a problem, we see it, or its effects, as lasting indefinitely.

For example, a school principal is aggressively challenged by a member of staff, in front of other colleagues. The incident is interpreted by the principal as something that neither he, nor the others, will ever forget. The principal also concludes, with conviction, that the damage to his authority and reputation will not be easily overcome. When a principal reacts to an incident on this basis the problem will escalate, the relationship will suffer, and the resilience of the principal will be eroded. If, on the other hand, the principal interprets the confrontation and its effects as being resolvable, then the response is more likely to include an appropriate challenging of the staff member's behaviour, and a proactive attempt to find and resolve any underlying and contributing issues or problems.

When we interpret a problem in terms of its pervasiveness, we see the worse possible consequences of it, and of its effects.

For example, the deputy principal in a school has applied for the position of principal. In her interview she was asked a question on a legal dimension of the role. She had no idea of the answer, and could not even hazard a guess. She was stressed and devastated after the interview and agonised in her conviction that everyone on the interview board, including her present manager, would think her stupid, ill-prepared, and totally unfit for the position. Those with a more positive explanatory style would be in a better mind-set to counteract their failure to answer the question, with an assessment that few applicants would be familiar with such intricate legal details. They might also be able to focus positively on the many questions that they had proficiently and competently answered. Bonanno (2004) proposed that we make ourselves more or less vulnerable or susceptible to stress, depending on how we think about the things that happen to us.

That is not to suggest that we can always prevent ourselves from being negatively affected by upsetting or challenging encounters. What it does suggest is that those with resilience have the ability to regain their equilibrium, and return to healthy functioning after such encounters (Bonanno, 2004). Examining our own explanatory style is an important first step in maximising positive interpretations and minimising negative ones, and, in the process, increasing personal resilience.

● Learned Helplessness

Unfortunately, there are those who perpetually interpret events negatively. They develop what Seligman calls 'learned helplessness'. Consequently, they feel that they have no control over what happens to them, have no confidence in their ability to undertake certain tasks, and are very intimidated and powerless in terms of undertaking new challenges. Learned helplessness is self-perpetuating, and seriously impacts on a person's resilience in overcoming obstacles. The 'I could never do it' attitude prevents people, generally, from doing things like speaking in public, standing up for themselves, learning to swim, overcoming their fear of flying, and a range of other challenges that they avoid like the plague.

> **The 'I could never do it' attitude prevents people, generally, from doing things like speaking in public, standing up for themselves, learning to swim, overcoming their fear of flying, and a range of other challenges that they avoid like the plague.**

In school terms, the imposition of challenging changes can lead to learned helplessness, where staff feel overwhelmed and disempowered in terms of complying with the expected changes. The effective management of change by school leaders, which includes adequate and open communication, meaningful consultation, and ongoing support, can empower and facilitate the change process and prevent staff members from developing a sense of helplessness and powerlessness.

School leaders can also develop a degree of learned helplessness when the demands on them, from both internal and external sources, exceed their perceived ability to comply and cope. Many school principals and deputy principals accept as inevitable the levels of isolation and aloofness that are attached to their role. In that context, they may be denied the support that they need to withstand problems and challenges. The importance of having a support network inside and outside the school cannot be overstated, particularly when school leaders feel stressed and overstretched. Their resilience in the face of adversity, however, is contingent on support, which, when school-based, is facilitated by leaders building positive relationships with their staff.

Relationships are alluded to not merely as being an important and necessary prerequisite for resilience, but as being at the very core of it. Jordan (2006) alluded to the engagement in mutually empathic and responsive relationships as a source of resilience. Despite some opinions to the contrary, teaching is widely considered to be one of the most challenging and stressful jobs. Resilience, in that context, is essential for staff, to enable them to maintain high standards of commitment and enthusiasm. The consistency of the support provided to them, and the quality of their relationships with others help them to keep going – especially when the going gets tough. When school leaders understand the importance of a high-quality school environment, and do everything possible to create and maintain such an environment, they provide the context that is most conducive to building and sustaining the resilience of the entire staff.

A. 2.5 Self Efficacy (Confidence) as a Positive Mind-set

Self-efficacy and confidence are strong indicators of the positive disposition of school staff, and are particularly relevant to educational workplaces. Much is written about the self-efficacy of teachers and its impact on student achievement, classroom management, and relationships in the school. The concept of self-efficacy was developed by Albert Bandura, and it refers to the self-belief and self-confidence that a person possesses in relation to their ability and capacity to perform effectively, and achieve desired and expected goals. Teacher self-efficacy is the belief and confidence that teachers have in relation to their effectiveness as educators. They are confident that they can influence the achievements of all students, even those who are considered difficult and unmotivated (Tschannen-Moran & Woolfolk Hoy, 2001).

> **"**
>
> **Despite the high volume of educational research that extols the merits and necessity of teachers employing a number of teaching methods, there are some who remain wedded to the didactic 'talk and chalk' method.**
>
> **"**

Self-efficacy is important because, as Bandura (1986, p. 129) stated, "people regulate their level and distribution of effort in accordance with the effects they expect their actions to have." In teaching terms, when teachers feel that students will engage in class and be motivated to persevere with difficult tasks as a result of their efforts, then their commitment will be consistent and high.

Confident and efficacious teachers are known to positively impact on the learning experiences of students. They are innovative, and use a variety of methods and approaches in order to cater for the various learning styles of their students. Despite the high volume of educational research that extols the merits and necessity of teachers employing a number of teaching methods, there are some who remain wedded to the didactic 'talk and chalk' method. This traditional method, which is formal and teacher-centred, involves students sitting quietly, paying attention, and listening. Minimal opportunities are afforded to students to interact with the teacher. This teaching style suits only a small number of learners and the remainder, to varying degrees, are disengaged, bored and frustrated. The attitude that the 'talk and chalk' approach reflects is one of 'take it or leave it'.

The introduction of new pedagogies has contributed to making teaching and learning experiences more interesting and fulfilling. For example, Ross (1994) made the link between increased teacher efficacy and the introduction of co-operative learning.

Some teachers need persuading to change their teaching methods. However, since the introduction of appropriate professional development opportunities, most of them have come around. Using innovative teaching methods and observing the benefits of them result in a rise in teachers' confidence and self-belief, and a significant increase in student participation and learning.

Efficacious teachers persist with students who are struggling, and criticise them less when they provide incorrect answers (Gibson & Dembo, 1984). They set attainable goals, and willingly provide special assistance to students who require it. In general they feel confident not only about their instruction, but also about their relationships with the students. Consequently, their students have higher levels of achievement and teachers have fewer behavioural problems with them. Tschannen-Moran and Woolfolk Hoy (2001) alluded to the enthusiasm and commitment of teachers with high self-efficacy, and also suggested that they are more likely to remain in the teaching profession.

● Sources of Self-efficacy

Self-efficacy presumes a certain level of self-belief that comes from childhood. It also presumes a certain level of knowledge and skills which, when built on, impacts positively on a person's confidence at work. Bandura (1997) cited four sources of self-efficacy as:

- mastery experience;
- vicarious experience;
- verbal persuasion;
- physiological cues.

> **"**
> **The more successes a person has, the more confident they become.**
> **"**

Mastery experience is gained through a person's accomplishments and successes, which in the aggregate boost self-belief and confidence. The more successes a person has, the more confident they become. Bandura (1997, p.80) suggested that "success builds a robust belief in one's personal efficacy."

Vicarious experience is gained through watching others perform well and achieve goals. Observing the effectiveness and success of others can increase a person's belief that she/he can be successful also.

Verbal persuasion is the encouragement and support that is needed to affirm a person's confidence and belief in their ability.

Physiological cues are the physical signals that one experiences prior to undertaking a task. The physical signals can enhance or diminish self-belief. Feeling energetic, for example, can instil in a person a belief that success is likely, whereas, feelings of nervousness or anxiety can contribute to a belief that success is unlikely. Paying attention to the signs of anxiety can help to alleviate it, and improve self-belief.

In relation to the four stated sources of efficacy, school leaders can reinforce the self-efficacy and confidence of their staff by consistently:

- acknowledging their achievements;
- encouraging collegiality among staff, and providing mentoring to new staff members;
- providing constructive feedback to staff members;
- offering assistance and support to those who are stressed or anxious.

Leaders will be unlikely to consistently engage in these types of behaviours unless they have a high degree of self-efficacy and self-confidence themselves. The four sources of self-efficacy, as outlined above, are equally applicable to enhancing the self-belief of school leaders. Particularly in relation to vicarious experience and verbal persuasion, leaders need to avail of professional development opportunities in order to share and learn, and to give and receive encouragement and support. Tschannen-Moran and Gareis (2007) found that the quality and relevance of the training available to leaders, to prepare them for their role, and the support that they received from others, contributed to developing their self-efficacy. In terms of the former, many school leaders openly admit that, when appointed, they were thrown in at the deep end, without adequate preparation or guidance.

The self-efficacy in school leaders manifests itself in their belief that they have the capacity and competence necessary to manage their team successfully and achieve the agreed goals of the school (McCormick, 2001). Bandura, 2000 alluded to the importance of self-efficacy for leaders particularly when they are faced with problems and challenges. It enables them not to be dissuaded from their course of action, and to redouble their efforts when the going gets tough (Bandura, 2000). Self-confidence is also an essential element of leader effectiveness. Confident leaders generally encourage their staff to take initiatives by facilitating their autonomy. If, as Bennis et al., (1997, p. 214) stated, "autonomy is the 'sine qua non' of creativity", then micromanagement is the antithesis of it. According to Bennis et al.,

(1997) great leaders trade the illusion of control that micromanagement provides, for the higher satisfaction of facilitating extraordinary achievements. A lofty aspiration, one might think, but possible to realise, under the stewardship of leaders who are confident enough to surround themselves with excellent people, and facilitate them in reaching their potential. McGregor's famous 'Theory Y' is one on which many other theories and philosophies of successful and effective leadership are based. It has, as its central plank, the necessity for leaders to:

● outline expectations for those who work with them;

● provide clarity and support in relation to what needs to be done;

● have the self-restraint and confidence to let people get on with it.

Genuine confidence helps the leader to understand that the effectiveness of his/her leadership is only realised when those around them are free to do exceptional work (Bennis et al., 1997).

● Confidence

Confidence is a realistic view of one's abilities that is backed up by skills and competence. Those who have genuine confidence are secure in their self-belief, and are not threatened by the confidence or competence of others. They are not afraid to admit to not understanding something.

A friend of mine related an incident, where she and a colleague had applied to provide training to a very large and well known organisation. The interview was going very well until a question was asked, the subject of which my friend had no knowledge of. She got somewhat tongue-tied as she tried to answer the question with vague generalities, in a bid to conceal her lack of knowledge. Her colleague, when asked the same question, simply said that she was sorry, but was unfamiliar with the concept alluded to in the question. My friend felt embarrassed by her own inability to be honest and upfront, and was really impressed by the honesty of her colleague. She realised afterwards that it took confidence to provide such an honest answer and that, compared to the stress that she experienced while trying to cover her lack of knowledge, her colleague's response caused much less stress and was much more liberating. Of course, my friend's ability to relate that story against herself, and her ability to learn from it, is evidence of her own confidence, which, by her own admission, she needs to work on and improve.

> **In positive schools with positive leadership, confidence grows and staff members are eager to learn new and innovative ways of doing things. They are rooting in the bags of newly qualified teachers for novel and creative ideas and methodologies. Unfortunately, this attitude does not prevail in all schools.**

In general, self-efficacy and confidence at work are positively related to engagement and persistence with the task, and to high levels of energy and enthusiasm. According to Watson (1991, p.203), there is a popular misconception that equates enthusiasm with, "peppy exuberance". He suggested that there is more to it than "superficial effusiveness" (1991, p. 203), which might appear glib and shallow, and that enthusiasm comes with sustained actions and hard work. Teachers with self-confidence are enthusiastic and persistent because they know that they are competent, and can do the job well. They are also generous, and more than willing to share their knowledge and experience with others. Supporting and helping others can be a great source of pleasure, and is also a natural motivator (Deal & Key, 1998).

● Building and Sustaining Confidence among Staff

In positive schools with positive leadership, confidence grows and staff members are eager to learn new and innovative ways of doing things. They are rooting in the bags of newly-qualified teachers for novel and creative ideas and methodologies. Unfortunately, this attitude does not prevail in all schools. The confidence and enthusiasm that new teachers demonstrate when they recount, in the staff room, a positive encounter with a student, or provide details of a lesson that went well, can be easily knocked out of them by the negative reactions of others. Verbal or non-verbal messages that effectively dismiss such enthusiasm as naivety, or something that will quickly evaporate once the harsh realities of teaching hit home, can result in the new teacher feeling deflated. At best, they will retain their confidence and enthusiasm solely for the classroom and, at worst, they will lose them altogether. A public endorsement, by a school leader, of the enthusiasm expressed by a new teacher will help to harness and sustain it. It can also minimise the adverse effects of negative comments, and hopefully help enthusiasm to become more widespread.

Teachers, who partake in postgraduate courses on which I teach, are often excited and enthused with the innovative ideas and approaches that they discover through the material being discussed, and through the focused group work that they engage in with fellow teachers. Many of them take copious notes on the outcomes of these discussions to relate to their colleagues. Others reluctantly admit that they could never presume to do such a thing. They suggest that it would be frowned upon and rejected and that they would be considered as showing off, or trying to indicate to colleagues that they were less competent. Self-efficacy and self-confidence are genuine reflections of abilities and competencies, which when appreciated and valued grow and improve. However, when they are disregarded and dismissed, they can be eroded and diminished.

The efficacy and confidence of a school's staff provide a positive psychological resource to a school. When combined with hope, optimism and resilience, the resource is multiplied. Leaders, who maximise this resource in their schools, unleash high levels of positivity. Their own role becomes more manageable and enjoyable as a result.

Key Points

- Those working in schools require resilience to withstand the pressures and challenges of the job, and to handle stress effectively.

- Resilience involves a set of skills that can be acquired and developed.

- Those who constantly interpret events negatively can develop 'learned helplessness', where they feel overwhelmed and unable to handle challenges.

- School leaders and staff with self-efficacy and confidence have high levels of self-belief in their ability to do the job well.

- Self-efficacious teachers support struggling students, and are generally enthusiastic and persistent.

- The self-efficacy of staff is enhanced by the supportive behaviour of school leaders who acknowledge their positivity, especially in the context of negativity expressed by others.

A. 3. Relationships that Contribute to Positivity in a School

The quality of the relationships is the biggest determinant of the levels of positivity in a school. Trust is a characteristic of all positive relationships. Trusting relationships between school leaders and their staff are essential to creating and maintaining a positive environment in a school.

A. 3.1 Trusting Relationships between School Leaders and Staff

Trust is contingent on one's belief in the other person, and a willingness to depend on him/her (Mayer et al., 1995). It is also defined in terms of the confidence that one has in the positive qualities of the other (Hoy & Tschannen-Moran, 1999).

Trust results from the interactions between a school leader and an individual staff member, and a willingness by both parties to engage in behaviours that are respectful, competent, supportive and honest. However, in the relationships between school leaders and their staff, the leaders have a responsibility to initiate these behaviours, in order for trust to be established.

● Respectful Behaviours of School Leaders

A school leader, who treats staff and students with respect, is held in very high esteem by both. Working with a respectful leader is one of the most important and motivating aspects of a person's job. Respectful behaviour by school leaders indicates a valuing of their staff, and is evident in the acknowledgement and appreciation of their contributions. People do not work for praise. However, they need to be appreciated. This is not a selfish, superficial craving for attention, but is reflective of "an authentic, deep seated desire to be deemed as worthy, when offering something of worth" (Deal & Key, 1998, pp. 47-48). Respectful school leaders seize every opportunity to give recognition for a job well done. They demonstrate their respect in many other ways including, for example, by:

● speaking to staff in a courteous manner;

● listening to what they have to say;

● trusting them to do their jobs;

● delegating responsibilities to them.

Leaders cannot lead those they do not respect and trust (O'Toole, 1995). When respectful behaviour is initiated by the school leader, it is generally reciprocated. Reciprocal respect builds and sustains trust.

● Competent Behaviours of School Leaders

A school leader demonstrates competent behaviour by using a wide variety of skills and competencies, and by participating in a range of relevant professional development initiatives. Leaders are trusted if the staff believe that they can do the job well. They trust someone who works hard, but is not a perfectionist or a workaholic. Workaholics often speak about their condition as if it were a virtue. They may even boast about it, for example, by letting

> **" Workaholics often speak about their condition as if it were a virtue "**

everyone know that they are always first to arrive in the morning, and last to leave in the evening. Workaholics are addicted to their work, and have no appreciation of the importance of a work-life balance. They expect everyone working with them to give the same level of commitment as they do. However, they get very stressed with overwork, which impacts negatively on those around them.

Perfectionists are never satisfied with what has been achieved by themselves or others. They run the risk of becoming obsessed with perfection, and are often critical of others to the point that their working relationships, and the good will of their staff, are seriously compromised. Although leaders who are workaholics or perfectionists often consider that they are highly competent, this view is rarely shared by their staff.

> **"**
> **Those who like to have a finger in every pie, and who are convinced that nothing will be done properly without their intervention, rarely delegate.**
> **"**

Appropriate delegation is an important leadership competency, and bears no relationship to the abdication of responsibilities. Delegation is a practice that some leaders find very difficult to engage in. Those who like to have a finger in every pie, and who are convinced that nothing will be done properly without their intervention, rarely delegate. They fail to have the trust in others that is required for delegation to take place. They miss the opportunity to utilise the skills and talents of their staff and as a result frustrate and disempower them. Many long term members of staff, in outlining their experiences of working with flapping and fussing leaders, suggest that when the leaders are absent, everything runs more smoothly and efficiently without them.

School leaders are considered competent if, for example, they manage people in a fair and just manner, and show no favouritism. They are also expected to have effective communication skills that will enable them to deal with difficult people, and difficult situations. Conducting what are euphemistically called 'the difficult conversations' about issues and problems takes courage and confidence, and gets the 'thumbs up' from those who do not like to work around the elephant in the staffroom. Having the ability to communicate in a way that does not escalate volatile or aggressive situations is one of the most valuable competencies of all. The competence of school leaders is also associated with initiating and facilitating innovative teaching and learning strategies. Motivating individual staff members by giving them regular constructive feedback is also a valued competence. Leaders who can manage change through communication and consultation are also considered to be competent.

> **"**
> **They keep staff fully informed of what is going on and resist the temptation to hoard information, and to drip feed it 'on a need-to-know basis'.**
> **"**

Leaders who are trusted are generally highly regarded for both their competence, and their credibility. Competence is easily identifiable, whereas credibility is built up slowly over time (Watson, 1991). Leaders' credibility is associated with their competence, and also with their integrity.

● Honest Behaviours of School Leaders

School leaders demonstrate that they have integrity by being open and honest in every aspect of their role, including their dealings with staff. Openness is a quality that is admired and respected. There is no difficulty spotting it in others, as it can be seen in everything they say and do (Watson, 1991). Leaders who are open and honest use straightforward communication that does not harbour hidden agendas. They are careful and considerate in what they say, and how they say it. They ensure that their message is clear and unambiguous. Their verbal, non-verbal and written communication is responsive and sensitive to the needs and feelings of others. They keep staff fully informed of what is going on and resist the temptation to hoard information, and to drip feed it 'on a need-to-know basis'. Information is power, however, leaders with integrity share power by sharing information. This sets an example that can enhance the general communication flow to:

- provide reasoning behind decisions and changes;

- encourage staff to seek help and support when they need it;

- keep leaders informed about issues and problems before they escalate into crises proportions.

If effective communication is to flow both ways, it starts with the leader. Information will not surge upwards if it barely trickles downwards (Bartolome, 1989). Honest and open leaders provide accurate and adequate information on all aspects of decisions, policies, proposed changes, and performance.

Above all else, staff members will not trust a leader unless they know where they stand with them. Leaders with integrity are fairly predictable, and place a huge emphasis on keeping their word and fulfilling their promises. They are known for saying what they mean and meaning what they say. They are not inclined to criticise colleagues behind their backs, betray a confidence, let colleagues down by withholding loyalty to them, or failing to support them. Staff members expect loyalty from the leader and also expect them to act in their best interest. However, a leader with integrity will not provide blind loyalty that includes ignoring, discounting, or rationalising the wrongdoing of a colleague.

Leaders also have high expectations that staff will be loyal to them, and to the school. There is a loyalty imperative in schools, with a commensurate expectation that leaders and staff will remain loyal to each other and to the school through good times and bad. When alluding to a requirement for loyalty, the leader must ensure that strict and unswerving allegiance is not demanded, as it can cause people to behave unethically for fear of been regarded as disloyal. However, if reasonable loyalty obligations are not fulfilled, feelings of betrayal can ensue. These often result in the disengagement of staff, the withholding of effort and commitment, and the destruction of trust (Grover et al., 2014).

When confidences are breeched, and people have their personal business divulged to others, it is extremely damaging to a relationship and to levels of trust. Those engaging in these behaviours may not realise what they are doing, or how much damage they are causing. However, their reputation for inappropriate disclosure and their loss of credibility is incrementally exposed, and becomes well known. Communication with them will generally be maintained, but it will be cautious and restrained, and involve very little self-disclosure. The offended person will be extremely reluctant to trust or confide in the offender.

If the perceived breeches of loyalty are not repetitious or intentional, trust is considered to be recoverable. A sincere apology and explanation can assuage the damage done (Grover et al., 2014), but it has a better chance of being further repaired if restorative actions follow, and are sustained.

● Supportive Behaviours of School Leaders

In a workplace characterised by supportive leadership, staff members feel cared-for and supported in everyday situations, and are confident of that support when

> **One can only imagine the isolation and exclusion that is felt by staff who work in schools where the voicing of an alternative point of view is regarded as a declaration of war.**

they encounter problems and when things go awry. The behaviour of supportive leaders incorporates compassion, kindness and consideration for others. Staff members feel supported when they get a sense that the leader is interested in them and what they have to say, and accepts them for who they are and what they think and feel. There is no better source of support than when you feel understood and accepted. Leaders who are gifted with being naturally supportive usually have high levels of social and situational awareness, which is an element of social intelligence. Albrecht (2006), describes this level of awareness as being able to read people and situations accurately. Those who have little or no social or situational awareness seem to always get the wrong end of the stick, and constantly put their foot in it. It creates a very stong feeling of not being supported when the other person does not get it, and does not get you.

Consistency is alluded to often as an essential leadership quality. It does not equate to rigidity or inflexibility. Being flexible and adaptable is not in any way incompatible with consistency. Flexible leaders are able to analyse the pros and cons of a situation, and make appropriate changes if necessary (Yukl & Mahsud, 2010). School leaders, who do not feel threatened by the expression of a view or opinion that is contrary to their own, facilitate and encourage staff members to speak their minds, and they feel supported when they know that what they have proposed will be given genuine consideration. One can only imagine the isolation and exclusion that is felt by staff who work in schools where the voicing of an alternative point of view is regarded as a declaration of war.

Leaders who are flexible and adaptable are able to match strategies and behaviours to the specific skills and needs of staff. Some staff members will need more assistance and reassurance from the leader, and when it is forthcoming they feel supported and motivated. School staff feel frustrated when the poor performance or lack of commitment of other staff members impacts negatively on them, or on their students. For example, when colleagues renege on their responsibilities and others have to pick up the pieces for them, they can feel used and abused, especially when the school leader ignores the behaviour. Leaders who have adaptive skills anticipate, are alert to, and deal with these and other problems.

Staff members feel supported when problems are tackled and resolved. When the resolution strategies are characterised by support, solutions are easier to find, and the relationship between the parties involved are less likely to deteriorate. Teachers expect to be supported by school leaders when they have an issue or a dispute with a parent. It is also necessary that the teacher has an understanding of the vulnerabilities of the parent, and has the skills required not to be defensive when challenged. Supportive leaders promote the acquisition of these essential skills, and encourage staff to diffuse rather than escalate confrontations. The leader could also adopt preventative strategies by engaging the support of parents in school activities (Bryk & Schneider, 2003). Supportive leaders get to the bottom of things by reaching out to others, and by talking things through. However, as Bryk & Schneider (2003) suggested, without trust, genuine conversations will not happen.

Trusting relationships between leaders and staff that are built on respect, competence, honesty and support, contribute significantly to the quality of the work environment in schools. However, the quality of the relationships between members of staff, and between staff and students, also contribute to creating and maintaining a positive environment in schools.

A. 3.2 Collegial Relationships between Members of Staff

Relationships between colleagues that are truly collegial have the best chance of impacting positively of the quality of the work environment in schools. The understanding and appreciation of collegial relationships have gradually improved, and consequently those relationships have become more interactive and supportive. Traditionally, the job of teaching was both physically and professionally isolating, and was characterised by teachers working in almost total seclusion in their classrooms. There were many disadvantages to this individualistic approach to teaching. Teachers were deprived of the support and encouragement needed to sustain their commitment and effectiveness. They were also curtailed in the opportunities available to them to share ideas, resources, and problems with others. Teachers were, to a large extent, left to their own devices, without intervention or question. Standards and methods of teaching and teacher behaviour varied greatly depending on the individual. Whereas innovative teachers found ways and means to interact informally with colleagues on professional matters, others had no interest in, or inclination to, engage in professional discourse. Some became increasingly entrenched, and deeply resented any intrusion into their domains.

Collegiality is now more widely recognised as having numerous benefits for school effectiveness and staff well-being. Collegiality is not merely a denotation of colleagues working together in the same school or teaching the same subject. It is a reflection of their working relationships, and the behaviours that constitute those relationships. Real collegiality is collaborative and participative, and presumes a valuing of diverse personalities, approaches, and beliefs. Positive consideration of the input of a diverse range of contributions ensures that a 'group think' mentality is avoided, as colleagues work well together in the common interest of providing a high-quality educational service. The hallmarks of collegial relationships are: mutuality of respect and support; and the prevalence of honest and open communication. Being encouraged and facilitated to share ideas, experiences and challenges, lessens feelings of isolation or inadequacy, and builds and sustains effectiveness.

● Competitiveness that Prevents Collegiality in Schools

Although many workplaces profess to value team work and collegiality, they continue to set the staff against each other in internally competitive environments. Ranking and rating of employees, and favouritism in the allocation of positions and resources, remain prevalent in a variety of organisations. Individualism, where it is every man for himself, results. Far from engaging in collegiality, ideas are guarded and sharing is limited. In these situations, secrecy is rife, and jealousy and sabotage often raise their ugly heads.

Thankfully these prohibitive and internally competitive conditions are not commonplace in schools. It is more likely that when collegiality between teachers is hampered, it is as a result of more parochial factors. Despite variations in competence and personality, teachers were traditionally viewed as being more knowledgeable than the average citizen. There was a respectability attached to being a teacher. The teaching profession had to guard and protect that image, and practitioners could not be seen to admit to not knowing something. The praising of another teacher's success or achievement was tantamount to admitting that they

> **"**
> **Democratic relationships are achieved when the rights of both the teacher and the students are mutually respected.**
> **"**

could not do it as well themselves. In this environment teachers were deprived of support, as they sought neither help nor advice.

Whereas those days are almost past, the residue lingers, and impacts negatively on collegial behaviours and relationships in schools. Proactivity on the part of the school leader is required to overcome residual resistance to building an interdependent community of sharers and learners among staff. The effectiveness of staff members is not simply an individual trait, but a capacity that arises through the interactions between people in the organisational context. It is enhanced by reciprocal support that improves motivation and performance.

A. 3.3 Democratic Relationships between Teachers and Students

The quality of the relationships between staff and students has a significant bearing on the quality of the environment in the school. When teachers build healthy relationships with students, the classroom environment improves. Student interest and engagement increase, and this impacts positively on the quality of teachers' working environment. Relationships that are democratic have the best chance of building mutual trust between teachers and students, and stand both in good stead when issues or problems arise. Democratic relationships are achieved when the rights of both the teacher and the students are mutually respected.

Whereas a teacher's role incorporates a degree of authority, it should not include authoritarianism, control, or disregard for the opinions and feelings of the students. There is no hierarchy of importance in a democratic relationship, and there should be no sense of superiority emanating from the teacher. The vast majority of teachers are aware that students are their partners, and not their subjects, but for those who do not realise this, reminders from school leaders are not only advisable, but are obligatory. How else, apart from the example of their own relationships with students, are school leaders to achieve consistency in the quality of relationships between teachers and students? In schools where expectations are not clearly outlined, it is the luck of the draw whether students are treated in a respectful and fair manner or not. In a democratic relationship both teacher and student become aware of the benefits accruing to them, and have a vested interest in sustaining the dynamics and quality of the relationship. The experience of the teacher and the student is more enjoyable, productive, and less stressful as a result.

Key Points

- The quality of the various relationships determines the levels of positivity in schools.
- Trusting relationships between school leaders and staff are reflective of respectful, competent, supportive, and honest behaviours, which are initiated by the leaders.
- Collegial relationships between staff involve colleagues working collaboratively, sharing ideas, and supporting and appreciating each other.
- Democratic relationships between teachers and students are built on equality and mutual respect.

A. 4. The Role of Leaders in Creating a Positive/Effective Work Environment in Schools

The importance of having a positive work environment in the school cannot be overstated. However, the creation of such an environment should never be at the expense of the overall effectiveness of the school. The school's primary function is the provision of a consistently high quality of educational service to all students, irrespective of their ability. Schools, like all organisations, have task and people dimensions, and it is widely acknowledged that the task dimension in schools, i.e. the teaching and learning, cannot be effectively fulfilled without the efforts of a motivated and committed staff.

> **Successful and effective school leaders are totally aware of the need to balance the task and people elements of their role. They are also acutely aware that it can be very challenging at times.**

Securing the sustained commitment and effort of staff members is contingent on the extent to which they are valued, respected and supported on a daily basis. How they are treated determines how well the job gets done. The general rule is that an equal emphasis should be placed on the task and people elements of the job. It goes without saying that at certain times the emphasis will shift and be more imbalanced. When a whole-school evaluation or important exams are imminent, the focus on the task will inevitably increase. And, when the school is celebrating success or dealing with a tragedy, the focus will be balanced in favour of the people.

The task element of the workplace, in other words getting the job done, was often referred to as the 'hard stuff', as opposed to the relationships in the workplace, which were referred to as the 'soft stuff'. Commensurately, there were the 'hard skills' and the 'soft skills'. I have always been deeply uncomfortable with those labels, as in some way they implied that the 'hard skills' were of superior importance to their poor relations, the 'soft skills'.

School leaders who are obsessed with having the best school with the best results, but who have little or no interest in looking after the needs and feelings of their staff, dismiss the 'soft stuff' as superfluous and optional. The negative consequences of this attitude, and approach to leadership, causes damage to both the reputation and the success of the school.

Successful and effective school leaders are totally aware of the need to balance the task and people elements of their role. They are also acutely aware that it can be very challenging at times.

A. 4.1 Task and People Leadership

As far back as the 1950s, research on leadership has focused on the task and people elements of the role. These elements were frequently referred to as the task-oriented and the relations-oriented leadership behaviours. Despite a wide array of leadership theories having emerged since, that have added significantly to the dimensions and interpretations of leadership, the task- and relations-oriented behaviours still constitute essential elements of leadership. In particular, Blake and Mouton (1982), through their managerial grid model, focused on leadership styles in terms of the leader's concern for people and concern for task. The Blake-Mouton grid has stood the test of time, and is still used to assess the task and people behaviours of leaders.

The grid is divided into five possible leadership styles, all of which focus on task and people elements. The five styles are:

- Country club
- Impoverished
- Middle of the road
- Authoritarian
- Team/Collaborative

The Country Club Style

James is a 'country club' school leader. Above all else, he likes to be liked and get on well with everyone. He uses clichés such as, 'I aim to please', and, 'It's nice to be nice'. He is always obliging and gives staff time off when they need it, but never considers the fallout or consequences of his generosity. Decisions on issues such as class allocation and timetabling are made through a lottery system, in order for him to appear fair, and to avoid being blamed for staff disappointment or annoyance. He regularly provides lunches and cakes for the staff, and takes them out to dinner for any occasion that he considers as warranting celebration. He continuously alludes to the fact that he allows staff to get on with their jobs, without interference from him. He also alludes to the importance of his staff being 'happy campers'.

James is really uncomfortable with any form of discontent or disagreement. He likes to keep staff meetings short and sweet, and discounts any issues or problems that are raised with comments such as, 'Don't worry about it', or, 'I'll get back to you on that'. However, he never does. The staff find it very difficult to get a discussion or debate going on any area in need of change and improvement. The feeling they get from him is that they are stirring things up, and upsetting the lovely cosy consensus.

The 'country club' or *laissez-faire* style of leadership, (high on people, low on task), is primarily concerned with creating a friendly, comfortable and easy-going work environment. Every effort is made to avoid any type of conflict or disagreement. The raising of problems or difficult issues is discouraged and disapproved of. Negative feelings and emotions are masked by bland and agreeable public faces (Jackall, 1983). Minimal attention is paid to the quality or effectiveness of the work being done. The 'country club' style suits some staff members, while most find it deeply frustrating.

The Authoritarian Style

Paul is an 'authoritarian' school principal. He runs a very tight ship. He stands at the door every morning with a stern face, berating any student who errs in relation to his/her uniform, general appearance, or behaviour. He addresses students in an aggressive manner, and always uses their surnames. He pointedly looks at his watch, and repeatedly pokes his finger at it, when staff members are even a minute late. He refuses to listen to an explanation or reason. He appears suddenly into classrooms without knocking or announcing his arrival, and instructs the teacher to continue. He comments negatively on details of the teaching content and delivery in front of the students. He is obsessed with the reputation of the school, but always relates his expectations in that regard to high grades in exams, and successes in sporting and other competitive activities. He works very hard, and is in the school from very early in the morning until late in the evening. He places a huge emphasis on the documentation surrounding policies and procedures. He demonstrates very little empathy to teachers who have problems or issues, and rarely provides praise or encouragement to staff or students. To varying degrees, both are afraid of him.

The 'authoritarian' leadership style, (high on task, low on people), is associated with formal and rigid authority. Staff are micromanaged because of a belief that, if left to their own devices, they could not be trusted to do their jobs. Results and achievement are the main focus, with control used to attain associated goals. A high priority is afforded to strict adherence to rules and regulations. Minimal concern is demonstrated for the feelings, needs, or welfare of staff or students. The 'authoritarian' leader's behaviour is generally dogmatic, cold and dispassionate. The 'authoritarian' style causes stress and distress to staff and students alike.

● The Impoverished Style

Mary is an 'impoverished' school leader. She always appears as if she is merely going through the motions in her school. There is an air of disengagement and disinterest in her demeanour. She shows little enthusiasm for her work, or the work of her staff. She makes herself unavailable if problems or issues arise, and has a habit of disappearing during the school day. She is polite and courteous to everyone, however, the staff have a sense that while she likes the position, she does not want to do the work that goes with it.

The 'impoverished' style, (low on task, low on people), is associated with a lack of competence, efficiency and effectiveness. Minimal attention, effort or interest is afforded to either the task, or the people at work. The 'impoverished' style is deeply resented by staff.

● The Middle of the Road Style

Helen is a 'middle of the road' school leader. She is a happy-go-lucky person, and has a general rule of letting staff get on with their jobs. She likes the quiet life, and is very reluctant to get involved with conflicts between teachers, or between staff and students. She encourages staff to sort problems out themselves. She facilitates staff who wish to engage in professional development, but does not get involved herself. She has a habit of saying, 'If it ain't broke, don't fix it' in relation to proposed changes or improvements. She certainly does not obstruct innovation or initiative, but offers no incentive or encouragement to anyone trying to introduce new ideas, or improve their practice. She gets on well with the staff, but does not see her role as one of motivating or challenging them.

The 'middle of the road' style is generally associated with maintaining the *status quo*. The logistics and the essentials of the task are attended to, but without a vision of the potential for increased effectiveness and innovation. There is a respect for staff and a general regard for their needs and welfare. However, their potential is neither appreciated, nor utilised. The 'middle of the road' style is usually regarded as safe, but not exciting or challenging. It suits some staff members, but adversely affects the enthusiasm and motivation of those who value, and want, change and innovation.

The examples of the four least effective leadership styles as outlined above, are included merely to provide an idea of how each of the styles manifests in the school context. It is worthy of mention also that as the leadership styles are generally considered to be gender-neutral, there is no gender significance attached to the examples, two of which allude to male leaders, and two to female leaders. Some elements of each of the four styles will be included in the leadership practices of most leaders. However the collaborative leadership style is considered to be the most effective.

● The Collaborative Style

'Collaborative' school leadership is associated with maximising the quality of the teaching and learning in schools, while encouraging and supporting the staff. 'Collaborative' leaders place a high and equal emphasis on both the task and the people elements of their role. They know that both are inextricably linked, and that in order to have high-quality teaching and learning, they need to build and maintain high-quality relationships with the staff. They understand and accept their role and responsibility for ensuring, in as far as possible, that each member of their staff is satisfied and fulfilled in their jobs. They also know that this can only be achieved when individual staff members feel valued and are treated well. 'Collaborative' school leaders really value their team. They share information, resources, time, knowledge, and credit with them. Thankfully, the number of 'collaborative' school leaders is on the increase. This is due to a combination of factors, including:

- higher expectations in relation to the range of competencies required by school leaders, that are reflected to a greater extent than before, in the selection and appointment process;

- greater awareness among applicants and newly-appointed school leaders of what constitutes effective and collaborative school leadership;

- increased focus on, and availability of, professional development opportunities for serving school leaders;

- increasing numbers of aspiring and serving school leaders enhancing their knowledge and skills through acquiring postgraduate qualifications in leadership and management.

The 'collaborative/team' style combines the task-oriented behaviours and the people-oriented behaviours. Although many leadership behaviours straddle the task and people categories, a school leader's task-oriented behaviours are generally associated with, for example; planning, organising, documenting, administrating, conducting meetings, clarifying, compiling, assigning and monitoring. School leaders' people/relations-orientated behaviours are generally associated with, for example; respecting, trusting, valuing, facilitating, motivating, challenging and caring. In terms of the Blake-Mouton model, the 'collaborative' approach is considered to be the optimal leadership style.

> **"**
> I define a positive/effective school environment as one that provides the highest quality of educational service to every student, in an atmosphere of respect, openness, collegiality and equality.
> **"**

'Collaborative' leadership, which places an equal emphasis on the task and people elements of a school, is the surest way to create a positive/effective environment. Consequently, I define a positive/effective school environment as one that provides the highest quality of educational service to every student, in an atmosphere of respect, openness, collegiality and equality.

Reflective questions for school leaders.

1. How would describe your leadership style?

2. What elements of your leadership style would you consider to be collaborative?

3. What improvements do you need to make to become a more collaborative leader?

4. How do your staff rate you leadership in terms of being collaborative?

Key Points

- Providing a positive/effective work environment in schools is contingent on leaders placing an equal emphasis on the task and people elements of their roles.

- In terms of the balance between the task and the people dimensions in schools, there are five styles of leadership, four of which are considered to be ineffective.

- The collaborative style of leadership in schools acknowledges that a high quality of educational service cannot be provided without gaining and maintaining the commitment of the staff.

A.5 Conclusion

The quality of a school environment is determined by the behaviours of, and the relationships between, all those working and studying in the school. Most members of staff in schools are positive and enthusiastic, and they contribute significantly to the quality of the environment. However, even one or two negative members of staff can have a serious and adverse affect on the quality of the environment in schools. School leaders make a significant contribution to the quality of the environment in their schools. They are responsible for ensuring that their own behaviours and relationships are consistently positive. It is also important that the positive behaviours of others are acknowledged and encouraged, and that negative behaviours are consistently and appropriately addressed and challenged. The task and people elements of a school leader's role are equally important in the provision of a positive/effective school for both staff and students.

Section B

Emotional Intelligence (EI): A Requirement for Leadership

B. 1. Introduction

I teach on an educational leadership and management postgraduate course. The students comprise educational professionals, including school leaders and aspiring school leaders. Consistently, the subject that attracts the most interest is the area of Emotional Intelligence. Particularly in the context of a realisation of the importance for leaders and managers of self-awareness, and building positive relationships, the 'post-grad' students are increasingly keen to learn about emotional intelligence and to acquire the associated skills and competencies. However, more generally there is a realisation that, in the context of the leadership role of the teachers and other professionals working in schools, their levels of emotional intelligence are also pivotal to overall effectiveness. This section, therefore, while focusing mainly on the emotional intelligence of principals and deputy principals, places a considerable focus also on the role that emotional intelligence plays in the leadership of teachers in the classroom.

The surge of interest in Emotional Intelligence has more than likely emanated from the popularisation of the construct from the 1990s onwards, and by the claims made in relation to the many and various benefits of EI for individual and organisational success. Goleman (1995), for example, claimed that EI could be as powerful – and at times more powerful – than IQ as a predictor of success. He also claimed that 67% of the abilities considered essential for high performance in leaders could be related to levels of EI (Goleman, 1998). These claims, and many others made by Goleman in relation to the elements and attributes of EI, have been the subject of some scrutiny and criticism by researchers and recognised experts on the subject of EI. Notwithstanding this criticism, Goleman can be credited with bringing the construct of EI to the attention of the general public, and with focusing attention on the increasingly acknowledged implications of EI for individual and organisational success.

Whereas many school leaders attach considerable significance to EI in terms of their own effectiveness, there are others who dismiss it as superfluous. Comments such as, 'I don't do emotions,' capture both their dismissal of EI and their lack of understanding of emotions generally. It is important to alert those who share this view that, irrespective of whether they do or don't 'do' emotions, all humans are emotional creatures by nature, and every day – indeed, more accurately every moment of every day – a wide range of emotions is impacting on their moods, their attitudes, and their behaviour (Bervovich & Eyal, 2015). Whether they acknowledge it or not, emotions are central to their work and their lives.

It is true that emotions and feelings are not in the vocabulary of many people, particularly those who have grown up in homes where emotions were not understood, discussed or expressed. Suppression of emotions is widespread in such circumstances. When emotions are suppressed their energy does not disappear but merely subsides (Sky, 2002). "Emotions are entities that build up and escape or leak out of the body in various ways" (Fussell, 2002, p.7). They are inextricably linked to the way people think and behave. They inform moods and behaviours specifically, and the quality of relationships more generally. Emotions are also essential sources of information about our core needs, and the core needs of others. Habitual suppression of emotions has serious consequences for a person's mental and physical health, and for their general happiness. The more we suppress our emotions, the greater the negative impact on our levels of enthusiasm for life and the quality of our basic human relationships (Sky, 2002).

> **It is true that emotions and feelings are not in the vocabulary of many people, particularly those who have grown up in homes where emotions were not understood, discussed or expressed.**

Of course, people differ in terms of the degree to which they are aware of the emotions they experience, and the degree to which they can express their emotions to others (George, 2000). Chang, (2009) suggested that inconsistency between the emotions one feels and the emotions one displays is a sure predictor of emotional exhaustion, with all the personal and professional implications it brings with it. Suppression of emotions is costly to an individual's well-being, as it causes serious damage to the body, mind and spirit (Sky, 2002). Being able to express emotions accurately contributes significantly to an individual's ability to communicate effectively with others in their lives and work, so that they can have their own needs and the needs of others met (George, 2000). Suffice to say, emotions are dismissed or ignored at our peril.

> **Suffice to say, emotions are dismissed or ignored at our peril.**

B. 2. Emotions and Emotional Intelligence

"Emotions are high-intensity feelings that are triggered by specific stimuli, either internal or external to the individual" (George, 2000, p.1029). They involve the release of chemicals throughout the body and mind. They are not merely something that we feel, but also a powerful source of information about what is going on inside us (Moore, 2009). Irrespective of whether they are negative or positive, there is a reason for them. They act as signals for us and they need to be acknowledged, understood and managed. Anger, fear, sadness and happiness are generally thought to be the four main basic, or primary, emotions. Love, shame, grief, surprise and disgust are also cited by some psychologists and researchers in their compilations of basic emotions.

Emotions are generally thought to be of very short duration, and Freedman (2015), proposed that they may only last for about six seconds. This insight has proven to be an invaluable resource in understanding and regulating emotions. The breakdown of the chemical process of emotions into its minute elements, as provided by Freedman (2015), is scientific and convincing. It suggests that, as emotions only last for a very short time, if we are feeling something for longer than that, then we are, at some level, choosing to recreate or refuel the original emotion. In other words, we are consciously or unconsciously holding on to the emotion.

B. 2.1 Holding on to Negative Emotions

Interestingly, Roseman and Smith (2001) suggested that emotions occur as a result of the interpretation of events, rather than the events themselves. How often have we heard someone who is very angry with another person say that, 'Hell will freeze over before I forget this,' or, 'If I live to be a hundred I will never speak to her again.' These sentiments suggest that the person has interpreted the incidents that provoked the anger as being very serious, and as a result is determined to remain angry indefinitely. Chang, (2009), proposed that different emotions, and different levels of emotion, result from how we view a situation or event. The degree of importance, that we attach to an incident may determine how we respond (Chang, 2009).

> **"**
> Not understanding that we can have input into managing and regulating our emotions renders us very vulnerable, particularly in challenging situations and difficult relationships.
> **"**

Those who are experiencing anger towards another person often say that they would not give them the satisfaction of suspending their anger towards them. This is an indication that they are aware of the potential impact of their anger on the other person, but almost certainly unaware of the impact that holding on to that anger has on them. A person who is experiencing hurt or distress can often be heard to say that they will never get over it. This sentiment indicates that they believe they have no control over how they feel and consequently, albeit unconsciously, they hold on to those feelings – sometimes for weeks, months, or even years.

Not understanding that we can have input into managing and regulating our emotions renders us very vulnerable, particularly in challenging situations and difficult relationships.

B. 2.2 Managing Emotions

The regulation of emotions includes the conscious and controlled reappraisal of situations in order to decrease unpleasant emotional experiences, and increase pleasant ones (Gross, 2002). In other words, through our thinking we can hold on to positive emotions and let go of negative ones. Who would have thought that we could possibly input into our emotional states to that extent? Rethinking and reappraising situations from a more positive view and perspective can:

- change how we feel;
- help us to respond to situations in a more measured way;
- impact positively on our mental well-being.

Many people try to regulate their negative emotions by suppressing them. This is done automatically and unconsciously, as suppression becomes a habitual method for those who are trying not to acknowledge or feel their emotions. Suppression has little impact on a person's negative emotions, in terms of decreasing or eliminating them (Gross, 2002). Rather, it consumes huge amounts of energy in a vain attempt to keep emotions at bay, when all the while they are

> **"**
> Negative emotions can be held onto for periods ranging from hours to years without the person being aware of it, and without realising how and to what extent they are being adversely affected.
> **"**

weighing the person down, like a bag of rocks. Negative emotions can be held onto for periods ranging from hours to years without the person being aware of it, and without realising how and to what extent they are being adversely affected.

> **A focus on understanding emotions and their impact is not an optional extra for people, but is essential to the quality of their lives.**

People also differ considerably in the degree to which they are able to express their emotions. Some are aware of them and would like to express them, but, for a variety of reasons, often fail to do so. There are also those who are totally and utterly incapable of communicating their feelings to others.

A focus on understanding emotions and their impact is not an optional extra for people, but is essential to the quality of their lives. As individuals, we are thinkers and feelers. We need to devote as much of our energies to studying how we feel, as we do to how we think (Muchinsky, 2000). Also, in order to understand our own behaviours as well as the behaviours of others, we must first understand emotions.

By understanding and handling emotions effectively we have the potential to:

- take charge of our responses to the everyday situations that we encounter;
- manage our moods;
- impact positively on our relationships with ourselves and others.

That, in a nutshell, is what emotional intelligence is about.

B. 2.3 Defining Emotional Intelligence

Emotional intelligence "is the ability to effectively join emotions and reasoning, using emotions to facilitate reasoning and reasoning intelligently about emotions" (Mayer & Salovey, 1997). Those skilful in dealing with emotions are considered as having high emotional intelligence (Moore, 2009). The term emotional intelligence is used, particularly in popular literature, to describe a wide range of abilities, behaviours and personality traits. It is also credited with having an extensive range of benefits and predictive powers – some of which are considered to be exaggerated and unsubstantiated. Locke, (2005) suggested that a number of the claims made in relation to EI were "preposterously all-encompassing" (2005, p. 428).

However, Mayer and Salovey (1997), consistently define EI as involving a series of mental abilities that enable a person to perceive and manage emotions in themselves and others. Whereas they have tweaked their definition over the years, the essence and clarity of it remains the same. Adopting their somewhat narrow definition for the purpose of exploring EI in this section does not limit the possibilities for broadening the discussion in relation to its elements. Neither does it inhibit discussion of, nor elaboration on, the numerous benefits associated with EI – especially in the context of leadership.

> **The workplace was historically considered as a setting that should be void of emotions. There was an expectation and an unspoken understanding among employers and employees that emotions and emotional 'stuff' would be left at home**

> **❝**
> **The notion of a teacher shouting at a child is now generally considered totally unacceptable by the vast majority of those who work in schools.**
> **However, it does still happen.**
> **❞**

B. 2.4 Emotions in the Workplace

The workplace was historically considered as a setting that should be void of emotions. There was an expectation and an unspoken understanding among employers and employees that emotions and emotional 'stuff' would be left at home. In actual fact, there was very little discussion about emotions, particularly as they were considered to be unwanted influences in the workplace. Furthermore, those considered to be emotional were often deemed to be weak or even unstable. Any display of emotions would certainly not have been encouraged from any member of staff, and would have been particularly frowned on if it emanated from leaders.

Of course, these expectations applied to some emotions more than others. In workplaces that were formal, hierarchical and authoritarian, emotions such as happiness and joy were rarely expressed, and equally, the expression of emotions such as sadness or distress was considered inappropriate. However, anger was more acceptable, and was frequently expressed, in an inappropriate manner. Angry outbursts from managers and leaders were, if not commonplace, certainly not exceptional. In many instances managers, who were known for losing their tempers and hurtling abuse at everyone around them, went unchallenged. They were often seen as being tough and getting things done, and were in many cases rewarded with promotion. In the teaching profession, some teachers were also associated with displaying anger, through shouting and even screaming at students.

Discussing these behaviours in the past tense belies the fact that there are still a considerable number of workplaces, including schools, that remain formal, hierarchical and authoritarian, and still a number of leaders and staff members who express anger in the workplace in very aggressive ways. The notion of a teacher shouting at a child is now considered unacceptable by the vast majority of those who work in schools. However, it does still happen.

Emotions are currently much more widely recognised as being central to experiences in workplaces (Rajah et al., 2011). Schools are intensely emotional workplaces that bring out a wide variety of emotions, both positive and negative, in everyone who works and studies in them. Positive emotions, such as enthusiasm, happiness, fulfilment, pride and hope, when they occur, can be very gratifying, whereas negative emotions such as worry, frustration, guilt, anger, fear, vulnerability and disappointment can cause stress and upset.

Key Points

- Emotional Intelligence is now widely acknowledged as being essential to effective leadership.

- Emotions are a source of information that alert people to what is going on inside them. Ignoring them is detrimental to health and well-being.

- Managing and regulating emotions impacts on peoples' moods, the quality of their relationships, and their responses to everyday events.

- The ability to perceive and manage emotions is referred to as Emotional Intelligence.

- The expression of emotions in workplaces was traditionally discouraged. Emotions are now increasingly recognised as being central to workplace experiences.

B. 3. Emotions in the Teaching Profession

Although teaching is recognised among educational professionals and researchers as one of the most emotionally demanding occupations, it is often perceived by the wider community as an easy option, in terms of career choice. While acknowledging the benefits of the longer-than-average holiday periods that teachers enjoy, these benefits do not negate the effects of the intensity and emotionality of the job of teaching.

"Teachers' emotions change, day by day, class by class and sometimes even moment by moment" (Chang, 2009, p.203). Their emotions impact on their own behaviour, as well as on the behaviours of those who observe them. Emotions spread directly from the expresser to the observer via what is described as emotional-contagion (Van Cleef, 2009). The emotions of teachers are frequently sensed and caught by their students, and the shared emotions, depending on whether they are positive or negative, influence for the better or worse the quality of teaching and learning in the classroom (Hargreaves, 1998).

It is important therefore, that teachers tune into their emotions and manage and express them appropriately, particularly because of the associated interpersonal benefits that impact positively on a teacher's:

- quality of communication and relationships with others;
- levels of empathy;
- acceptance of others;
- assertiveness;
- levels of disclosure.

The lesser-known intrapersonal (self-related) benefits are equally important, and impact positively on a teacher's emotional and behavioural self-awareness, self-esteem and self-acceptance, frustration tolerance and anger management, stress and well-being.

The 'self' and 'social' elements of Emotional Intelligence are inextricably linked, and are essential for the development of the associated social and emotional competencies and skills. Social and Emotional Competencies (SECs) are at the very core of effective teaching.

B. 3.1 Emotional Dimensions of Teaching

There is an emotional dimension to every aspect of the work taking place in schools. There are, however, some potentially highly-charged dimensions of dealing with students. Managing student behaviours, and gaining and maintaining student engagement in particular, require effective intervention. Notwithstanding the major leadership role that each and every member of staff in schools undertakes on a daily basis, neither of those two tasks should be left totally to the discretion of the individual teacher. It is important that there is a consistent approach across the entire school. School leaders need to be aware of how best to respond appropriately to difficult and demanding issues with students. They also need to promote an emotionally intelligent approach by teachers to dealing with these issues, and to resolving problems when they arise. This empowers

> **The emotionally intelligent teacher will be much more likely to engage positively with students, and to have the emotional and social competencies (SECs) necessary for responding to the challenges that the emotionally charged dimensions of their role bring.**

those with EI to effectively manage the emotional dimensions of their work, and encourages others to become more emotionally aware. The emotionally intelligent teacher will be much more likely to engage positively with students, and to have the competencies necessary for responding to the challenges that the emotionally-charged dimensions of their role bring.

B. 3.2 Managing Student Behaviours

Managing students' disruptive behaviours is one of the most challenging aspects of the job of teaching. It can severely test patience, provoke frustration, anger and upset, take up inordinate amounts of time and energy, and cause physical and emotional exhaustion. When behaviours are particularly disruptive and provocative, and when they thwart the teacher's ability to get on with the job of teaching, it is inevitable that teachers will experience a range of negative emotions.

It is the ability to regulate and express those emotions appropriately that gives the emotionally intelligent teacher the advantage in managing challenging behaviours. This is easier said than done, even for the emotionally competent teacher, particularly when they are in the middle of a class and have no realistic chance of escaping. However, they will be more aware of the consequences of losing control of their emotions and expressing them in dysfunctional ways. They will also be more aware that, in those circumstances, there is a strong possibility that:

- the behaviour will further escalate;
- the relationship between the student and themselves will deteriorate;
- they will lose the respect, not only of the offending student, but also of the other students in the class.

All behaviours have an emotional context. Dealing with the inappropriate behaviours of students, without considering the context in which they occur, is a superficial approach that will not have a real or sustained impact on improving behaviour. Teachers high in EI have a better insight into the emotions that might be driving the students' behaviours. They 'don't poke the polecat' by immediately reacting in a negative or aggressive manner. They don't rush to judge the behaviours as disrespectful, but seek to establish what is behind them. They try not to attribute motives of destructive intent to the student. They steer well clear of using the threat of punishment, or the promise of

> **Teachers high in EI have a better insight into the emotions that might be driving the students' behaviours. They 'don't poke the polecat' by immediately reacting in a negative or aggressive manner. They don't rush to judge the behaviours as disrespectful, but seek to establish what is behind them. They try not to attribute motives of destructive intent to the student.**

rewards, to endeavour to change and improve their behaviour. Rather they use supportive and measured responses to help students to identify and regulate their underlying emotions, and to ascertain what is causing them.

When the teacher gains some insight into what is behind the behaviours, it enables them to respond more compassionately to the students, and work with them to redirect their behaviours more positively. Irrespective of how skilled the teacher is, dealing with difficult and challenging behaviour takes its toll on them. Therefore, the focus should always be on preventing the behaviours from occurring in the first place. The skill of assertiveness is associated with the social dimensions of EI, and is essential for establishing and communicating boundaries in relation to behaviours.

B. 3.3 Assertiveness in Managing Student Behaviours

Teachers who are assertive are clear and unambiguous in outlining their rights and needs. While focusing on having their rights and needs met, they ensure that they do not disregard the rights and needs of their students. One of our identified biological needs is to be free to choose (Glasser, 1998). Students who perceive themselves as having some freedom to make choices about their behaviours do not generally feel inclined to behave inappropriately. On the contrary, if behavioural expectations are imposed on them, with no opportunity or freedom to discuss and debate them, then they are much more likely to use behaviours that are disruptive and disrespectful.

Assertive teachers use a consultative and co-operative approach to involve students in the setting of boundaries and the outlining of expected standards of behaviours. Welcoming their input, and giving genuine consideration to what they suggest, gives students a sense of ownership in the management of their own behaviours. It is one of the best strategies for encouraging students to reflect on their behaviour, to assess their behaviour independently, and to become intrinsically motivated to behave appropriately.

When behaviour management relies on conditioning students to comply with, and conform to, teacher expectations only, and incorporates punishment or reward to achieve this, it effectively wipes out the intrinsic motivation of the student to manage their own behaviour (Hill, 1990). On the contrary, where there are agreed standards of behaviours, and a context of caring and supportive relationships with teachers, students are more likely to be intrinsically motivated to adhere to the standards. This makes the job of the teacher much easier. They don't have to spend time 'giving out,' or engaging in futile attempts at controlling behaviours.

The consistent employment of these alternative and more effective preventative strategies can be very difficult, even for emotionally intelligent teachers, when their colleagues or the school principal do not support them. The dismissal, disregard, and occasional ridiculing of their methods are often reflective of a school culture that promotes punitive control measures for dealing with students' misbehaviour, rather than authoritative and collaborative preventative measures.

B. 3.4 Preventing Inappropriate Behaviours

The 'School Rules Book' was frequently distributed to students as a means of making them aware of how they should and should not behave in the school, and of the consequences of breaching the rules. The rules related exclusively to the behaviours exhibited by students towards others. There was minimal, if any, focus of the behaviours exhibited by those in authority. An alternative document that outlines the expected standards of behaviours *for everyone in the school* is considered to be more effective in preventing and managing unacceptable behaviours. In compiling this document, it is important to clearly articulate the responsibilities of the principal, the teachers, and other staff members in relation to promoting positive behaviours. The responsibilities of the students should also be outlined.

A separate document, outlining the responsibilities of school leaders and staff in relation to behavioural expectations between the adults in the school, is an essential element of any 'dignity at work' initiative, and will be discussed in the section on workplace bullying. It is also worth reiterating that the behaviours of the adults in the school towards each other, and towards the students, have a significant impact on student behaviour generally. However, in relation to the document on managing student behaviours, it might include something along the lines of the following statements.

Everyone who works in this school is responsible for:

- caring for all students;
- treating all students equally;
- listening to students and hearing what they have to say, and taking their perspectives on board;
- ensuring that the school environment facilitates optimal learning opportunities for all students;
- doing their very best to keep every student safe.

Every student has a responsibility to:

- do their best, and make the most of their abilities and talents;
- treat everyone in the school with courtesy and consideration;
- treat school property and the property of others with care;
- assist those who need help;
- tell someone if they, or others, are being treated unfairly or being hurt.

When behaviour management is associated with catching students being good, as instead of catching them being bad, the incentive to behave responsibly is greater. The challenge for the teacher is to provide every opportunity for students to behave positively. Focusing on their strengths rather than on their failings, allocating responsibilities to them for doing things that they are good at, and graciously giving them praise and recognition for what they achieve, are powerful tools for increasing their self-esteem and preventing inappropriate behaviour. When their self-esteem is enhanced, students feel good about themselves and are motivated by these positive feelings to behave positively also. School leaders can reflect on the management of student behaviour in their schools by answering the following questions:

> **"When behaviour management is associated with catching students being good, instead of catching them being bad, the incentive to behave responsibly is greater."**

- Is there a consistent approach to managing student behaviours in your school?

- What sort of encouragement is provided to students to behave appropriately?

- Should the imposition of sanctions for breeches of rules, constitute a major element of the behaviour management guidelines in your school? What are your reasons for your answer?

B. 4. Managing Students' Negative Behaviours

When negative behaviours occur, teachers often feel frustrated and angry. Being emotionally aware does not prevent those feelings, but rather prevents the immediate and automatic negative reactions that many teachers can exhibit when challenged by disruptive behaviours. Emotionally intelligent teachers have learned to manage their frustration and anger to the extent that they have time to pause and think before reacting, and, consequently, they tend to respond more appropriately and effectively. If the goal of the teacher in managing behaviours is to teach responsibility, respect and self-control, it is obvious that they must behave responsibly and respectfully themselves, and maintain their own self-control.

> **"When severely provoked, teachers may lose control and say things that exacerbate, rather than alleviate, the situation."**

Being emotionally intelligent does not bring with it a guarantee that self-control will automatically and consistently be maintained. When severely provoked, teachers may lose control and say things that exacerbate, rather than alleviate, the situation. However, there is a better chance, through their self-awareness, that they will regret their actions and find it easier to apologise, thereby mitigating the worst effects of their behaviour on the relationship with the student.

Fear and control can, of course, temporarily reduce unacceptable behaviours of students, but they will always recur in one form or another. You can get students to do almost anything through instilling fear in them.

> **"Fear and control can, of course, temporarily reduce unacceptable behaviours from students, but they will always recur in one form or another."**

In my very early years as a student teacher in a

primary school, I remember a teacher telling me that he could leave his pupils sitting with their fingers on their lips, while he went on holidays for a fortnight to Majorca, and that they would be still sitting, with their fingers on their lips, when he got back. Witnessing the levels of fear in that classroom, I did not doubt it. It was a good lesson for me, at the beginning of my career, on how not to do things. I thought to myself, 'any idiot could do that'. It takes no skill, merely ignorance. However, it takes high levels of self- and social-awareness to engage in effective behaviour management.

Those who view the punitive approach to managing behaviours as appropriate and necessary often regard those who do not, as having a *laissez-faire* approach to dealing with behavioural issues. In reality, those who caution against punitive actions usually take a very proactive and assertive approach.

They consistently identify behaviours that are disruptive, aggressive and/or destructive. What they refrain from doing is identifying the student as bad or destructive. They know that when they separate the behaviours from the student:

- negative emotions are less likely to be stirred up;
- the intervention from the teacher is not taken personally;
- students can remain emotionally stable and are more likely to hear the message of the teacher in relation to their behaviour.

B. 4.1 The Win-Win Outcome

The aim in managing student behaviour is to have a win-win outcome, where the needs of both the teacher and the student are met. This, according to Bluenstein (2001), is one of the hardest ideas to sell to those in authority. They often fail to realise that their authority is not compromised by accommodating the autonomy needs of the student. Teachers make students lose when they humiliate, embarrass or denigrate them. I always wonder what makes those teachers think that they have a right to do that.

Recently I met a family on holiday. The parents have one little boy aged about 8 years. As I know the area where they live, I asked them, by way of conversation, what school their little boy attended. They named a school that was quite a distance from where they live. I asked them why they had chosen that particular school. They answered assuredly "We've heard they don't give out to the kids there." The line resonated so much with me, that I asked them to elaborate. "They don't shout at students and they don't scare them," was the explanation proffered. It was sufficient for me to respond by saying "That's a very good reason for choosing a school".

One might conclude that all of the above recommendations could be achieved by using a bit of common sense. However, without emotional intelligence, common sense in the context of appropriate management of student behaviour may not be that common.

The lack of common sense and emotional awareness also comes into play, when a teacher reacts to the reputation of a student rather than to their actual behaviour (Jordan & Le Metais, 1999). Making a student aware that you have heard from another teacher about his/her behavioural record, even before there is any evidence of current bad behaviour, is a recipe for disaster. It gives students a sense of being 'picked-on', and of the teacher having low expectations in relation to their behaviour. If students are labelled as disruptive, they are more likely to live up to that reputation. It is exceedingly de-motivating not to be given the benefit of the doubt, and it demonstrates a distinct lack of empathy on the part of the teacher.

> **"**
> Making a student aware that you have heard from another teacher about his/her behavioural record, even before there is any evidence of current bad behaviour, is a recipe for disaster.
> **"**

Teachers contribute significantly to student misbehaviour when they respond inappropriately, causing low-level disruptions to escalate into major issues (Murphy, 1986). When teachers respond negativity to the behaviour of students by:

- calling them names;
- blaming them for their own negative reactions;
- isolating or excluding them;
- speaking disparagingly to others about them,

it sends a very strong message to the student that the teacher does not like them or does not want to deal with them. Bluestein (2001) stated that when a student feels disliked or overlooked by the teacher, it has a real and serious impact on them. Feeling disliked impacts negatively on self-esteem and on the strength, commitment and inner resources that are needed to keep trying when nothing seems to be going right (Bluestein, 2001).

B. 4.2 Emotional Intelligence: Central to Managing Student Behaviour

The four essential elements of EI are:

- self-awareness;
- self-management;
- social awareness;
- relationship management (Goleman, 2000).

All four are central to managing students' behaviour appropriately, respectfully, and effectively.

Self-awareness enables the teacher to recognise the emotions that are aroused in them when a student is aggressive or disruptive. It enables them to reflect on their own behaviour, and accurately assess whether it is helping or hindering the situation.

Self-management enables the teacher to:

- manage their moods;
- maintain their self-control in trying situations;
- change their behaviour when it is not working;
- recover more quickly from personal comments or affronts.

Social awareness enables the teacher to:

- take on board how students might be feeling;

- understand and appreciate the underlying issues that may be affecting students' behaviours;
- listen to students and hear their perspective;
- strive to meet their needs.

Relationship management enables the teacher to:

- relate to students in a way that makes them feel valued, cared for and supported;
- address students' behaviours without personal and hurtful comments;
- place a consistent emphasis on catching them being good.

Self-awareness, self-management and social-awareness are all essential for managing relationships with students. Furthermore, building and maintaining quality relationships is widely acknowledged as the biggest single factor influencing student behaviour and student learning.

Key Points

- Teaching is an emotional profession.

- Leaders have a responsibility to be aware of, and encourage teachers to, appropriately manage the emotional dimensions of teaching.

- The emotional dimensions of teaching include the management of student behaviour and student engagement.

- Emotionally intelligent teachers are more successful at preventing negative behaviours, dealing constructively with negative behaviours when they occur, and managing their own reactions to provocative behaviours by students.

- The four elements of EI, which are self-awareness, self-management, social-awareness and relationship management, are essential to managing student behaviours.

B. 5. Gaining and Maintaining Student Engagement

The lack of engagement of students is a perennial problem in schools, and is caused by a variety of issues. Providing students with optimal learning opportunities is arguably the key role of school leaders. They need to be proponents of best practice in relation to student engagement and success. Their efforts will have a better chance of being rewarded when staff members have the levels of emotional intelligence necessary for gaining, and maintaining, student engagement. The emotionally intelligent teacher will be better equipped to maximise students' interest in, and engagement with, their subject, and minimise their levels of frustration, boredom and disengagement. Through their empathy, they will be tuned in to the needs of students, and will make consistent efforts to incorporate those needs into their lesson planning and delivery.

Irrespective of what subject is being taught, it is possible to devise ways of making it more relevant to students' interests and experiences. When this is done, it helps to engage students emotionally with the subject matter through what Rosiek (2004), calls 'emotional scaffolding'.

B. 5.1 Emotional Scaffolding

Teachers regularly use scaffolding as a teaching strategy. Scaffolding refers to the use of a variety of teaching techniques that encourage students to focus on the elements of a task that they feel comfortable with, and that are within their ability. This is done to facilitate them in gaining the confidence and the sense of achievement necessary for them to move to the more difficult elements of the task.

Emotional scaffolding encourages students to engage emotionally with the task by making it relevant to them and by helping them to connect with it. The emotional engagement then increases as the task progresses. If a maths problem, for example, is based on a football league table, or on the logistics of getting thousands of people into a rock concert, students can tune into the scenario and display an interest in, and engagement with, the task. If history lessons involve the use of drama, props and artefacts to visualise and act out historical events, students will connect and empathise with them. Examining the patterns of how history repeats itself by comparing, for example, the plight of the Jewish people during the Second World War to the plight of the millions who have since died in places like Darfur, Rwanda and Syria helps to sensitise students to the horrors of wars. Petitioning on behalf of people whose human rights have being breeched is an emotional exercise, from which can spring an understanding of human rights abuses down through the years. Debates, fieldtrips, role-play, music and art are all excellent means of making emotional connections to a variety of subjects.

> **"**
> If a maths problem, for example, is based on a football league table, or on the logistics of getting thousands of people into a rock concert, students can tune into the scenario and display an interest in, and engagement with, the task.
> **"**

Whenever a teacher can identify and use a strong emotional tie-in to lesson content, and allude to the emotional connection while teaching it, the content is more likely to be retained for longer, and with greater clarity, by the students (Sousa, 2009).

Emotional scaffolding can be used in all schools and colleges. I frequently use practical and relevant case-studies to engage students emotionally, to engender interest, participation and passion, and to maximise their commitment to the task in hand.

B. 5.2 Instilling Confidence and Self-Belief in Students

Students often disengage because of feelings of inadequacy, or inability to complete tasks. Emotionally intelligent teachers will be more likely to recognise and understand these feelings, and will endeavour to find ways to help students overcome them and improve their confidence and self-belief.

Introducing the concept of "possibility thinking" (Craft, 2007), to those who are despondent and disengaged often proves very helpful. It supports and encourages students to look at things in a more positive light, and move their thinking from what they can presently do, to what they could do. Possibility thinking is an imaginative means of replacing negative emotions with positive ones, so that the students can feel capable of trying new things, and finding new ways of approaching problems.

> **"**
> **Emotionally intelligent teachers do not focus on the disengagement through automatically blaming the student, rather, they seek the input of the student into finding out what is happening. They also put the microscope on their own performance; on the particular needs of the student; and on the relationships between themselves and the student.**
> **"**

B. 5.3 Responding to Students' Disengagement

Another indication of the levels of emotional intelligence in teachers can be found in how they deal with student disengagement. Emotionally intelligent teachers do not focus on the disengagement through automatically blaming the student; rather, they seek the input of the student into finding out what is happening. They also put the microscope on their own performance; on the particular needs of the student; and on the relationships between themselves and the students. Inadequate and unsupportive relations between teachers and students frequently cause students to have a dread or fear of coming to school. When this happens, they are more likely to have a sense of alienation and disengagement (Jennings & Greenberg, 2009).

Teachers with high levels of emotional self-awareness will regularly seek the views of students on what is working for them, and what could be changed and improved. If criticisms of the teacher's methods are expressed, they are equipped to dispassionately discuss the reasons for them, without reacting negatively or taking criticisms personally. Allowing students to have their say provides them with a degree of autonomy which is positively associated with persistence on task, and increased self-regulation for learning (Deci & Ryan, 1987).

Through lack of self and social-awareness, many teachers continue to exert high levels of control over all aspects of learning in the classroom. The social dimension of emotional intelligence is primarily about the ability to build supportive relationships. Jennings and Greenberg (2009) drew on the work of a number of researchers in proposing that, when teachers are warm and supportive, they give students a sense of connectedness to the school environment, and a sense of security that enables them to explore new ideas and take risks. These conditions are considered to be fundamental to learning (Jennings & Greenberg, 2009).

B. 5.4 Emotional Climate in the Classroom

Ultimately, it is the emotional climate in the classroom that has the biggest impact on student engagement, and the quality of the learning taking place. A positive emotional climate is associated with, for example:

- teachers' sensitivity to students' needs;
- warm and caring teacher/student relationships;
- students' perspectives being considered;
- encouragement and facilitation of co-operative practices, (including co-operative learning), among students.

In relation to co-operative learning, it has to be said that the widely proclaimed and proven benefits of this approach for student engagement, achievement, behaviour and self-esteem, are acknowledged by the many progressive schools that use it. However, schools with a highly competitive and individualised learning focus appear to remain oblivious to these benefits and successes.

> **"**
>
> **In relation to co-operative learning, it has to be said that the widely proclaimed and proven benefits of this approach for student engagement, achievement, behaviour and self-esteem, are acknowledged by the many progressive schools that use it**
>
> **"**

Student learning and achievement are considerably hindered by a negative emotional climate in the classroom, which is associated with, for example:

- Minimal regard, respect and connection between teacher and student;
- Lessons being planned and taught without consideration for the needs and capabilities of individual students;
- A controlling rather than an autonomy-supportive social environment;
- Teacher sarcasm and punitive practices.

In relation to the use of sarcasm by teachers, unfortunately, the practice is still ubiquitous. On the surface sarcasm may seem funny – and it can be, even when used by teachers in class – but only when it does not seek to demean or ridicule a student. One teacher I know would regularly say to the class 'Am I talking to myself? I ask myself', which was quite sarcastic, but also quite funny. However, it did not include a hint of anger, negativity or nastiness.

Sarcasm can cause negative emotions in students, and can be cruel and demeaning. So-called 'smart comments' in relation to a student being late, taking a long time to complete a task, not knowing the answer to a question, or submitting poorly presented work, can be undermining, upsetting or embarrassing. In the context of the teacher being unhappy with the progress of the entire class, the comment, 'take your books out and read the chapter for yourselves...I'm obviously wasting my time here', can be very unfair, and extremely frustrating for the students.

When a teacher uses sarcasm that ridicules or demeans either an individual student or an entire class, they risk losing the students' respect. Sarcasm damages a positive classroom climate. It can result in retaliatory comments being made by the offended student. When targeted by sarcasm, vulnerable students can feel even more vulnerable, and it can send messages to classmates that it is okay for them to sneer at, tease, or make fun of those targeted by the teacher. Sarcasm that includes putdowns of any sort has no place in a caring classroom.

A sense of humour and fun in a teacher is, however, not merely a bonus, but a must. Emotionally intelligent teachers generally do not take themselves too seriously. They are not, as I describe it, addicted to being affronted. They have the capacity to laugh even when the joke is on them. Bluestein (2001) recalled the advice of Ron Burgess author and teacher, who urged teachers to practice, "random acts of craziness". Bluestein further alluded to humour and a little silliness as a

> **"**
>
> **Sarcasm that includes putdowns of any sort has no place in a caring classroom.**
>
> **"**

means of holding students' attention, improving learning, reducing stress, increasing recall and shortening the school day. I could not agree more!

Key Points

- Emotionally intelligent teachers use a variety of means to gain, and maintain, student engagement.

- Emotional scaffolding helps students to engage emotionally with what is being taught.

- Seeking the input of students into how best to improve their levels of engagement is a progressive initiative, and an indication of the emotional intelligence of teachers.

- A positive emotional climate in the classroom is characterised by high levels of caring and encouragement of students, considerations of their needs and feelings, and a teacher's sense of humour and fun.

B. 6. The Emotionally Intelligent Leader

The emotional skills and competencies absolutely essential for leadership are increasingly being given the necessary attention in the research. In conjunction with this, the recognition of the importance of those skills and competencies is beginning to inform the appointment of leaders, leadership preparation, and professional development courses.

Over a long number of years, the main criteria for appointing school leaders were their experience, qualifications and seniority. This is quite apart from those who may have been appointed as a result of their:

- association with prominent or influential people;

- involvement in a particular organisation or church;

- affiliation to a political party.

Neither at interview stage, nor at pre- or post-appointment stages, would there have been a mention, of the emotional aspects of their role. Questions in relation to the levels of emotional self-awareness or self-management of the candidates, or their ability to manage their moods or behaviours, would generally not have been contemplated. Questions of that nature would have been regarded as being too personal, and outside the remit of the interview panel. In fact, it was generally considered that emotions and emotionality had no place in leadership. The social aspects of emotional intelligence, although they would not have been labelled as such, might have been alluded to in terms of questions on team building, or encouraging co-operation. However, ascertaining the competence of leadership candidates, in relation to building and maintaining positive relationships with staff and students, rarely formed part of the discussion in an interview process. However, the effects of the lack of these competencies in newly-appointed leaders were quickly evident in schools. It was often a matter of chance whether these leaders went on to influence for the better or worse the effectiveness of the school, or the quality of the school environment.

> "
> **There are many school leaders who are highly qualified, have high IQ, and are technically and/or academically skilled. However, if they are not socially and interpersonally competent, their qualifications etc. are of little value, in terms of dealing with and managing people.**
> "

This social dimensions of EI, sometimes referred to as social intelligence, are essential for school leaders to enable them to interact effectively with others, and to build quality relationships with colleagues and students. There are many school leaders who are highly qualified, have high IQ, and are technically and/or academically skilled. However, if they are not socially and interpersonally competent, their qualifications etc. are of little value, in terms of dealing with and managing people. They also "often come across as lacking in compassion and empathy and usually find it difficult to get others to co-operate with them and their agendas" (Ruderman, et al., 2001, p. 3). Many such leaders expect loyalty as a matter of course. Sometimes, they even demand it. As a result, they may get something – deference perhaps, or even compliance – but they will not get loyalty. Loyalty has to be earned, and will only be forthcoming if the leader forms a connection with, and an understanding of, the needs of those they work with.

Leaders high in EI will always focus on the needs of others, and will, as a result, be skilful in "influencing, inspiring, intellectually stimulating, and growing their staff" (Moore, 2009, p. 21).

Leaders, who do not have emotional intelligence, deny, ignore, or are generally oblivious to their own emotions. Even if they are somewhat aware of them, they find ways to suppress them, thereby giving power to their emotions to control their moods, behaviours, and ways of thinking. They remain ignorant of their capacity to change and improve how they think, feel and behave, and often believe it when they say, 'That's just the way I am, and that's just the way I'll always be'. They miss out on the opportunities that EI provides to change and become more effective in what they do, and to be more respected and admired.

It is hardly surprising that emotionally intelligent leaders are generally respected and admired, when one considers the characteristics that are associated with high levels of EI. These include being genuine, warm, persistent, well-adjusted and optimistic (Salovey & Mayer, 1990).

B. 6.1 Leaders' Moods

There are nuances of differences between moods and emotions. Notwithstanding this, George, (2000) reflected the views of many others, when he suggested that "EI is used broadly to refer to moods as well as emotions." (2000, p. 1033) Being aware of how you are feeling, as well as what you are feeling, are separate and important elements of EI. Everyone is entitled to be in a bad mood from time to time. School leaders are no exception. There are always going to be days when they are 'down in the dumps', or, 'like a bag of cats', or when they are 'ready to hit the roof'. If they use any of those exclamations in relation to themselves, it indicates a level of awareness of their moods, and an ability to express how they are feeling.

School leaders or staff, who are totally unaware of their moods, regularly bring them into school with them, without an inkling of the impact that they are having on themselves or others. Moods are extremely contagious. Peoples' moods drive their own behaviours, and also drive the moods and behaviours of those around them. Sometimes those in a bad mood do not even have to come into the school – they merely have to park their car in the car-park for their mood to shoot ahead of them, infecting all those in

> **There are always going to be days when leaders are 'down in the dumps', or, 'like a bag of cats', or when they are 'ready to hit the roof'. If they use any of those exclamations in relation to themselves, it indicates a level of awareness of their moods, and an ability to express how they are feeling.**

its path. Particularly if the school leader is generally moody or volatile, both staff and students check daily, to ascertain what kind of a mood he/she is in. This is because, at some level, they know that the mood of the leader will determine the quality of their day. Through their moods, school leaders have the power to create a school environment that is either positive and productive, or negative and toxic.

The elements and effects of mood-contagion are widely acknowledged in the literature. Indeed, moods are described as social viruses that spread like wildfire. Mood-contagion affects not merely the mood of the other person, but also their judgements and their behaviours (Barsade, 2002). In terms of leaders' moods, Golemen et al., suggested that, "the moods that start at the top, tend to move the fastest" (p. 47, 2001), and have a domino effect throughout the school. It is worth alluding to the fact that positive as well as negative moods are caught by others. Catching positive moods is associated with increased co-operation and competence (Barsade, 2002). It is also linked to the reduction of stress and distress among staff. Many leaders do not realise the influence they have over the emotions and moods of their staff. Among those who have some awareness, there are many who regard their role in managing group emotions as a peripheral task with little relevance to productivity. However, far from being peripheral, the spreading of positive moods and emotions is one of the main ways that leaders can impact on performance (Humphrey, 2002). Unfortunately, it has to be acknowledged that negative emotions are considered to be more contagious than positive ones.

> **School leaders, whose moods are unpredictable and who are often cranky and unreasonable, are not considered to be approachable.**

The adverse effects of mood contagion are associated with what we euphemistically call 'bad moods', or, 'being moody'. School leaders, whose moods are unpredictable and who are often cranky and unreasonable, are not considered to be approachable. Staff and students are cautious and fearful around them. They create a toxic environment that drags everyone down. The negative moods and emotions displayed by leaders result in the spread of negative energy among the staff. This has a significant and lasting effect on the relationships between leaders and staff (Barsade, 2000).

When emotionally intelligent leaders are having a bad day, they are aware of it. They are also aware that their moods will impact on others, and they use their skills to manage moods, and minimise any adverse effects. A symptom of low EI in leaders is a near total ignorance about their moods, and how they are regarded by others. They lack the primary element of EI, which is self-awareness, and this results in their own assessments of how they are regarded, being very far removed from reality. Challenging leaders with low or no self-awareness on their moods, and the effects of them, can be deeply resented, and regarded by them as an invasion of their privacy (Goleman et al., 2001). Consequently, they generally remain unchallenged and, indeed, unchanged.

> **"**
>
> **Leaders with EI will have a better chance of disciplining themselves to remain calm in the face of the provocation, caused by the perennial complainer.**
>
> **"**

Negative mood-contagion, although most powerful when it is top-down, can come from any member of staff, and can also cause a ripple effect of ramifications for group dynamics, morale and effectiveness. Chronic complainers, who are constantly negative about everything, present a major challenge for school leaders. Leaders with EI will have a better chance of disciplining themselves to remain calm in the face of the provocation, caused by the perennial complainer. While it would be expected that a leader might get 'a bit hot under the collar' by having every idea and initiative knocked and dismissed, those with EI can manage their anger to the extent that they do not 'fly off the handle', 'blow their top', or, 'lose it'. Any such loss of control provides a reason for the negative person to feel justified in their criticisms. It disappoints the onlookers, and discredits the leader and his/her authority.

Among those most in need of improving their EI are those with low impulse control (Ruderman et al., 2001). Poor impulse control is manifested in irresponsible and aggressive responses. On the contrary, good impulse control is associated with, for example, composure, patience, and coolness under fire (Ruderman et al., 2001). It is difficult to see how any leader would not be doing everything possible to acquire those universally-lauded characteristics, so essential for their own well-being, their effectiveness, and the quality of their interpersonal interactions and relationships.

Key Points

- Emotional intelligence as a central element of effective leadership must be a criterion in the selection and promotion of leaders.

- Leaders with emotional intelligence are aware that their moods are contagious, and impact on the moods and behaviours of others.

- Emotionally intelligent leaders manage their moods and control their impulses.

B. 7. The Four Dimensions of Emotional Intelligence

The four dimensions of emotional intelligence, are also central to effective leadership in a school. They include self –awareness, self-management, social awareness and relationship management (Goleman, 2000). Each of the four components will be discussed in terms of its relevance to leadership and in terms of how it manifests in leadership behaviours.

B. 7.1 Self –Awareness for Leaders

The first, and arguably most important, dimension of emotional intelligence is self-awareness. Self-awareness involves having an accurate picture of yourself overall, and a high degree of understanding and knowledge about the various aspects of yourself. Ultimately it is about getting to know yourself. Those with self-awareness have the ability to focus attention inward, and study themselves as though looking in a mirror (Ashley & Reiter-Palmon, 2012). The question is, what are they looking for?

● **Becoming Self-Aware**

Self-awareness has a number of dimensions, all of which constitute pieces of the jigsaw that make up the picture of who and what a person is. Self-awareness allows people to see themselves as others see them. It alerts them to the gaps between their self-evaluation and the evaluation of others. It helps them to align their actions to their words. And it facilitates them in understanding the impact that their words and actions can have on others.

> "
> Self-awareness allows people to see themselves as others see them. It alerts them to the gaps between their self-evaluation and the evaluation of others. It helps them to align their actions to their words.
> "

Anyone can improve their self-awareness. The two criteria are: seeing the need to do it; and wanting to do it. If levels of self-delusion are such that someone has little or no insight into discrepancies between how they see themselves and how others see them, or between how they think they are regarded by others, and how they are actually regarded, then they are highly unlikely to embark on a journey towards self-awareness. Unfortunately, peoples' tendency to speak one way and act in another is very common. When leaders do it, it does not go unnoticed. They are considered as inauthentic and insincere, and are generally – and justifiably – not trusted. When leaders are not trusted, staff members have negative expectations in relation to their leadership. There is more time spent on trying to figure out what is going on in the mind of the leader than on getting the job done.

Becoming self-aware enables leaders to represent themselves accurately and honestly to others. It requires a continuous reflective process in order to find the gaps, and make the comparisons, between self-evaluations and the evaluations of others.

● **The Johari Window**

One helpful means of getting to know oneself is by using the Johari Window. This is a psychological tool for enhancing self-awareness, which was named after the two psychologists, Joseph Luft and Harry Ingram, who invented it in 1955. The four panes of the window represent four aspects of the self. These are: the open self; the hidden self; the unknown self; and the blind self.

The Johari Window	

	Known to Self	**Unknown to Self**
Known to Others	THE OPEN SELF	THE BLIND SELF
Unknown to Others	THE HIDDEN SELF	THE UNKNOWN SELF

Based on the concept of the Johari Window *(Luft & Ingham, 1955)*

● The Open Self

The open self comprises the things you know about yourself, that others know about you also. For example, a leader may allude to a number of qualities when asked to provide an assessment of him/herself. If staff members allude to the same set of qualities in describing the leader, then those qualities are part of the leader's open self. They are known to the leader and also known to the staff. Ideally, in relation to enhancing self-awareness, the goal is to maximise the open self, so that what those around the leader see is what they get. Becoming self-aware involves having a strong desire for accurate self-knowledge and self-evaluation. The task of increasing the open self is predominantly concerned with making inroads into the hidden, the blind, and – to a lesser extent – the unknown self.

● The Hidden Self

The hidden self is the side of the self that is known to the self, and unknown to others. Everyone is entitled to, and has, a hidden self, where things about themselves are kept away from others. This is particularly true in the workplace, where certain personal and intimate details are rightly withheld. It is generally better for everyone if leaders, or other members of staff, do not bring 'the whole self' into work. On the other hand, it is not appropriate for leaders to have such a big hidden self that they bring little or none of themselves into work. It is often said, in relation to those with a very large hidden self, that they would not let the left hand know what the right hand is doing.

It is important for leaders to share a certain amount of themselves, as a degree of self-disclosure is an essential requirement for good relationships and trust. Self-disclosure is generally referred to in terms of a process of revealing aspects of the self to others. It is thought to be a desirable, healthy and beneficial exercise for those in leadership roles. For school leaders, self-disclosure does not mean bringing the 'whole self' in and sharing the minutiae of their private lives, their health and their relationships, with all and sundry. Those who do just that, risk creating a very uncomfortable environment for others. It is also often surmised and suspected about them, that if they are inclined to open up to that extent about those close to them, that they are not to be trusted to keep a confidence. 'Open books', who talk endlessly about everything, can also be naïve in not realising that they may be used, by their more cunning colleagues, as a source of information about others (Rosh & Offermann, 2013).

> " For school leaders, self-disclosure does not mean bringing the whole self in and sharing the minutiae of their private lives, their health and their relationships, with all and sundry. "

Notwithstanding these reservations, the appropriate disclosure of the self to others helps leaders to connect, and build rapport with those around them. Using examples from their own personal experiences to illustrate an approach, a practice, or indeed a flaw or failing, can be more supportive and empowering to staff members than merely telling them what to do, or what not to do. Being aware of the benefits of self-disclosure will help leaders to examine their own hidden self and adjust it to the level that is appropriate for healthy, open and trusting relationships.

● The Unknown Self

The unknown self is the side of the self that is unknown both to the self and to others. The advice, as I always understood it, was that the unknown self is best left alone, unless there is a requirement for psychoanalysis or some other probing mechanism. Recently, however, it has been suggested in a number of articles that within the unknown self there may be valuable information about previously undiscovered talents and proficiencies that could, and should, be unleashed. Good luck with that, one might say quite cynically – particularly in the context of how difficult it is for some to get in touch with the more accessible sides of the self.

● The Blind Self

In the context of the current discussion on self-awareness, the blind self is arguably the most important and relevant side of the self to understand, and to amend. The blind self is the side of the self that is unknown to the self, but known to others. Whereas people can be partially or totally unaware of the attributes or behaviours that characterise them, others can see them clearly. These characteristics can be positive or negative. Those with either low or inflated high self-esteem can fail to identify either good, or not so good, attributes or behaviours in themselves.

All leaders should consistently seek feedback from others on their strengths and areas in need of improvement, in order to become more self-aware. The feedback is generally ineffective unless it is truthful, and is not taken on board unless it is tactful, constructive and supportive.

A leader should never underestimate how big his/her blind self can be. Recently a colleague of mine was asked by the Board of Management in a school, to work with all the school staff, to try to facilitate a resolution of a breakdown in relations between the principal and the other staff members. As part of an agreed process, my colleague asked each of the staff members to identify the top five strengths that they perceived the principal to have and the top five areas in need of improvement. The principal was also asked to identify what he considered to be his top five strengths, and his areas in need of improvement. It is hardly surprising, given the levels of dissent in the school, that the lists did not tally. However, a strong indication of the size of the principal's blind self emerged through all five attributes, which he listed as strengths, being included on the lists of his areas in need of improvement, as provided by the staff.

In schools where relations are harmonious there will generally be more overlap resulting from this type of exercise. However, there are almost always surprises included, some containing positive affirmations, and some highlighting practices or behaviours that are deemed to warrant improvement. Seeking feedback in this form or another is always a worthwhile exercise for leaders. It takes courage, but it is the best means of seeing the self from the vantage point of others, and achieving greater congruence between the staff's evaluation of the leader, and the leader's self-evaluation. Ultimately it helps to reduce the size of the blind self.

Drucker (2005) suggested that most people think they know what they are good at, and that they are usually wrong. He makes a number of recommendations in relation to increasing the self-awareness of leaders. He suggested that, when a leader makes a decision, that, after a period, they should review the consequences and effects of their decision, to ascertain if the actual results tally with their expectations. In comparing the real-outcome with the ideal-outcome, they can identify what they have got right, and indeed what they have got wrong. It is one thing for a leader to recognise what they have done wrong. However, Drucker (2005), also stated that it is equally essential to work on remedying the bad habits that are unearthed in the real-self/ideal-self exercise as outlined above. A leader's self-awareness in relation to performance can also be improved by setting goals, and bench-marking progress to identify obstacles. A review and reassessment by the leader, of the approach and behaviours that they are presently using, can lead to positive change and improvements. However, no one can amend their ways without the self-awareness required to see what needs to be amended. Through self-awareness, one comes to really understand one's strengths, weaknesses, and values in the multi-faced and multi-facetted self (Gardner et al., 2005).

B. 7.2 Becoming Emotionally Self-Aware

Once leaders begin to get to know themselves better by:

- seeking out and taking cognisance of the feedback and appraisal of others;
- reducing the gaps between how they see themselves and how others see them;
- identifying their positive and negative attributes,

they can then begin to get to know their emotional selves also.

The literature on EI refers to emotional self-awareness as the ability to recognise emotions as they occur, and to differentiate between them. It also refers to the ability to understand what has caused the emotions, and to be aware of why, how and to what extent they impact on one's moods and behaviours, and on one's relationships with others. There are occasions when school leaders feel the need to fake emotions.

For example, if something is said at a staff meeting that causes them to feel hurt or upset, they may ignore how they feel and pretend to be fine. Impression management is often the motivation for this practice, where the leader does not want to give the impression of weakness. Those who are emotionally self-aware tend to be more authentic. They manage to keep inconsistencies between felt and expressed emotions to a minimum. They

> **Being aware that the process of changing established behavioural responses is a very slow, rigorous, and onerous one, can help leaders to persevere in finding more creative responses.**

find ways to share their feelings appropriately, rather than displaying insincere ones, a practice which is generally spotted by others.

That practice may sound very challenging for any leader, and indeed it can be. However, it is virtually impossible for those who know very little about themselves, or those whose view of themselves is very far removed from the reality of who they are. A focus on general self-awareness would appear to be a prerequisite for the difficult task of getting in touch with the emotional aspects of one's self.

As various situations and interactions take place during the day, school leaders should try to notice and register how they feel and how they behave.

For example, in a hypotetical situation where a number of teachers, for the fourth day in a row, remain in the staff-room ten minutes after the coffee break, it is helpful for school leaders to reflect on how they would feel about that and what they would say or do in that situation. Examining the link between the feeling and the action, and determaining if something different and more effective could be said or done, creates an awareness in relation to how the impact of emotions on behaviours can be managed and controlled.

In another hypothetical situation, a teacher comes into your office on the morning that she is returning to work after a number of days off sick. She is very appreciative and thanks you for your supportive tone when she initially called to say that she would not be in. Reflecting on how you would feel in the face of the appreciative comments, and how that feeling might impact positively on future similar situations, is another emotional awareness strategy.

Learning how emotions impact on your behaviours, and how you need to modify some behaviours and enhance others, is a central element of emotional awareness. However, when leaders are in stressful situations and, despite their best efforts to respond effectively, they frequently revert to old habits of behaviour. Being aware that the process of changing established behavioural responses is a very slow, rigorous, and onerous one, can help leaders to persevere in finding more creative responses. Boyatzis and Van Oosten (2002) suggested that in order to integrate new responses into our repertoire of behaviours, we need to first identify what they are, and then make a conscious and sustained effort to use them.

Noticing when you become angry or upset, and monitoring the length of time that you hold onto those feelings, provides important information for helping the process of letting negative emotions go. Also, noticing when you feel happy, and monitoring the length of time that you remain happy, is the type of insight needed to help in holding on to positive emotions. Awareness in relation to our potential to manage and control emotions is particularly beneficial in the context of a tendency, on the part of most people, to hold onto negative emotions and let go of positive ones. 'My colleague was exceedingly rude to me at the staff meeting last month, and I'm still very annoyed about it', is an example of the holding on. And, 'I looked out the window just now, and was happy to see the sun shining brightly. However, I'm not getting my hopes up, as, it will surely be raining in an hour', is an example of letting go. Being emotionally aware will help to reverse the above responses, and facilitate the letting go of the negative and the holding on to the positive.

Emotionally aware leaders are in touch with their inner feelings, and with the effects that they have on themselves and on others. This awareness is a fundamental element of emotional intelligence, on which all other elements are dependent.

Key Points

- Becoming self-aware is a prerequisite for developing emotional intelligence.

- Self-awareness involves having an accurate picture of yourself, and seeing yourself as others see you (more or less).

- The Johari Window, which represents the four sides of a person, provides a useful means of becoming self- aware.

- The blind-self is the side of yourself that others see, but that you do not see. Minimising the blind-self facilitates self-awareness.

- Observing yourself, and seeking feedback from others, helps the process of becoming self-aware.

- Emotional self-awareness is also essential element of Emotional Intelligence.

B. 7. 3 Self-Management for Leaders

Self-management as the second dimension of emotional intelligence involves the appropriate expression and regulation of emotions and moods.

Leaders who regularly express positive emotions are much better regarded and liked than those who regularly display negative ones. Positive emotions in leaders are associated with many positive outcomes, such as high performance, levels of enthusiasm, and reduced stress among staff. On the contrary, negative emotions in leaders are associated with negative outcomes, such as anxiety, fear, missed opportunities and underachieving staff. That is not to say that the emotionally intelligent school leader will always be in a good mood. That would be impossible, especially when one considers the pressures that school leaders are exposed to on a daily basis. Berkovich and Eyal (2015), in their review of empirical evidence in relation to educational leaders and emotions, alluded to those pressures in terms of causing leaders to experience negative emotions such as fear, anger and emotional stress.

They referred to the changing dimensions of the role of educational leader, and the excessive pressure to perform, combined with the perceived lower levels of autonomy and support. They also attributed their negative emotions to the sense of isolation felt by school leaders, and cited the external demands of parents and the internal disagreements with staff, as causes of negative emotions also. Workload and long hours are also alluded to as contributing factors, as were resistance to change and improvements, students' misbehaviour, and underperforming teachers. With all that to contend with, it would appear that reasons to be cheerful are minimal. However, there are a number of mitigating factors worth considering here.

Firstly, those who are appointed as school leaders are expected to bring competencies with them to match the challenges of the role. Their emotional competencies are pivotal to managing those challenges.

Secondly, because of the contagion of positive and negative emotions and moods, they have a responsibility to maximise positive emotions and minimise negative ones. Maximising positive emotions and moods does not mean that school leaders are constantly chirpy and happy. However, they do need to be aware of the many beneficial outcomes associated with their positive moods, and to consciously make efforts to up-regulate and savour them where possible. Up-regulation involves attending to, enhancing and prolonging the positive emotion, in order to maximise its effects (Bryant et al., 2011). The most effective leaders display moods and behaviours that are generally optimistic and good humoured. They are also sensitive to the moods and behaviours of those they work with, and are measured in relation to not overdoing the positivity in the face of those who are feeling low, or are down in the dumps.

> **"**
>
> **The most effective leaders display moods and behaviours that are generally optimistic and good humoured. They are also sensitive to the moods and behaviours of those they work with, and are measured in relation to not overdoing the positivity in the face of those who are feeling low, or are down in the dumps.**
>
> **"**

On the other hand, minimising negative emotions does not mean that they will not occur, but rather that when they do, they are either expressed appropriately when necessary, regulated, or simply let go.

● Appropriate Expression of Negative Emotions

Telling others that you are angry or upset can be very difficult for a school leader, especially in the context of the expectations that leaders appear rational, even when they are feeling emotional. As Crawford (2007) suggested the tensions between being professional and being able to show that you are human can be very difficult. It often results in school leaders feeling that it is neither acceptable, nor safe, to display their real emotions. This can result in what O'Connor, (2006, p. 47), called the "façade of superficiality", which leaders display, "while keeping the real self well hidden" from others. This façade can involve hiding negative emotions, and stating that everything is okay, and that they are fine. It can further involve them faking being upbeat and happy, when they are far from it. This is called emotional labour, and is much more prevalent than we might think among school leaders. According to Lazanyi (2009), the genuine emotions of leaders are, more often than not, different from those they display. "Emotional labour is experienced most strongly when individuals express emotions that clash with their inner feelings" (Brennan & Mac Ruairc, 2011, p. 136).

Emotional labour is a common phenomenon among service providers, such as airline staff or shop assistants. They are expected to keep the sunny side out, irrespective of how they feel. While faking or pretending always takes a toll on people, it is not particularly impactful if the relationships with those they are dealing with are temporary and transient. However because of the centrality of the relationships between school leaders and others in the school, emotional labour, (faking), on a grand scale is inappropriate, and is seen as insincere and inauthentic. It also causes emotional exhaustion, and eventual burn-out, to the leaders who feel the need to constantly keep it up.

A balance between presenting a public face, and being able to let those you work with know how you feel, demonstrates emotional intelligence and maturity. In other words emotional intelligence is not about emoting all over the place, as its detractors would like to portray it. It is the judicious and appropriate expression of emotions to others, in order to enhance and strengthen working relationships with them.

● Regulation of Negative Emotions

Every situation and event, both positive and negative, has an emotional reaction. Those with an interpersonal dimension cause the most intense reactions. Reactions are involuntary, and feed into how we respond to the contributing situation. Contrary to what those who lack emotional awareness generally believe, we can override our immediate and instinctive 'action tendencies', and input positively into our behavioural responses.

Considering the number of situations and events that a school leader encounters in the course of every school day, one can begin to understand how central and important the role of managing and regulating emotions is to their leadership. It is also worth reiterating the associated health-related benefits. For example, the ability to regulate emotions contingently and flexibly has been widely associated with indices of mental well-being and psychological resilience. (Cote et al., 2010; Gross, 2007)

The emotional response to an event or a situation is determined by the appraisal of the situation, rather than by the situation itself.

For example, a school leader comes into the staffroom to make an important announcement. Just as he/she begins to speak a staff member takes up the newspaper, and proceeds to read it. The school leader can immediately feel annoyed and angry. However, it is the interpretation of the action of the staff member that determines how angry the leader gets, and how she/he responds to that action. If the action is interpreted by the leader as a threat to his/her authority, or as a deliberate attempt to embarrass, undermine or discredit him/her, the anger and annoyance will be exacerbated, and will be reflected in the response.

The following are two of the most common responses to this negative interpretation, neither of which is appropriate or effective. The school leader may express his/her anger in an unrestrained manner, through what is commonly known as venting. Venting was often thought to be a cathartic and good way to let another person know, in no uncertain terms, what you think about their action. However, a great deal of research demonstrates that venting prolongs, rather than reduces, negative emotions (Tice & Bratslavsky, 2000). For example, if the principal explodes in anger, the other person will likely respond angrily, thereby escalating the angry exchanges. Also, when people are venting, they are making their points by continuously feeding into their anger and what is causing it. This is very unlikely to allow them to regulate or reduce the negative emotion. Furthermore, venting by a principal is considered by onlookers to be embarrassing and inappropriate, and it takes a long time for the episode to be forgotten.

The second of the two inappropriate responses involves the school leader feeling angry at the staff member who is reading the paper, but ignoring the action, and pretending not to be affected. The denial of feelings, and the inability to express them, does not reduce them, but rather contributes to a 'bottling up' of those feelings. Unexpressed and 'bottled up' emotions can have adverse short and long term effects. They can tax the body over time, and can result in physical illness including higher blood pressure and cancer (Grandey, 2000). Quite apart from those serious health considerations, 'bottled up' emotions often result in retaliatory action being taken against the person perceived to have caused the negative emotions. Leaders who ignore negative emotions, and who pretend not to be affected by negative actions, even when it is obvious that they are, disappoint and disillusion other staff members, and are judged by them to be weak and ineffective in their leadership.

The first and most important step in regulating emotions is the ability to alter our appraisal of events and situations. How we think about situations determines how we feel about them. Humans regularly use thoughts to alter their emotions (Hartley & Phelps, 2010). There are many methods of reappraising situations, including taking a more benign view of what has happened, changing the significance of the situation, and/or altering how we engage with it. By manipulating the appraisal process, one can alter the emotional response (Hartley & Phelps, 2010).

In the scenario of the school principal who felt angry at the staff member, for reading the paper as he/she was making an important announcement, a benign appraisal of the situation would be enabled by not taking the action personally, and by not attributing intentionality to it. The significance of the negative action might also be ameliorated by focusing on those who are listening, and by a realisation that, whether the errant staff member is reading or not, the follow up action will have to be taken by all the staff members. Engaging with what has just happened might involve a simple but assertive reminder that the message requires the attention of all staff members. If that intervention is not heeded, a firm but polite request for the staff member to cease reading the paper until the details of the announcement are outlined could prove effective.

> **Even the occasional rant or loss of temper can cause long lasting damage to the reputation of, and regard for, the leader.**

In the face of the impulsive reactions that people generally have to negative emotions, such as anger, the above reappraisal strategies will appear difficult, if not impossible. However, the essential nature of regulation of emotions involves overriding one's impulses with alternative strategies. These new strategies need to be repeatedly practiced in order for them to become habitual, and easier to enact over time (Hartley & Phelps, 2010). They are particularly important for school leaders whose anger reactions tend to be volatile and unpredictable. Even the occasional rant or loss of temper can cause long-lasting damage to the reputation of, and regard for, the leader. I have heard it said about some school leaders that they are great at their jobs, but you wouldn't want to cross them. This is a contradiction in terms, as it almost excuses the potential for explosion, in the context of the otherwise good leadership. It is also an inaccurate reflection of what most people, who work with this type of leader, really think about their leadership. More frequently, staff members are constantly vigilant around the unpredictable and inconsistent leader. The hyper-vigilance affects the quality of their work environment, as there is always an air of worry, fear and anxiety prevailing.

Regulating emotions is also vital for the school leader who holds onto bad moods and resentment for long periods. These tendencies do not go unnoticed by staff and students.

Apart from the aforementioned reappraising and reframing of a situation to place it in a better and more manageable light, there are other helpful suggestions for the regulation of emotions and moods.

> **Leaders who bring negative emotions home with them, to engage in what Scott (2009) called "the emotional wake", find no respite, and also have little or no boundary between their personal and professional lives.**

Attentional Deployment is a good strategy for improving moods, and involves distracting attention away from the negative elements of the difficult situation, or even moving away from the situation, altogether (Gross, 1998). It also involves making a concerted effort to focus instead on something that makes you happy, or something you really like to do. As it is our thinking that prolongs our emotions, it is very helpful to try to think good and happy thoughts by way of distraction.

This is especially powerful to prevent and minimise the rumination that most people engage in after a particularly difficult interpersonal situation, where they obsess about the incident, and where details of what happened are replayed in the mind over and over again, thereby prolonging the adverse effects. Leaders who bring negative emotions home with them, to engage in what Scott (2009) called "the emotional wake", find no respite, and also have little or no boundary between their personal and professional lives.

A principal teacher in a large second level school related to me that for years he had been bringing the residue of difficult situations home with him, on an almost daily basis, and allowing it to adversely affect his mood and his relationship with his family. He genuinely believed that this process was an inevitable consequence of the job, and was outside his control. Having latterly discovered his power in relation to managing emotions and having learned and practiced the associated regulation skills, he now no longer allows "negative emotions to lodge, rent free, in his head."

There are, of course, many times during the course of the working day, when leaders do not have the luxury of being able to put negative emotions to one side. Often they have to engage proactively with them, and with the situation that caused them. In these circumstances, it is always helpful to have a trusted other to share your emotions with. This is a good way to help regulate them – as the mantra says, a trouble shared is a trouble halved. It can also provide another perspective on the situation, help to focus on a more positive interpretation, and assist in finding an appropriate response. Regulation of emotions and moods is only possible in the context of:

- being able to first identify them;
- appreciating the benefits of regulating them;
- understanding what regulation entails;
- practicing a variety of regulation strategies;
- monitoring how you are doing.

The attention that school leaders pay to regulating emotions and moods, and the standards they set themselves in terms of the expression and regulation of both their own and others emotions and moods, is reflective of their levels of emotional intelligence.

Reflective Questions:

- When you feel angry or upset, what do you do to regulate those feelings?
- How often do you tell others when you are feeling angry or upset?

● Letting go of Negative Emotions

Thankfully, most school leaders, whether they are emotionally aware or not, keep the excesses of their negative emotions in check. Intuitively, or of necessity, they, generally refrain from 'blowing their tops' when angry and screaming or ranting. They also, by and large, either through faking, suppressing or regulating, keep their bad moods to a minimum. Unfortunately, there are some exceptions. These school leaders have, what is euphemistically called, 'anger management issues'. In other words, they just let fly when they are angry. They generally justify the outbursts through feeling provoked, and through blaming someone else. They don't appear to have any awareness of the need for them to control their anger.

There are others who seem to be always on their marks for the next bout of moodiness. Even the most innocuous remark can push them into a sulk, Everyone knows something is wrong with them, but they steadfastly refuse to enlighten others. Instead, those around them are forced to guess. Sulking and huffing is considered to be one of the most ineffective means of communicating. It involves the suspension of verbal communication, and it is deeply frustrating and confusing for those on the receiving end of this treatment. They know the person is upset or annoyed with them, they don't know why and they feel helpless and powerless in terms of resolving the situation. Tice and Baumeister (1993), suggested that many of those who adopt these tactics seem to get some kind of perverse pleasure out of "wallowing in their negative moods and in indulging themselves by acting cranky, depressed, irritable, and so forth" (Tice & Baumeister, 1993, cited in Tice and Bratslavsky, 2000, p. 156).

Whatever about that rather harsh analysis and notwithstanding the fact that we all know people who do exactly that, those who are persistently moody are demonstrating emotional immaturity at best, and emotional ignorance at worst. They usually take comments and incidents far too personally, and they generally take themselves far too seriously also. They need to be made aware of the inappropriateness of their emotional reactions, and of the impact they have on those around them. They also need to be made aware of their responsibilities in relation to building and maintaining positive relationships in their school, rather than disrupting and destroying those relationships.

I have worked with a number of leaders who have been made aware of the need to amend their tendency to engage in angry outbursts, or their propensity to sulk and hold grudges for long periods. Most of them claim that they cannot control their impulses. However, they must be made aware of their own input into the negative emotional reactions that they display. Reminding leaders that an emotion only lasts for a very short time, as little as six seconds, and that they can then decide what to do with it, is a helpful first step. Making them aware, that they have a choice – whether to hold on to their emotions, regurgitate them, and allow them to feed into their moods and behaviours, or to simply let them go – is quite a revelation to some. Belief in this ability, and practice, improves this amazing skill which, if the feedback is anything to go by, is both effective and liberating.

Key Points

- The pressures that school leaders are under contribute to myriad negative emotions.

- All school leaders experience negative emotions. Emotional competencies enable them to express those emotions appropriately, regulate them, and minimise their effects on themselves and others.

- Emotional labour, which involves hiding emotions by faking or pretending, is prevalent among school leaders.

- Emotional labour can have serious implications for leaders in terms of how they are perceived by others, and in terms of emotional exhaustion and burnout.

- Altering appraisals of difficult situations helps leaders to regulate their emotions, and respond appropriately.

- School leaders who are moody, who take things personally and who are very easily offended, frequently hold onto negative emotions, and behave in a negative way.

- Letting go of negative emotions is easier said than done. When achieved, it prevents rumination and stress, and provides a sense of liberation.

B. 7.4 Social Awareness and Relationship Management for Leaders

The third and fourth dimensions of emotional intelligence are the interpersonal elements of social awareness and relationship management, which are often referred to as social intelligence. Whatever banner they are considered under, they are both absolutely essential for leaders, and involve:

- sensing and being sensitive to the feelings, needs and concerns of others;

- acting in ways that maximise the positive emotions and moods of their staff;

- helping and supporting staff in regulating negative emotions when they occur.

Sensing and Being Sensitive to the Feelings, Needs and Concerns of Others

As far back as 1920, and long before the acknowledgement of emotional intelligence, Thorndyke referred to social intelligence as the ability to act wisely in human relations. That definition still resonates, and is something that every leader should aspire to in terms of building positive relations with those they work with. What better way to do this than to be able to sense and be sensitive to the feelings, needs and concerns of others. Those who have the ability to understand and respond appropriately to others are commonly referred to as having social awareness. They generally:

- get on well with others;

- make others feel the better for an encounter or interaction with them;

- demonstrate tact, fairness, care and compassion.

Those who lack social awareness frequently put their foot in it, say the wrong and unhelpful thing, and leave others feeling the worse for an encounter with them.

Social awareness is particularly important when a school leader is faced with a staff member who is angry or upset. Thinking about the range of possible responses under the apathy, sympathy or empathy headings gives an indication of which ones constitute acting wisely, and which ones constitute putting your foot in it.

Apathy is often associated with a 'couldn't care less', 'talk to the hand', or, 'tell someone who cares' attitude. However, even in its more innocuous forms, apathy demonstrates a lack of interest in, or concern about, the feelings and needs of others. An apathetic response to the staff member who is upset might include comments such as: 'Pull yourself together'; 'Don't be silly.... she would never do that'; 'You're too sensitive altogether'; or, 'You're making a spectacle of yourself'. All of the above are condescending, and disregard and dismiss the concerns of the other person. They are neither tactful nor helpful, and they do absolutely nothing to give the other person the impression that the leader cares a whit for them.

Sympathy is defined as feelings of pity or sorrow for someone else's difficulties or misfortunes. A sympathetic response to the staff member might include comments such as, 'Oh you poor thing', 'That's just terrible', or, 'No wonder you're so angry'. Many leaders think that these types of comments constitute helpful and supportive responses. However, they often have the opposite effect. They can give the impression to the other person that the problem is even worse than they previously thought, and can be disempowering and unhelpful.

Being aware of and understanding another person's emotions is generally referred to as having empathy. Empathy, a contributor to emotional intelligence, enables the leader to put themselves in the shoes of others, in terms of understanding how they are feeling and what their needs are, rather than doing the walking for them. Having an empathic insight involves seeing things from the other person's perspective, and genuinely relating to their feelings and needs. This gives the leader a much better idea of what to say and do, in order to help the other person.

An empathic response to the angry or upset staff member might involve acknowledging how they are feeling, inviting them to talk about what has angered or upset them, and working with them to find out what can be done to alleviate the negative feelings. Using phrases such as, 'I can see you are very upset', 'I am free now, if you would like to talk about what is bothering you?', 'How can I help?', and, 'I'm sure we can find a solution', all give the other person a sense of connectedness so that they feel listened to and cared for. A show of empathy is always empowering to the other person. The leader does not have to come up with the solution. They merely have to demonstrate to the other person that they are on their wavelength, and are prepared to work with them to find one. Empathic leaders generally do not put their foot in it. It is much more likely that they will leave the other person feeling the better for the interaction with them.

> **The leader does not have to come up with the solution. They merely have to demonstrate to the other person that they are on their wavelength, and are prepared to work with them to find one.**

Reflective Questions:

- Can you think an example of when you gave an empathic response to an angry outburst by a colleague?
- What was the response of the colleague?

- Can you think of an example of when you put your foot in it when dealing with a colleague who was very upset?

- What was the response of the colleague?

Acting in Ways that Maximise the Positive Emotions and Moods of Staff

In all schools, it is the leader who has the most power to influence the emotions of others, and to establish the prevailing emotional climate of the school. The optimal emotional climate is one where the positive emotional experiences outweigh the negative ones. According to Fredrickson's (2001) 'broaden and build' theory, positive emotions broaden people's ways of thinking and behaving and, over time, build their enduring personal and social resources. High rates of positive to negative emotions are associated with the ability to 'flourish' – in other words, to live optimally and enjoy the good things of life. In all dimensions of our lives including work, positive to negative emotion ratios of greater than 3:1 are considered to be indicators of well-being (Frederickson & Losada, 2005). The accumulative positive emotions of the leader and the staff contribute to a climate of positive emotions in the school and "encourage empathy, sensitivity and care" (Arnaud & Sekerka, 2010).

There are many leaders who retain the belief that actively managing the moods and emotions of their staff is outside the remit of their role. While some leaders regard it as irrelevant and even unprofessional, the majority feel totally ill-equipped to undertake such a task (Barsade & O'Neill, 2016). Without a full understanding of the influence of emotions on personal and organisational outcomes in the school, it is difficult to see how those attitudes can be addressed and changed. The link between positive emotions and individual well-being is generally acknowledged, however, the extent of the impact on individual and organisational performance is far from fully appreciated. Staw et al., (1994) alluded to the link between positive emotions and increased task activity and perseverance. In terms of the latter, those experiencing positive emotions and moods have increased power to persevere even under difficult circumstances, such as problems with students and colleagues. They generally take an optimistic view of their ability to influence the outcomes of problems. They also have higher expectations and anticipation of success in resolving problems (Staw et al., 1994). With reference to the 'happier and smarter' studies, Staw et al., (1994) also reported that positive emotions and moods are indicators of efficiency, creativity, better decision making and more accurate information processing. What leader would not want to stimulate such valuable qualities in his/her team?

Most leaders are insufficiently aware of how much influence they exert over the quality of the emotional climate in their schools. They are responsible for some of the most important and frequent determinants of the emotions experienced by their staff (Kaplan et al., 2014). Therefore it is imperative that they consider the task of inducing positive emotions as an essential element of their job, and

> **"**
>
> Whereas there are a number of key behaviours that leaders should engage in to maximise positive emotions, exhibiting caring, calm and considerate behaviour in everyday interactions makes a big difference to how staff feel.
>
> **"**

prioritise it at every opportunity. Kaplan et al., (2014) drew on the research of a large number of authors to highlight the key practices and attributes necessary for leaders to positively impact on the emotions and moods of others. Whereas there are a number of key behaviours that leaders should engage in to maximise positive emotions, exhibiting caring, calm and considerate behaviour in everyday interactions makes a big difference to how staff members feel. When there is an informal environment in the school, in which leaders use humour and fun, it can really lift the mood of everyone. Regular small acts of kindness do not go unnoticed, and are appreciated and enjoyed. Kaplan et al., (2014) stated that seemingly small mood inducements, in the aggregate, affect employee well-being, emotional climate and group productivity.

Considering the established linkages between positive emotion and performance, it is hardly surprising that the provision of praise and recognition is among the most powerful instigators of positive emotions. When provided consistently and genuinely, the benefits are more fully realised. Support and solidarity are also shown to be among the most common sources of positive emotions. As previously stated, supportive behaviour empowers people to do their jobs well, and assists and supports them when things go wrong. This does not mean that leaders will always support the actions of their staff unconditionally, but, rather, that they will always behave in a respectful, supportive and fair way towards them. Staff members also feel supported when leaders are aware of, and responsive to, any negative emotional reaction that is generated, as a result of something they have said or done. When leaders take the opportunity to explain what they meant, rephrase the message, point out that the impact was unintentional, and apologise as appropriate, the negative emotions can be ameliorated. Kador (2009) alluded to the courage needed to apologise, but stated that when offered it is an indication of the value one places on the relationship with the other person. An apology increases positive emotions and decreases negative emotions in those who have been transgressed against or offended (Lazare, 2004). There are very few things in life that are more powerful than an apology. For some people of course, there are very few things in life that are more difficult to do than to apologise.

Open communication and the provision of adequate information are also alluded to as enhancing positive emotions. Particularly in times of uncertainty and change, members of staff need to be fully informed. Doing this demonstrates respect and consideration for them and helps them to prepare for, and adjust to, what the future may hold.

Maximising positive emotions in staff members has many benefits. The advantages that accrue to working with those who bring a positive attitude into the school are obvious. Their positivity is contagious, they are easy to work with, are generally liked, and are more helpful and supportive to others (Staw et al., 1994). Resourced by positive emotions, staff members are more likely to engage constructively with colleagues and build trust between them. They are also much more likely to rebound from the problems and difficulties that are part and parcel of school life. Frederickson, (2003) hit the nail on the head when she suggested that positive emotions help people to survive and thrive.

Every school leader will spend an inordinate amount of time counteracting the effects of negative emotions and moods, and it would be a terrible shame if they did not realise and utilise the enormous power that they have to cultivate and maximise the positive ones.

● Helping Others to Regulate their Emotions

It is difficult to conceptualise the complexities of the relationships, and the multi dimensions of teaching and managing in schools, without considering the influence of emotions. Managing both individual and group emotions is one of the main ways that leaders influence performance (Humphrey, 2002). They also have an important role in helping staff to contain and regulate their negative moods.

For example, if a teacher consistently displays negative moods, is critical of everything, and upsets both colleagues and students, it is the business of the school leader to let him/her know that the negativity is unacceptable. It is also important to point out how it is impacting on others. The school leader may be tempted to tell the teacher to snap out of it. This approach, while understandable, is rarely helpful, because it fails to deal with the underlying cause of the negative moods. The teacher will likely feel totally unsupported, and the bad moods will more than likely continue and worsen. An emotionally intelligent leader will be aware that negative emotions and moods never occur in a vacuum but are generally fuelled by underlying problems.

The cause of the problems may or may not be school-related. However, by engaging with staff to find and deal with underlying causes, they are more likely to feel supported rather than criticised. When staff members' expectations are met in relation to feeling supported, they are much more inclined to:

- take a more benign view of the underlying problem;
- see their own coping potential;
- engage with the leader to find a solution;
- understand, the leader's imperative to contain negative moods.

These suggestions do not provide a panacea for addressing the negative emotions and moods of staff. They do, at the very minimum, provide some insight into the complexities of dealing with them. While the school leader does have a major role in keeping the emotions and moods of the staff members in check, they must not stifle all expression of negative emotions. If they do, they miss the opportunity that appropriately expressed negative emotions provide, for bringing attention to, and airing, underlying school problems.

Key Points

- Social awareness and relationship management skills, as elements of emotional intelligence, are essential for school leaders.

- Leaders who lack social awareness find it difficult to read and respond to situations.

- A positive emotional climate in a school is one where positive emotions outweigh negative ones. School leaders play a significant role in the creation of a positive emotional climate.

- The effective management by leaders of the individual and group emotions in a school impacts positively on the quality of relationships and on performance.

B. 8. Conclusion

Schools are complex organisations, and emotions are integral to every aspect of school life, including the processes of teaching and learning, the various relationships and the many aspects of management. The job of the school leader is multi-dimensional, time-consuming, and sometimes overwhelming. It is above all else an emotionally demanding role, that leaves very little time to concentrate on personal fulfilment and well-being (Sackney et al., 2000). Because of these constraints and pressures, and because of the desire, on the part of the vast majority of school leaders, to do a good job, they need every bit of help that they can get. Developing emotional intelligence and becoming adept at managing their own and others' emotions, is guaranteed to make the leader's role more manageable, and to reduce the stresses that are associated with it. Emotional intelligence, and the associated competencies, can be acquired by everyone. Small wins that result from, for example:

- letting a negative emotion go, and holding on to a positive one;

- breaking an old habit of how you would normally react or behave in emotional situations;

- understanding the emotions of others, and showing empathy to them,

can encourage a leader to explore the further possibilities that emotional intelligence and competence can provide for the quality of their leadership. As Crawford (2009) suggested, it is within the emotional context that all the other aspects of leadership and management take place.

Section C

Conflict in Schools

C. 1. Introduction

When conducting professional development courses in schools, I regularly provide staff members with a simple work-environment survey, designed to gain their perceptions on the strengths and areas in need of improvement in their schools. The survey lists ten characteristics of a positive/effective school environment, and asks for a score from 1-10 on each of the elements. With very few exceptions, staff members have consistently provided a low rating, to "discussion and resolution of conflict". They have also consistently cited "discussion and resolution of conflict" as the characteristic most in need of improvement in their schools.

In my work with principals and deputy principals, they repeatedly cite dealing with conflict, particularly interpersonal conflict, as their most difficult and challenging task. The types of conflicts that appear to cause most of the problems in schools emanate from differences or disagreements that are not appropriately aired or properly discussed, and that consequently lead to resentment and hostility. How seriously one perceives the difference or disagreement to be, and how they are responded to, determines the levels and extent of the ensuing resentment and hostility.

> **Toxic and unresolved conflict is one of the biggest causes of trouble and strife in a school.**

One stray and thoughtless comment made in the staffroom can be interpreted by the recipient as being insulting or demeaning, and can, in the absence of discussion and clarification of the issue, result in an escalating conflict. Relationships between the two colleagues can deteriorate, or even disintegrate. Verbal communication is often suspended between those involved, and tension is felt by all who work with them. The general atmosphere becomes increasingly tense, and frequently neither the principal, nor anyone else raises or addresses the issue.

Toxic and unresolved conflict is one of the biggest causes of trouble and strife in a school. These types of conflict cause stress and distress, which is contagious and spreads, eventually affecting everyone in the school. The morale and motivation of the staff are adversely affected. Standards of effectiveness and productivity are lowered, and relationships become increasingly dysfunctional and hostile. School principals spend an inordinate amount of time dealing with the fallout from negative conflicts. Yet, in the majority of cases – and often by their own admission – they find it exceedingly difficult, if not impossible, to understand, manage or resolve these divisive, and often utterly destructive, conflicts.

C. 2. Understanding Conflict

It is true that the vast majority of people do not like conflict. When conflicts do arise, most people immediately feel stressed and uncomfortable. However, because of the myriad potential negative consequences of unresolved disputes in schools, there is an onus on school leaders to endeavour to understand the various dimensions and effects of conflict, and to learn to deal with and manage conflicts when they occur.

C. 2.1 Causes of Conflict

There are numerous causes of conflicts in schools. Low-level conflict can arise from the interpersonal irritants – such as an unwashed cup being left in the staffroom sink, or someone eating the last biscuit. More serious conflict can result from events that have widespread implications, such as the imposition of major changes without adequate consultation or explanation.

When the everyday behaviour of a school leader or a staff member is negative and defensive it can cause on-going and recurring conflicts. Frustration and annoyance can result, which can be manifested in either overt or covert reactions.

The lack of what is referred to as 'common courtesy' can be at the root of many conflicts in schools. This is characterised by a paucity of basic greetings, acknowledgements or recognition, such as: 'Good morning'; 'Please'; 'Thank you'; or, 'Well done'. Ill feeling and upset can be sparked by these oversights or slights, which if unattended can grow and worsen.

A perceived lack of sensitivity and consideration can also result in conflict. For example, if a school leader has extremely high expectations in relation to staff commitment and performance, without due regard for the impact on them or on their work/life balance, resentment can be deeply felt.

Any evidence of unfairness, or a perception of unfairness, can be a significant cause of conflict. When a member of staff fails to secure a promotion, despite meeting the required criteria, it can result in disappointment and disgruntlement. The absence of open, honest and detailed feedback and communication, in relation to all aspects of the selection process, is guaranteed to produce convictions of unfairness and injustice. The resulting conflict can be prolonged and bitter. Often, it is the successful candidate, and/or the person responsible for the selection decision, that can be targeted and ostracised.

Any show of favouritism on the part of the school leader is quickly spotted, and can result in negative behaviours such as back-biting, exclusion, withholding of effort and even sabotage. Whether or not the perceptions that there is an in-group and an out-group are based on reality, cliques can form, and cause both minor and major conflicts. Cliques are described as informal fraternities where the members agree with each other, irrespective of the rights or wrongs of the particular situations (Field, 1996; Everand & Morris, 1990). They usually contain a clique leader, and a group of 'yes people'. The clique leader generally makes the metaphorical snowballs, which other clique members throw, willy-nilly, to discommode and disrupt.

> "
> **Change blockers, who resist with dogmatic determination any encroachment into their work practices, can be the bane of an innovative school leader's life.**
> „

One principal described how the presence of a clique in his school made his life very difficult on a daily basis, through constant undermining of him, and his attempts to make changes and improvements. Resistance to change is a constant cause of conflict. Change blockers, who resist with dogmatic determination any encroachment into their work practices, can be the bane of an innovative school leader's life.

Unchallenged deficiencies in the performance of one or more colleagues, that impact on the team's overall efforts and achievements, can be deeply resented by those who are consistently dedicated and comitted. Deficiencies in performance specifically, and incompetence more generally, can cause destructive conflicts among staff members, and between the staff and the leader.

Any perception or evidence of dishonest or unethical practices carried out by a school leader can be the cause of serious conflict, particularly if individuals feel pressured to engage in behaviours that run contrary to their own personal values. When school admissions practices are ambiguous or dubious, some staff members are very uncomfortable with them. Where students are refused entry, ostensibly on ethos protection and maintenance grounds, but with undertones of religious, or racial discrimination, staff can be very disapproving, and can often feel compromised and overruled. Conflicts that arise in these situations can simmer away under the surface, and manifest in lowered morale, withholding of commitment, as well as strained and unhealthy relationships.

Academic 'cherry picking' is an unsavoury and unenlightened practice, which is relatively rare in schools. When it does occur, it usually emanates from schools with a highly competitive ethos, where there may be a hierarchy of regard for students, based, for example, on their academic success or their sporting prowess. Teachers and other educational professionals who value the more co-operative, inclusive and equitable systems are very disillusioned in overly competitive school environments. The differing attitudes can cause long-running conflicts in those schools. When the prevailing competitive focus wins out, disillusioned staff may feel compelled to disengage, or seek employment elsewhere.

Internal factors are the more usual causes of conflicts in schools. However, external factors can also play a significant role. Deterioration in pay, conditions, resources and a general feeling of not being appreciated, can cause deep frustration for school staff. Disagreements and disputes can occur among members of staff, as well as between staff and management.

Conflict is inevitable, particularly between those who are thrown together and who have to interact with and depend on each other. Understanding the causes of conflict in schools and discussing them openly can help leaders and staff to become aware of how their own behaviours can contribute to those conflicts. Becoming aware of the potential for escalation of even the most minor of conflicts may encourage early intervention to manage and diffuse them.

C. 2.2 Responses to Conflict

There are various ways that people respond and behave when in conflict. It is important to be aware of these differences, and the reasons for them, in order to better understand and manage conflict. Reactions to conflict are based on our own habitual conflict styles, which have been learned and practised, and have become the only way we know how to behave in a conflict situation. Thomas and Kilmann (1974) have written extensively on what they considered to be the five main conflicts responses. These are the avoiding, competing, accommodating, compromising and collaborating responses. They have discussed the five responses in terms of their functional and dysfunctional aspects, which demonstrate that all the styles have merit in particular circumstances, but only the collaborating style is consistently effective in workplace conflicts. An examination of these five styles, later in this section, will certainly shed light on one's prevailing conflict style.

From my experience of observing conflicts in schools, and from the many accounts of conflict that I have been made aware of, it appears to me that only a very small minority of those involved in conflict use a constructive, positive and effective response in dealing with it. Rather, the majority appear to get it wrong, by using what, in broad terms, would be deemed to be the 'fight or flight' response.

> "
>
> **Those with low self-esteem frequently employ passive, accommodating behaviours. They justify these behaviours to themselves by confusing their passivity with 'just being nice'. They are loath to offend, upset, or discommode others.**
>
> "

The fight response is generally associated with aggressive behaviours, and is characterised by a prolongation, an escalation, or a repetition of the conflict. The flight response, on the other hand, is generally associated with passive behaviours, through which conflicts are neither discussed nor dealt with, and are, to all intents and purposes, pushed under the carpet, where they fester, and result in simmering and on-going resentment.

In order for school leaders to have any hope of dealing effectively with, and managing, conflict in their schools, they need to have an appreciation of how they and others, respond to conflict, particularly interpersonal conflict.

● Role of Threats and Self-Esteem in Conflict Responses

People generally evaluate conflict based on how threatening they perceive it to be. Physical threats are thankfully rare in school staffrooms, although they can occasionally occur in conflicts between students, students and teachers, and between parents and teachers. Interpersonal conflicts are more generally associated with social self-threat – "threats to one's social value or standing" (Gruenewald et al., 2004, p. 915), or ego-threat – threats to one's personal ego or sense of self-importance, rather than the physical self. Perceived threats to the social-self are interpreted and responded to with various behaviours, primarily depending on the state and level of the self-esteem of those who feel threatened. Soloman et al., (1991) suggested that a great deal of our behaviour seems to be guided by the need to maintain and defend our self-esteem.

● Low Self-Esteem and Passive Behaviours in Conflict

Self-esteem is defined as "a person's appraisal of his or her value" (Leary & Baumister, 2000, p. 2), and those with low self-esteem have a low or poor appraisal of their own value and worth. In conflict situations, they often allow others to have their way at an unreasonable cost to themselves. Acceding to other's demands is often done to prevent themselves from being viewed as unreasonable or selfish. It is part of their effort to be accepted and liked. Those with low self-esteem frequently employ passive, accommodating behaviours. They justify these behaviours to themselves by confusing their passivity with 'just being nice'. They are loath to offend, or discommode others. Perceived threats to their social-self in conflict situations may stir up and reinforce previous negative evaluations that they have received from others (Soloman et al., 1991). The renowned sociologist Charles Horton Cooley, (1902) put forward the notion that our opinions of ourselves are hugely influenced by our interactions with others, and that to a large extent our assessments of our own value and worth are based on the judgements of others. Therefore, those with low self esteem are very concerned about social-evaluations, and they try to avoid negative reminders or reinforcements of their own low appraisal of their worth and value.

Social-evaluations and criticisms are part and parcel of conflict situations, and therefore it is highly probable that those with low self esteem will avoid the threats that conflicts present, either by ignoring or withdrawing from conflict, or by giving in to, and accommodating, the demands of others. The fundamental need to belong and the fear of having their "social exclusion activated" (Heatherton & Vohs, 2000, p.726), are also strong motivators to avoid interactions that are conflicted and that have a negative effect on them (Baumeister & Leary, 1995).

They are very reluctant to engage in conflict because of the "imminent danger of being rejected" (Heatherton & Vohs, 2000, p. 726). Instead, they prefer to keep the peace at all costs and engage, as a rule, in behaviours that are characterised by caution, restraint and malleability (Tice, 1993). In conflict, they unwittingly allow themselves to be taken advantage of. Consequently, they do not have their own needs met, and they feel a sense of frustration and injustice. Becoming aware of their own conflict style, the consequences of it, and the underlying contributing factors to it, can be the first step for them in improving their self-esteem, and responding more assertively in conflict situations.

School leaders need to ask themselves, 'Do I constantly try to avoid conflict or constantly give in to others in conflict situations?' If they do persistently engage in those passive responses, they need to be aware that they are often perceived as being weak and ineffective. Also, they do not have their own needs, or the needs of others who depend of them, met. Ultimately, this has a serious impact on the stress levels and general well-being of themselves, and of others.

● High Self-Esteem and Behaviours in Conflict

Many teachers work consistently to help and support students to enhance their self-esteem. Programmes designed to raise self-esteem are common in schools. High self-esteem is regarded as something that students are encouraged to aspire to. This is in the belief that high self-esteem generally refers to a favourable, yet realistic, view of their own value and worth. It also presumes that those with high self-esteem will also have a favourable, yet realistic, view of the value and worth of others. In transactional analysis terms, a theory which was developed by Dr Eric Berne in the 1950s, they would have an 'I'm ok, you're ok' perspective. In other words, whether they had anything in common with another person or whether they liked them or not, they would maintain a view that others had worth and value, just as they themselves had. Those possessing this type of genuine and healthy high self esteem are much more likely to behave assertively and reasonably in conflict.

● Unhealthy High Self-Esteem and Aggresive Behaviours

Most people regard high self-esteem as invariably positive and something for everyone to aspire to. This view has proven to be rather one-sided and limited,

> **“**
>
> **Viewing high self-esteem as an exclusively positive state, that is characterised by confidence, assuredness and empathy, appears to be somewhat misguided and ill-informed, particularly as it does not take account of its more negative connotations.**
>
> **”**

69

particularly in the context of how it has been critiqued and challenged over the past number of years. Whereas, in the minds of many, high self-esteem remains associated with a myriad of good and positive outcomes, the research evidence increasingly shows that it does not warrant the level of advocacy that it previously enjoyed. Viewing high self-esteem as an exclusively positive state, that is characterised by confidence, assuredness and empathy, appears to be somewhat misguided and ill-informed, particularly as it does not take account of its more negative connotations.

The down-side of high self-esteem is associated with superiority, conceitedness, grandiosity and narcissism (Baumeister et al., 1996). This negative side is also variously described as inflated, exaggerated, unrealistically positive and even malignant. For the purpose of understanding conflict and conflict responses, it can be stated, without much fear of contradiction, that those with inflated and unrealistic high self-esteem have a tendency to engage in aggressive and hostile behaviours in conflict situations.

They have a self-protective approach and are unwilling to tolerate any feedback or evaluation that fails to confirm their favourable self-regard (Baumeister et al., 1996).

At some level they really believe that they are superior to others, and that their views and perspectives are superior also. However, because their favourable self-appraisal is often very unstable, they can become very defensive and aggressive when they feel challenged. The person on the receiving end of their aggression may have done nothing more than disagree with them, or express a contrary point of view.

Those with inflated self-esteem are very difficult to deal with in conflict situations. However, understanding the vulnerabilities behind their behaviours may help leaders not to 'get hooked' on their aggression and respond in kind, but rather to diffuse the situation, and use more effective strategies to resolve the conflict. Remaining calm is the first and most effective response to aggression.

Key Points

- Unresolved conflicts cause multiple negative and on-going problems in schools.

- There are numerous causes of conflicts in schools, most of them are internal to the school, and are interpersonal.

- Generally those in conflict adopt either a 'fight or flight' approach, and do not respond constructively or effectively.

- Self-esteem has a major influence of how individuals respond to conflict.

C. 3. Behaviours, Emotions and Communication in Conflict

Having some understanding of what causes conflict and how those involved respond to conflict, facilitates an appreciation of the complexities of the conflict process. However, the process is significantly and further complicated by the dynamics of conflict which are determined by the behaviours and emotions exhibited by those involved. Unresolved conflicts put a severe strain on the communication between those directly involved and also among those witnessing the conflict.

C. 3.1 Behaviours in Conflict (Aggressive Behaviours)

When people are regularly aggressive and angry in conflict, one can be reasonably sure that their anger is not specifically related to the current conflict, or indeed to any one individual. Keeping this thought in mind can help a leader to remain composed when communicating with those who are aggressive. Encouraging the angry person to outline the specifics of their point of view is usually a good intervention. Allowing them to speak uninterrupted and listening for anything that sounds reasonable or rational, rather than focusing on their personal, negative or insulting comments is difficult but helpful in diffusing anger. Speaking slowly and quietly when discussing or clarifying the contentious issues raised, helps to prevent an escalation of the anger displayed.

Only after a more conciliatory tone is achieved should leaders find an opportunity for a private discussion with the aggressor, to communicate how they feel when they are subjected to angry outbursts. The 'I' rather than the 'You' statements give a better guarantee that the sentiments will be heard. 'I feel upset and annoyed when you shout at me, and it is very difficult to get issues resolved', is an example of an 'I' statement, and is much more effective than an alternative 'You' statement, an example being, 'You upset so many people in the staffroom today, and you made me so angry with your shouting and roaring', or, even worse, 'You really let yourself down today, and that is no way for a professional to be carrying on'. You may feel that those two 'You' statements are a more accurate reflection of how you feel, and of what actually happened. However, undoubtedly, if uttered, they will merely escalate the situation.

School leaders need to ask themselves, 'Do I become aggressive when challenged and do I react aggressively when someone is aggressive with me?' If the answer is yes, then they need to know that when they use aggressive behaviours in conflict, they are regarded as being totally insensitive to the needs and feelings of others. Although staff members feel frustrated and annoyed with aggressive leaders, they are very wary of them and rarely challenge them. They often fear and obey them, but they never respect them.

● Passive/Aggressive Behaviours in Conflict

The manifestations of both passive and aggressive behaviours in conflict are fairly easily identifiable as the 'flight or fight' response of withdrawal or domination, respectively. However, those who respond passively to conflict, in order not to draw criticism or disapproval on themselves and to avoid further arguments or conflict, often also engage in behaviours that include disengaging, pretending, and even lying. 'Whatever you all decide is ok with me', they may say when it is not. 'I'm fine with the smaller classroom', they may say when they are not. 'I wasn't paying attention to the various arguments', they may say when they were, and, 'I'm not bothered one way or the other', they may say when they are.

If these dishonest responses are accompanied by indirect hostility, such as back-biting, blaming and sulking, then they constitute passive/aggressive behaviours. These are dysfunctional behaviours in terms of dealing with conflict, and they are also disingenuous and disrespectful. Dealing with passive/aggressive behaviours can be frustrating and annoying, as they are usually insidious and difficult to decipher. Understanding the insecurity and low self esteem that underpin them may help to lessen the negative reactions to them, and encourage more positive and collaborative engagement with those who behave in this manner.

Those who openly use aggressive behaviours in conflict may also engage in the more subtle and indirect passive/aggressive behaviours. They may alternate aggression with appearing agreeable and friendly, in a Jekyll and Hyde fashion. The outward show of friendliness is often a false and insincere façade, which obscures and belies the undermining behaviours taking place behind the scenes.

A teacher related his experience of working with a colleague who is invariably aggressive in getting his point of view across. If he does not get his way, he leaves the room with an exasperated air about him. Later, he acts as if nothing had happened and according to his colleague is 'as sweet as pie'. However, there is always a sting in the tail. It invariably comes in the form of either passive resistance, where he remains totally silent and makes no contribution at departmental meetings. At other times, he reads the newspaper or texts persistently during staff meetings, or in-service courses. When asked a question by a visiting facilitator, he generally responds with a shrug of his shoulders, much to the embarrassment and discomfort of his colleagues and the school leaders. Sometimes his resistance is more obstructionist, when, for example, he gives last-minute notice of his intended absence from student supervision or other commitments, leaving others to shoulder the extra work or responsibilities. He has also boycotted social events and student outings without explanation, and despite having given a commitment to attend.

Passive/aggressive behaviours, in whatever form they take, are destructive and cause distress and dissent, as well as further escalating arguments and conflict.

Being aware of the myriad behaviours that are involved in conflict, and having some understanding of the underlying reasons for them serves to highlight the complexities of conflict, and also facilitates a realisation that in order to manage conflict, school leaders need to employ a range of specific and targeted responses, which will be outlined later in this section.

C. 3.2 Emotions in Conflict

The previous section of this book provided a comprehensive examination of the role that emotions and emotional intelligence play in schools. It may be difficult for the reader to understand the need for further discussion on the subject of emotions in this section. However, it would be impossible to explore the dynamics and management of conflict without reference to the emotional dimensions that permeate every aspect of a conflict situation. Runde and Flanagan (2012, p. 69), who have written widely on the subject of conflict-competence, suggested that "conflict is all about emotions." The problems that childhood conditioning, societal norms, organisational culture, and/or lack of emotional intelligence cause, in terms of ignoring, denying and dealing inappropriately with emotions, are considerably exacerbated when people are in conflict with others.

Those in conflict frequently experience an amalgam of emotions, such as fear, anger, frustration, discontent, upset, distress, disappointment, resignation and even hopelessness. However, the conflict dynamics make it much less likely that they will be able to:

- recognise and acknowledge these feelings in themselves or in others;
- express these feelings reasonably or honestly;
- deal rationally with the irrational expression of these emotions by others.

Some may disguise their emotions and keep them hidden and, although they may feel extremely angry or upset, they will not or cannot share these feelings. Suppression of emotions in conflict might be justified if it helped to regulate and manage them, but usually they merely fester and bubble away under the surface, leaking out bit by bit in the form of tense facial expressions and body language, that leaves no one in any doubt that something is wrong. The suppressor may protest that 'they are fine', and refuse to engage with others about how they really feel.

> **"**
> Their emotions can be 'filed and saved as', to be dealt with later, and usually through negative behaviours. Hurtful and cynical comments, that are often totally unrelated to the conflict, can be delivered, when least expected, and with the accuracy of scud missiles.
> **"**

Their emotions can be 'filed and saved as', to be dealt with later, and usually through negative behaviours. Hurtful and cynical comments, that are often totally unrelated to the conflict, can be delivered, when least expected, and with the accuracy of scud missiles. Staff can suspend verbal communication with others and may not speak to them for periods of weeks, months or even years. Suppressed and pent-up emotions can become wound up like a spring, only to snap, and explode in the form of angry or distressed outbursts.

On the other side of the coin, there are those who lose total control of their emotions at the first sign of disagreement and conflict, and who habitually explode in anger, indignation or distress. All manifestations of failure to recognise, manage and express emotions cause conflicts to continue, escalate, and remain unresolved.

Managing your own emotions, and those of others, in conflict situations is a key skill for leaders, and will be explored later in this section.

C. 3.3 Communication in Conflict

Faulty and dysfunctional communication, involving misinterpretation and misunderstanding, is characteristic of unmanaged and escalating conflict. Normal interactions can be flawed and faulty but when conflict occurs the communication problems seem to be exacerbated and worsen. In some schools, there is very little understanding of how to communicate in an inclusive, respectful and professional manner, but, whatever understanding there is, can become totally obscured by the incompatibilities and disagreements that are associated with conflict.

When in conflict, people have a very firm and fixed notion of what is right and fair. Unfortunately, their assessment of fairness is often skewed and distorted. If, what others say during a conflict confirms their beliefs of what is right and fair, then they usually interpret the messages accurately. However, when what others communicate refutes or disputes their own firmly-held views, it is often misinterpreted and dismissed. According to Thompson and Lowenstein (1992, p.

130), "individuals in a dispute may distort the facts of the case or the significance of those facts in a manner that favours their own positions." How often have you heard two people, who have just had an argument, separately recount what occurred? They invariably present two very differing accounts, and are absolutely convinced that their take on the argument is accurate and correct.

Communication in conflict is often tense and strained. It is very easy for people to completely misunderstand each other, and only hear what they want to hear or what they expect to hear. They jump to conclusions and react negatively to others based on those conclusions, especially when they perceive what has been said or done as a display of disregard for, and disrespect towards, them. When they attribute intentionality to those engaging in the behaviours, the negativity intensifies. People in conflict are, very often, wrongly convinced that the other person has set out to upset or hurt them.

Negative interpretations of the words, actions and omissions of others are often made as a result of cognitive distortions. These are biased and inaccurate ways of thinking. We all engage in cognitive distortions from time to time, when we view and judge what is said and done in ways that do not match the reality of the situation.

Some of the more common cognitive distortions in conflict situations include:

- Catastrophising, which involves making a negative and disastrous prediction of what will occur, and thinking that the very worst that could happen will happen or has happened;

- 'All or Nothing' thinking involves having a distinct, rigid and absolute black and white view of a situation, with no regard for, or consideration of, a grey area or a middle-ground explanation;

- Mind-Reading involves thinking with certainty that you know what others are thinking, without considering a range of options for what they might actually be thinking;

- Mental-Filtering involves selectively taking certain details out of context, while neglecting to look at the full picture, and focusing on the negatives while ignoring the positives;

- Personalising and Blaming involves assuming guilt for something that was outside your control, or, on the contrary, avoiding personal responsibility by attributing guilt to others, because someone always has to be blamed. (Burns, 1980; Beck, 1995)

Of course, one cannot rule out the possibility that, occasionally, negative interpretations are a reflection of the reality, of the intention or the behaviour of others. However, it is widely recognised that even when someone is convinced that his or her interpretation is correct, it is, in fact, very often distorted, exaggerated and frequently completely wrong.

Nevertheless, those in conflict ruminate on everything that has been said or implied, and they replay it over and over again in their heads, generally reinforcing or exaggerating

> **"**
> ...those in conflict ruminate on everything that has been said or implied, and they replay it over and over again in their heads, generally reinforcing or exaggerating their negative interpretations and perceptions.
> **"**

their negative interpretations and perceptions. According to Rentzenbrink (2015, p.15), "memory is altered to the point of destruction by overplaying."

When people relate their version of what occurred during a conflict, it often bears little or no resemblance to what was actually said or intended. In schools where the parties to conflict – staff, students, parents and/or management – are totally interdependent in terms of communication and relationships, and where agreements and settlements of disputes are mutually beneficial, it is always perplexing and surprising that conflicts so often degenerate into unnecessary impasses.

Thompson and Loewenstein (1992) provided an interesting insight into why this might be. They suggested that as conflict situations are typically complex and ambiguous, multiple interpretations of what is a fair and equitable agreement or settlement occur. The various interpretations, combined with a range of ineffective and inadequate responses to conflict in schools, ensure that conflict-management for school leaders can be a very difficult and daunting task, and one which they frequently avoid.

In order for school leaders, who are involved in a conflict themselves or who are trying to resolve a conflict between other parties, to have any hope of a successful outcome, they need to bend over backwards in not only being fair but also, in being seen to be fair. This can be a very time-consuming exercise, involving checking and explaining, but is worth every minute spent on it. Being seen to be fair is not only invaluable in conflict resolution, it is also essential in every aspect of the role of school leader.

Key Points

- Whether passive or aggressive in conflict, many people use subtle and insidious passive/aggressive behaviours, which are difficult to identify and deal with.

- Emotions are always prevalent in conflicts.

- Suppressed emotions have a habit of leaking out in one form or another.

- Misperceptions and misinterpretations are characteristic of conflict.

C. 4. Managing Conflict

It is not surprising that conflict management is one of the most, if not the most, difficult and time consuming of the school leaders' tasks. It is suggested in a number of studies that 30-40% of a manager's daily activities are devoted to dealing with some form of conflict, and that they are involved in up to five disputes a day (Runde, 2014). Because conflict is largely misunderstood and feared, it is also not surprising that in many schools, like in many families, every effort is made to suppress and avoid it. Leaders, who adopt this avoidance attitude, regard conflict merely in terms of negative and destructive outcomes.

Conflict was historically, and still is to a large extent, regarded "as being undesirable and something to be avoided" (Lee, 2008, p.12). The notion that conflict can have positive potential has not previously been seriously contemplated or subscribed to. "Classical organisation theorists believed that conflict produced inefficiency... and was detrimental to the organisation and should be eliminated or at least minimized to the extent possible" (Lee, 2008, p.12). When one recalls the causes of conflict, as cited at the beginning of this section, and the damage that can result from even the most innocuous of disagreements, one might be inclined to agree with the traditionalists that conflict should be avoided at all costs.

Increasingly, however, conflict is viewed as an inevitable and natural occurrence in families, workplaces, and communities such as schools. It is also more widely recognised as a necessary part of the growth and development of individuals and communities. Conflict at work – the existence of incompatible positions – is considered as normal and unavoidable. It is also regarded as "a positive indicator of organisational management" (Lee, 2008, p. 12). Through dealing with and managing conflict appropriately, opportunities are created to:

- build and improve relationships;
- encourage people to articulate their needs in an open and honest manner;
- facilitate and support people in balancing their individual needs with the needs of the wider group;
- enable people to face up to and address problems and issues when they arise.

It is also worth alluding to the fact that the cost of resolving conflict is negligible, relative to the cost of leaving conflicts unresolved (Belak, 2004). In order to further enhance the confidence of school leaders in tackling conflict, it is also worth keeping in mind that something can always be done to improve the situation. Whereas not all conflicts can be resolved, the vast majority of them can be moved along a constructive path through a productive response (Mayer, 2000).

Armed with these positive perspectives, it is hoped that school leaders will gain the necessary confidence for dealing with conflicts in their schools. A willingness to work towards resolving conflict, where possible, is an important first step in moving from a conflict-avoiding to a conflict-managing attitude and approach.

C. 4.1 The Conflict-Competent Leader

Notwithstanding the fact that there are many school leaders who already manage conflict successfully, the concept of a conflict-competent leader is a relatively new one. It has been gaining some momentum of late, and is an integral part of many educational leadership and management courses, including the ones that I teach on. This inclusion is probably due to the increasing recognition and acknowledgement that conflict-competence is one of the most essential and invaluable skills that a leader and manager can have and use.

Runde and Flanagan, (2012) have provided a comprehensive insight into what is entailed in conflict-competence, and in particular what leaders are required to do to become conflict-competent. They suggested that, "individual conflict-competence involves developing cognitive, emotional and behavioural skills" (Runde & Flanagan, 2012, p. 8). The range of diverse skills alluded to suggests that attaining conflict-competence might well be a complex and arduous task. However, the skills can be learned. Leaders, who believe in the value of managing and resolving conflict and have the motivation to become skilled at doing it, are well on their way to attaining the necessary competence.

Practice and perseverance will then enable them to tackle the three main elements of conflict-competence, which are:

- the ability to constructively manage conflict and interpersonal problems between themselves and other parties, rather than ignore them or make them worse;

- the ability to facilitate, support and promote a conflict-competent climate in their schools, where conflict of opinions is welcomed, and where conflict that has a destructive or nasty side to it is talked about, resolved or simply let go;

- the ability to coach and mentor staff members to constructively manage conflict and interpersonal problems between themselves and others.

C. 4.2 Examining how Leaders Respond to Conflict

The conflict-competence of individual leaders is, to a great extent, influenced by how they normally respond to conflict. Conflict management styles refer to the specific and habitual behavioural patterns that individuals use when dealing with conflict (Moberg, 2001). As previously mentioned, the five recognised conflict styles are: avoiding; obliging/accommodating; compromising; competing/dominating; and collaborating/integrating (Thomas & Kilmann, 1974; Rahim, 1983).

● Avoiding Style

The leaders who adopt an avoiding style are aware that conflict is taking place but invariably they do not deal with it. They sidestep problems, pretend they are not happening, and maintain a 'least said, soonest mended' attitude. They find if difficult to raise concerns, even when conflicts are impacting severely on relationships and on the school environment. If a conflict kicks off in the presence of serial avoiders, they become terrified, withdraw, and even absent themselves, in the guise of having something pressing to attend to.

Their lack of assertiveness renders it almost impossible for them to challenge or disagree with others. The behaviour of extreme conflict avoiders has usually developed over a long period, and its source can very often be found in their childhood. Being exposed to aggression or violent behaviour can instil a lifelong fear of retribution for standing up for oneself or for others. More frequently, the source may be family norms, values and expectations, which discouraged and disallowed any form of disagreement or argument. Leaders who consistently adopt an avoiding style are considered by others to be lacking in courage. Conflicts may be rendered dormant when they are ignored or avoided, but they are never resolved.

● Obliging/Accommodating Style

Those adopting an obliging/accommodating style usually maintain a 'keep the peace at all costs' approach, by giving in to the demands of others, especially those who are aggressive. They generally regard conflict as a disruption to what they view as an otherwise harmonious and agreeable environment where everyone gets on well with each other. They really dislike and feel very uncomfortable with conflict, and they use every opportunity to minimise, discourage and dismiss it. Through their 'don't mention the war' attitude, they endeavour to agree with and accommodate everyone in the interest of a quiet life.

● Compromising Style

Those adopting a compromising style in conflict generally want to get the conflict dealt with as quickly as possible. This quick-fix approach, involving concession and consensus, is regarded, by those who habitually use it, as an effective means of resolving conflict. Indeed, in certain circumstances – of limited time, for example – it may well be, but, generally, it entails only a partial solution where each party sacrifices some elements of their needs. Those habitually employing this consensus approach of limited effectiveness may not fully understand the merits of pursuing and supporting a more collaborative approach. They also may not have the relevant skills to facilitate the more effective/multidimensional approach, which takes time and effort, and involves a thorough discussion of issues and perspectives.

● Competing/Dominating Style

Those who adopt a competing/dominating approach to conflict use their power and control in order to break down opposition and accomplish their own objectives. They have a must-win attitude and show no regard for, or interest in, the needs of others. They are generally defensive in conflict and often take things personally and become affronted and angry. They act and appear tough, and frequently elicit larger concessions at the expense of others (Sinaceur & Tiedens, 2006). However, there is a cost to those who are angry and aggressive in conflict. They are feared, distrusted and disliked by others, which adversely affects the quality of their relationships with colleagues. Also, conflicts involving those who think only of themselves and their own needs have a tendency to recur and escalate.

> **"**
> One conciliatory comment, for example, can have the effect of instantly changing the course of an entrenched conflict, as it is the sticking to one's guns that causes the entrenchment.
> **"**

● Collaborative/Integrating Style

The collaborative approach is widely considered to be the most effective conflict-management style. Those employing this integrating approach use creative thinking and problem-solving strategies to arrive at a solution that is mutually acceptable, and reflects the needs of all parties, while maximising the gains for all involved (Trudel & Reio, 2011). What is encouraging, for those leaders who are endeavouring to change their conflict styles, are the small wins that they achieve, while on the way to adopting a more collaborative and effective response to conflict. One conciliatory comment, for example, can have the effect of instantly changing the course of an entrenched conflict, as it is the sticking to one's guns that causes the entrenchment. Managing conflict collaboratively will ultimately yield many and varied benefits to the leader, and also to the entire school community.

● Conflict Styles and the Blind Self

Many school leaders are appointed to their posts without having adequate conflict-management competence, and rely on their existing conflict styles when conflict occurs. These styles are developed over a long period, and are influenced by an individual's personal history (Mayer, 2000). Gradually, they become unconscious and automatic, and are therefore not easily acknowledged or amended. It is exceedingly difficult to objectively identify one's own patterns of behaviour that have developed from childhood onwards. The behaviours often become part of a person's blind self. The four sides of a person, as presented in the 'Johari Windows' model, were explored in Section A, and include the open self, the hidden self, the unknown self, and the blind self. The blind self is the side of the self that others see clearly, while the person in question does not (Hase et al., 2000).

In conflict situations, those with a big blind self may say that: they don't let things get to them, or that conflict runs off them like water off a duck's back. However, all and sundry see that they redden in the face when challenged or disagreed with. They often either refuse to engage in any further discussion, blow their tops or storm off, banging the door on the way out.

They may also say that: they always consider the views of those presenting a different perspective to them. However, they do not draw breath when arguing their case. Eventually, when the other person does get a chance to speak, their point of view is quickly and forcefully dismissed.

> " How often have we heard people saying that they could not tell a lie to save their life, when it is widely acknowledged that they concoct and fabricate stories at the drop of a hat? "

Finally, those with a big blind self may say that: they always speak their mind and express their opinion. However, it is well known that as soon as any disagreement takes place they run for cover, hide behind the newspaper and only speak to sanction what has been decided, irrespective of whether they agree or not.

The lack of self-awareness in relation to our behaviours is frighteningly prevalent in people who do not make a conscious effort to get to know themselves. In general terms, they may say 'far be from me to gossip', when it is widely known that they could not be trusted to keep even the most minute detail of a conversation to themselves. How often have we heard people saying that they could not tell a lie to save their life, when it is widely acknowledged that they concoct and fabricate stories at the drop of a hat?

Self-awareness is essential to become familiar with aspects of ourselves that we are not in touch with. In the conflict context, self-awareness may be facilitated by asking a trusted and honest friend or colleague what they perceive your conflict style to be. If asking someone for their candid opinion, it is important that you make them aware that you really want a true assessment, even if it is not very complimentary. It is also helpful to observe how others handle conflict in order, by comparison, to become clearer in identifying and acknowledging your own style, and to become more attuned to the advantages and disadvantages of the various other conflict responses. With increased levels of awareness, and willingness to change, school leaders can alter and improve their old conflict habits, and embrace new and more effective responses.

● Conflict Scenario

The following scenario is fairly typical of the type of conflict that occurs between two colleagues in a school:

Mary and Eileen have been teaching in the same school for twenty and twelve years respectively. They became good friends very soon after Eileen arrived. They generally sat together in the staffroom, and seemed to have a lot in common. Mary has had a Post of Responsibility for some years and, at the beginning of this year, Eileen was given a new post which involves organising the Transition Year Programme. She regularly, enthusiastically shares her plans with her colleagues during lunch breaks. She is asked questions in the staffroom, and seems to be more involved with her colleagues than previously. During this period Mary has appeared disinterested in what Eileen has to say, and often makes dismissive comments under her breath. She frequently leaves the staffroom as Eileen is speaking. She also moves away if Eileen sits down beside her. For the last few weeks, she has refused to speak to Eileen at all. The atmosphere in the staffroom is very strained, with colleagues not knowing what, if anything, they should say or do. The principal has been approached by another senior colleague, who has asked her to do something about the situation.

Which of the following responses would you be most likely to use?

Do you:

1. Go immediately to Mary and tell her that the staff are upset and annoyed by her childish and unprofessional behaviour, and that it should immediately stop. Tell her that you have more to be doing with your time than dealing with these kinds of issues, and that you hope you won't have to mention it again?

2. Tell the senior staff member who has expressed concerns about the problem that these types of disagreements are part and parcel of school life and that you think it would be better not to draw attention to it, and to let Mary and Eileen sort it out themselves?

3. Thank the senior member of staff for bringing the concerns to your attention. Call Eileen into the office and compliment her on the work she is doing as part of her post of responsibility. Tell her that Mary may be feeling a bit left out, so it might be better if Eileen would inform you about what is happening in relation to transition year, and that you will relay it to the staff?

4. Call Mary and Eileen into the office together and explain to them that you have noticed that they are not speaking to each other, and that Mary frequently leaves the staffroom when Eileen is speaking. Tell them that these problems are impacting on the atmosphere in the staffroom, and that you would like them to resolve their differences. Suggest to them that they might try to resolve the issue themselves but that, if they are unable to do this, you will intervene to help get the problem solved?

5. Call Mary and Eileen into the office separately and suggest to Eileen that she only discusses elements of the Transition Year Programme on one day every second week, and that anything else that needs to be shared can be done by speaking to the teachers individually. Tell Mary that Eileen will only be speaking to the staff in relation to transition year issues on every second week, and that you would like her to be there for those information sessions?

Each of these responses is somewhat reflective of one of the five conflict styles. Which one do you think reflects which style and why?

Response Number 4, as outlined above, is suggestive of a collaborative style. It very clearly describes, without embellishment, the details of the problem, the consequences of it, and the need for a solution to be found. It also provides Mary and Eileen with an opportunity to resolve the issue themselves, while making it clear that other avenues for resolution will be made available to them if necessary. It sets the collaborative tone for a process of resolution.

Response Number 1 as outlined above is suggestive of a competing/dominating style. It evaluates the behaviour of Mary, rather than merely describing it. It has an angry and blaming tone, demonstrates no interest in establishing what has caused the problem, and no understanding of the need to find an effective solution. The conflict will likely continue, but may take on more subtle and insidious manifestations for fear of provoking further aggression from the leader. .

Response Number 2, as outlined above, is suggestive of an avoiding style. It demonstrates a 'hands-off' approach by the school leader, who tries to minimise the problem, and believes that neither she, nor indeed anyone else, should intervene to address it. There will be no imperative for the conflict to be resolved as a result of this response, and it will very likely continue and escalate.

Response Number 3, as outlined above, is suggestive of an obliging/accommodating style. This style is often also referred to as the smoothing style. It demonstrates a desire by the leader to keep everyone happy. It attempts to gloss over the inappropriate behaviour that is taking place, and provides a solution that will very likely cause more problems than it will solve.

Response Number 5, as outlined above, is suggestive of a compromising style. It offers a quick-fix solution which does not examine or deal with the underlying issues of the problem. Because this response does not get to the nub of the problem, it is likely to cause offence or upset to either, or both, of the two people involved.

Whereas both the accommodating and the consensus styles of handling conflict are considered to have merit in certain circumstances, it is interesting to note that they both, almost always, have an avoiding dimension to them, which is not conducive to resolving conflicts in schools.

It goes without saying that the collaborative response to the scenario as outlined above is merely a first step in a collaborative process that has the best chance of resolving the conflict between Mary and Eileen. However, it is an essential first step, as it clearly outlines the inappropriateness of the impasse, and the necessity to resolve the underlying issues. If that vital first step is not taken by the school leader, there is absolutely nothing to stop the conflict from continuing and worsening.

Key Points

- Conflict is inevitable and unavoidable in schools, and has many potential benefits.

- Conflict competence is an essential skill for school leaders.

- The conflict style of a school leader determines how they respond to conflict.

- A school leader has to first identify his/her individual conflict style in order to change and improve how they respond to conflict.

C. 5. Conflict Management Skills

There are specific and specialised skills involved in managing conflict effectively. In terms of dealing with, and resolving, conflicts in schools, leaders are required to:

- Manage their own emotions and the emotions of others;
- Use positive and appropriate behaviours;
- Engage in an effective process for finding solutions.

C. 5.1 Managing Emotions in Conflict

Emotional Intelligence is a prerequisite for conflict competence in leaders, and it is widely acknowledged that those with higher levels of emotional intelligence will resolve conflict more productively and collaboratively than those with lower levels (Jordan & Troth, 2002). "Conflict is replete with emotion" (Runde, 2014, p.27). "Emotions fuel conflict but they are also a key to deescalating it." (Mayer, 2000). The ability to be aware of and manage

> " If someone loses their temper and engages in an angry tirade against you, the first instinctive reaction is often to lose control of your own anger and to give as good as you get, thereby escalating the conflict. "

emotions facilitates functional rather than dysfunctional conflict-resolution (Jordan & Troth, 2002). Many leaders appear to regard the managing of emotions in conflict merely in terms of diffusing the anger or upset of others, whereas they also need to be conscious of identifying and managing their own emotions as they occur.

Managing the Emotions of Others in Conflict

Being able to elicit and acknowledge the emotions of others, particularly when locked in conflict with them, is invaluable in breaking the impasse. Leaders also need to be able to manage the moods of others, and to diffuse negative and impulsive outbursts, which are characteristic of many interpersonal conflicts. A highly-charged conflict situation can be diffused and transformed into something more positive when a leader has the ability to convey to the other person that they understand their feelings. However, understanding feelings that are negatively expressed is easier said than done. If someone loses their temper and engages in an angry tirade against you, the first instinctive reaction is often to lose control of your own anger and to give as good as you get, thereby escalating the conflict.

Those with high levels of emotional intelligence have learned to pause and think in these situations, and not to get hooked on the anger of another. They know that by acknowledging the anger of the other person with a simple 'I can see you are very angry,' they can diffuse the situation somewhat. This facilitates the other person in expressing their anger in a more measured manner that is more likely to be heard and heeded.

School leaders have a particular responsibility to take the initiative in diffusing anger in conflict situations. Similarly, teachers, as leaders, have a responsibility to diffuse the anger that a student may express aggressively during a conflict with them.

I have often witnessed teachers getting hooked on the anger of a student and reacting equally aggressively, only to escalate the situation up to the status of an international incident. When in conflict with a student, it is always advisable not to get into the boxing ring with them. In order to diffuse rather than escalate the situation, it is essential to acknowledge the student's anger, address their behaviour, seek out their perspective on what has happened, and find a solution as quickly as possible. Emotional intelligence is the key to seeing the benefits of this type of approach, and the key to making life easier for teacher and student alike when conflict occurs.

The skill of identifying and dealing with the emotions of others can be learned and utilised successfully, when one is favourably disposed towards it, and with the aid of a number of practical and workable strategies. When someone displays emotions in a negative way, however, either by expressing them aggressively, or through sarcasm, condescension, silence and/or some other negative non-verbal leakages, it is extremely difficult to empathise with them or feel inclined to behave positively towards them. You may feel that it would 'stick in your craw' to engage constructively with them, or that 'you would not please them or give them the satisfaction' of acknowledging their perspective. Unfortunately, whereas this attitude may be an understandable human reaction, it is counter-productive and certainly not one that a school leader can afford to adopt in the context of resolving a conflict.

There are a number of points worth contemplating in terms of adopting a more effective response to dealing with those who behave negatively in conflict:

1. The only way you can change the offending behaviour of another person is by changing your own behaviour in relation to them. This suggests that, even if you feel like telling them what you think of them in no uncertain terms, a better strategy is to listen to them, show them respect, and try to elicit from them what their perception of the problem is.

2. Holding on to resentment towards others punishes you, as much as it does them and further damages the relationship.

3. If resolving conflict is about anything, it is about pulling with, instead of pulling against, the other party. This is the essence of the win/win approach, and the only chance of success in finding a solution.

Notwithstanding the points made above, it is also very important to acknowledge that difficult and negative behaviours cannot be condoned or ignored. However, when school leaders can manage the emotions of others, and their own emotions as well, they have a much better chance of challenging that behaviour in a measured and appropriate way.

● Managing your own Emotions in Conflict

Like most people, school leaders can find in very difficult to manage their own emotions when in conflict. Becoming aware of emotions, and finding ways of expressing them and regulating them, particularly in the heat of argument and in the face of things said that are upsetting and hurtful, is particularly difficult. Yet, expressing and controlling emotions is one of the most vital, albeit challenging, aspects of resolving conflicts.

Hiding or suppressing emotions – for example, anger – can lead to on-going and festering resentment and hostility, in the face of which, any agreement reached will tend to be superficial and temporary. Problems will invariably recur regardless of what the agreement is (Johnson & Johnson, 1995). Additionally, suppressing and repressing anger often leads to emotional explosions that are very difficult to recover from, especially for a leader who is expected, at the very least, not to be temperamental or volatile.

People are wary of, and vigilant around, those who lose their temper. Even one explosion can be remembered for a very long time, can intensify conflict, create new conflicts, and can rekindle old ones in destructive ways (Johnson & Johnson, 1995). An explosion of anger can also provoke similar reactions from the other party, contributing to what Dana (2005), calls the retaliatory cycle. This is, in effect, a whizzing merry-go-round of destructive words/actions and reactions, sparked by out of control emotions that serve to escalate and intensify a conflict.

A characteristic of the start of every destructive conflict is one sharp comment or insult, followed by a negative reaction, as the retaliatory cycle begins. A loud and angry rebuke by A might be retaliated to by B, with a phrase, such as; 'How dare you speak to me in that tone of voice?' which in turn might provoke the reaction from A of; 'Well, someone needed to tell you the truth, you talk too much and you never give anyone else a look in', to which the retort from B might be; 'At least I bring up some good points, we would be waiting a long time for you to make any helpful suggestion' – and so on, and so on – as insults get worse, and tempers flare.

There is a very long way to travel back to anything approaching equilibrium, after that round of tit-for-tat retaliation. The secret is to recognise the pattern of retaliation quickly, and intervene with a conciliatory gesture to break the retaliatory cycle, and replace it with a cycle of conciliation. Dana (2006) cited apologising, taking responsibility, conceding, self-disclosure, the expression of a positive feeling to the other person, and initiating a win-win outcome, as examples of conciliatory gestures. In the above scenario, after B has said, 'how dare you speak to me in that tone of voice', A could have made a conciliatory gesture by:

- Apologising: 'I am sorry for shouting at you like that, it was very insensitive';

- Self-disclosure: 'I really wanted to make a suggestion at the meeting and when I did not get a chance, I felt very angry';

- Expressing positive feelings for the other: 'I know that you are always willing to take on the lion's share of the work after our meetings'.

After A has said, 'well someone needed to tell you the truth, you talk too much and you never give anyone else a look in', B could have made a conciliatory gesture by:

- Conceding: 'I did have a lot to say today, and I should have asked others if they wished to contribute';

- Owning responsibility: 'I will remember the next time to make sure that everyone gets a chance to speak';

- Initiating a win-win outcome: 'I think we should sit down and try to work out a solution together'.

> " It goes without saying that, for the conciliation gesture to have the desired reciprocal effect; it needs to be sincere and genuine. "

Emotional intelligence and associated emotional competencies are major contributing factors in helping those in conflict to pause, think, and choose to make a conciliatory gesture, rather than 'flying off the handle' in an automatic reaction. It goes without saying that, for the conciliation gesture to have the desired reciprocal effect; it needs to be sincere and genuine.

The ability to regulate anger, and remain calm when provoked, can positively impact on the emotional response of the other party, and enhance the chances of a mutually beneficial resolution being achieved. For those who have developed emotional competencies, the regulation of emotions in conflict becomes easier and more frequent, as does the appropriate expression of those emotions. Johnson and Johnson (1995), suggested that by expressing your feelings to the other party in conflict, you can actually clarify those feelings for yourself, provide information about what is going wrong between both of you, and begin a dialogue that will improve your relationship with the other party.

Key Points

- In order to effectively resolve conflicts, school leaders need to be able to mange their own emotions, and the emotions of others.

- Being able to identify and acknowledge the emotions and moods of others is essential to managing people.

- Diffusing the negative emotions of others, rather than getting hooked on them, moves conflicts towards constructive resolution.

- The appropriate expression and regulation of their emotions is essential if school leaders are to effectively resolve conflict.

- Breaking retaliation cycles and replacing them with conciliatory cycles is a necessary step in conflict resolution.

C. 5.2 Leadership Behaviours for Managing Conflict Effectively

The management of conflict was previously thought of, primarily, in terms of discouraging and preventing it in the first instance, and by reducing it and eliminating it when, and if, it did occur. This was often achieved either by stamping conflict out forcefully, or by avoiding or ignoring it and hoping it would go away. Conflict is now widely recognised as inevitable and potentially beneficial in workplaces. The focus of managing conflict has changed and moved towards using constructive and effective communication and behaviours to render the conflict functional, rather then dysfunctional, and to maximise the benefits of conflicts. These benefits include:

- the facility to raise and discuss issues and problems;

- the capacity to build better relationships;

- the opportunity to prevent conflicts from becoming nasty and destructive.

Rahim (2002) suggested that conflict management is about minimising negative outcomes and maximising positive ones.

If the leader is party to the conflict, then they have a particular responsibility to initiate a problem-solving approach, as soon as possible; to remain open to views and perspectives that are different to their own; to change their perspectives when appropriate. Some school leaders regard changing their positions or their views as being tantamount to a dissolution of their power, control and authority.

However, done in the context of an innovative, inclusive and problem-solving approach, it generally serves to enhance rather than undermine their credibility, and to increase the levels of respect and admiration in which they are held.

The acceptance by the leader, of an agreement that constitutes the best solution for everyone, but that runs contrary to aspects of his/her previously stated position, is really appreciated, and is often reciprocated with increased collegiality and co-operation.

A principal of a school in a famous hurling county was hell-bent on producing hurlers who would eventually make the county team. He insisted that the exclusive sports focus be maintained on coaching and promoting the game of hurling. Quite a number of students were very interested in playing soccer, and in response to this interest, a number of teachers were enthusiastic about including it as an official option for students The principal was adamantly opposed to this move, fearing a negative impact on the standard of hurling. A bitter and divisive conflict ensued which resulted in some teachers withdrawing from coaching and involvement in any sporting activity. After the intervention of a wise and trusted senior member of staff, the principal could see that his passion for the game of hurling, combined with his ambition for success for the school, was blinding him to the needs of others and was destroying the good will of his staff. He called a meeting and garnered the views of everyone. All opinions were discussed and considered and a solution emerged that included retaining hurling as the number one sport, while introducing a number of other options for students. The principal graciously accepted the solution, despite his reservations and concerns. I cannot provide an exciting finish to this story, in terms of the numbers of county players or international soccer stars that have emerged from the school. Suffice it to say, the impasse was quickly resolved, to the relief of everyone, and that the actions of the principal were acknowledged and appreciated.

In more general terms, leaders with a collaborative/integrating approach to conflict pursue and endeavour to ensure a win-win outcome, by attaching the same importance to the views and perspectives of others as they do to their own. The win-win objective is widely considered to be, by far, the most successful outcome to a conflict situation. Yet the prevailing myth that 'if you win, I lose', combined with a lack of understanding of the dynamics and effects of the win-win option, prevents many leaders from going for it. In managing conflict, as in all other aspects of the leadership role, a healthy 'other-centred' rather than an exclusively 'self-centred' perspective is a key determinant of the depth of expertise of the leader's management (Johnson, 2003).

> **"**
> The acceptance by the leader, of an agreement that constitutes the best solution for everyone, but that runs contrary to aspects of his/her previously stated position, is really appreciated, and is often reciprocated with increased collegiality and co-operation.
> **"**

● Listening

Demonstrating regard for others in conflict is manifested in empathic and inclusive behaviours that involve listening, considering the other person's perspectives, and adapting one's own views and behaviours where appropriate. Runde and Flanagan (2013) elaborated on the first of these behaviours, in terms of their manifestations and effects in conflict. They suggested that listening for understanding, as opposed to listening to respond, is essential in conflict.

Most people listen to respond when they are in conflict, and often cannot wait for the other person to stop speaking so that they can start. Those who are totally focused on what they are going to say next have a tendency to interrupt others in mid-sentence, usually to dismiss or contradict what they have just said, or to take exception to their tone or inference. This evaluative type of listening is always counter-productive in trying to manage and resolve conflict. If, as a leader, you can tick the boxes on the above characteristics of evaluative listening, then you are like most people – many of whom unfortunately will never even consider how they listen when in conflict. However, once you begin to think about the quality of your listening, you can start to appreciate the benefits of the more effective type of listening as outlined below.

Runde and Flangan (2013) suggested that listening for understanding is what is required, and they define it as listening with the sole intent of grasping fully what the other person is saying. "The goal is to comprehend" (Runde & Flangan, 2013, p.176). Listening for understanding is not easy, especially in conflict situations where we become so focused on convincing, controlling or changing the other person that we cannot hear what they have to say. The skill of active listening needs to be practiced, in order to achieve the desired outcome of capturing what the other person has said. Belak (2004) suggested that "the art of listening requires submersion of the self and immersion in the other" (Belak, 2004, p. 3). He further stated that when you listen with a minimum of defensiveness, criticism and impatience, you give the gift of understanding, and earn the right to have it reciprocated. (Belak, 2004)

Reciprocation is important to the listener, who also needs to have an equal opportunity to be listened to and understood. However, someone has to initiate the process, and that responsibility rests with the leader.

Runde and Flanagan (2013) offered a number of suggestions to help in the art of listening for understanding, some of which are adapted here for leaders and include:

- listening as if you had to summarise what the other person just said for everyone on the staff;

- demonstrating that you are listening, by asking for clarification or elaboration on points that you have not fully understood;

- checking after the other person is finished speaking to make sure that you have understood, by restating what you have heard and saying something like, 'so what I think you are saying is …is that right?' This allows the other person to confirm or correct your understanding.

> "
> **People in conflict have a very strong need to be heard and understood. When they have a sense that this has occurred, their levels of frustration, intransigence and anger are lowered, and their ability to engage constructively in a collaborative problem-solving effort is greatly enhanced.**
> "

It is also recommended that, when you disagree with what the other person is saying, it is better not to interrupt them, but rather to wait until they are finished and then, instead of telling them that they are wrong, to focus on the different perspective that you have.

People in conflict have a very strong need to be heard and understood. When they have a sense that this has occurred, their levels of frustration, intransigence and anger are lowered, and their ability to engage constructively in a collaborative problem-solving effort is greatly enhanced. It is only when leaders begin a practice of listening for understanding that they can fully appreciated the benefits for themselves, and for others, in everyday social interactions, but particularly in conflict situations. Effective listening improves relationships immeasurably, uses much less energy, and alleviates stress.

● Perspective-Taking

Perspective-taking, combined with listening for understanding, "are two of the most powerful behaviours that help to move conflict towards constructive, satisfying and mutually-agreeable outcomes" (Runde & Flanagan, 2013, p. 179). However, perspective-taking, like listening, is not easy for a leader in conflict, especially when they are convinced of, and committed to, their own perspective.

Perspective-taking is an 'other-centred' behaviour that involves putting yourself in the other person's position, and seeing the conflict from their point of view, while also being able to capture and articulate the essence of how the other person feels in relation to the issues involved in the conflict (Runde & Flanagan, 2013). Seeking to understand another's perspective suggests to them that both perspectives are valid. "It is not whether one view is right and the other is wrong, it is that both views matter" (McConnan & McConnan, 2008, p. 27).

The opposite of perspective-taking is what Johnson and Johnson describe as "egocentrism" (Johnson & Johnson, 1995, p.61). This is reflected in a failure to recognise that other perspectives exist, and are worthy of consideration. It also involves an inability to recognise that one's own view of a conflict situation is always incomplete and limited (Johnson & Johnson, 1995). Those who only give consideration and credence to their own perspective often try to change the other person's perspective to fit theirs. They run the risk of implying to the other person that they are wrong, resulting in them becoming offended and annoyed, and responding with defensiveness and further argument.

It is vitally important to consider the other person's perspective, endeavour to accurately understand it, and then convey to him/her that you do understand it. Only then can the conflict begin to move collaboratively towards a mutually beneficial agreement.

> **It is really difficult to articulate an alternative perspective when the leader's point of view is stated as a fact. On the contrary, phrases like, 'in my view', 'from my perspective', 'I think', or, 'I feel', are less definitive, and facilitate others in hearing your point of view, but also in presenting a different one.**

While acknowledging and understanding the other person's perspective is important, it does not mean that you have to agree with it. From a practical, logistical and effectiveness point of view, it is important for leaders to allow others to give their perspective first. The genuine encouragement and invitation to others to share their perspective, combined with the provision of a blank canvas on which to lay out their stall, affords a powerful opportunity for them to voice their point of view. It is particularly empowering for those who normally behave passively, and are reluctant to give their perspective. Also, affording the time and space to those who have a tendency to behave aggressively, to express their views, considerably lessens their inclination to be dismissive of, and inconsiderate to others.

Those in leadership roles are perceived as having a degree of authority and power and, therefore, they may be perceived as having an unfair advantage in the sharing of perspectives, particularly if they articulate their perspective first. When leaders do get the opportunity to define the problem from their perspective, it is important to ensure that they do not state their opinions as facts. This is seen as an aggressive way of insisting that what you have to say is the only way of seeing and doing things. For example, 'We have tried other ways, but this is the one that works best', 'There will be all sorts of problems if we don't stick to the tried and tested', or, 'We tried that last year and it was a total disaster'. It is really difficult to articulate an alternative perspective when the leader's point of view is stated as a fact. On the contrary, phrases like, 'In my view', 'From my perspective', 'I think', or, 'I feel', are less definitive, and facilitate others in hearing your perspective, but also in presenting a different one.

It is also helpful for leaders to be concise, lest the impression be given that they are trying to hammer home their point of view, or that they are endeavouring to convince the other party/parties that they are right, and by implication, that others are wrong.

It is worthy of note that a considerable body of research suggests that very often those in a position of power find it more difficult to understand how others see, think, and feel, as they themselves become disproportionately wedded to their own status-related perspective on issues (Galinsky et al., 2006). Leaders, who are aware of this tendency, are more conscious of sharing power, rather than holding on to it and letting it go to their heads. They are, also, less inclined to get carried away by their own importance.

For a variety of reasons, perspective-taking is a powerful elixir for helping to manage conflict, however it is not a panacea. When conflicts have remained unresolved for a considerable length of time, and have become extremely toxic, and when the opposing parties are increasingly entrenched and polarised, it is very difficult to listen to or understand the perspective of the other party, or indeed to feel empathy for their position. It is also difficult for those in conflict to consider the perspective of others when they firmly believe that their own perspective is a reflection of the reality of the situation. It is worth remembering that, in conflict, there is rarely an objective truth. In order to have any hope of getting anywhere near the full picture, everyone has to hear everyone else's point of view.

Perspective-taking can have huge benefits in effectively managing conflict, particularly when initiated by a conflict-competent leader, and employed as part of a collaborative approach to dealing with and resolving conflict.

● Adapting

Adapting is the third of the behaviours that Runde and Flanagan (2013), alluded to in terms of effectiveness in managing conflict. It is grouped with listening for understanding and perspective-taking, under an 'other-centred' behaviour heading. They interpreted adapting in two ways:

- being flexible, and making adjustments in the context of ensuring the success of any agreed solution to the conflict;

- adopting a positive attitude, and remaining optimistic that a good outcome is attainable and possible.

Both of these elements of adapting are necessary in conflict-management, with optimism playing a leading role in every aspect of it.

> **As Oscar Wilde so irreverently and accurately put it,**
> **"Between optimist and pessimist the difference is droll:**
> **The optimist sees the doughnut and the pessimist sees the hole."**

Optimism is regarded as an element of successful adaptation. Being optimisic is not to be confused with having unrealistic expectations. Rather it entails weighing up the pros and cons of conflict situations in order to seek out and find optimal solutions (Deutsch, et al., 2006). Optimists adopt a 'can-do' attitude to problems, and persist when the going gets tough. They retain a sense of positivity and enthusiasm when faced with challenges, and they are less likely to be fazed by the 'bolt from the blue' comment or intervention. Pessimists, on the other hand, are oblivious to these and other positive insights. "By lamenting, they indulge in increasing the burden of conflict rather than lessening it" (Deutsch et al., 2006). As Oscar Wilde so irreverently and accurately put it,

> "Between optimist and pessimist the difference is droll:
> The optimist sees the doughnut and the pessimist sees the hole."

A further insight into the differences between optimists and pessimists was provided by Seligman (1991). He suggested that optimists generally view difficulties as temporary, specific, and external to themselves.

For example, a teacher frog-marched a student down to the principal's office, barged in the door without knocking, and demanded, in a very aggressive and angry manner, that the student be severely punished. The teacher claimed that the student had displayed gross insolence and disrespect to him. A principal's optimistic response, through externalising the problem, would include an assessment that the anger displayed by the teacher was likely caused by either something the student may or may not have done, or something totally unrelated to the incident, but aggravated by it. She would then be able to regard the teacher's anger as being inadvertently and not purposefully, directed at her, and be less inclined to retaliate. Separating the teacher from the student by inviting the teacher into the office is a good initial step in diffusing the anger. Providing the teacher with an opportunity to provide details of the alleged incident also helps to diffuse anger, (specific). Getting the student's perspective will help the principal to come up with a recommendation that she believes to be fair to both. Presenting the proposed solution to the teacher will give him an opportunity to discuss the pros and cons of it in a measured manner so that an agreed and equitable solution can be found, (temporary and resolvable problem). Seeing conflict as external, temporary and specific to a particular issue or indeed a set of issues, encourages and facilitates a positive attitude of resolvability in relation to tackling a problem.

> **When one gets hooked on negative behaviours, and reacts with counter negativity, the focus shifts from the specifics of the conflict issue to the wider and more sensitive personal dimensions, which are much more emotive and difficult to recover from.**

Many people in conflicts put the behaviours of others through the narrow filter of how those behaviours affect themselves, their feelings, and their positions. School leaders who work on seeing conflict as external rather than personal are better able to focus outside themselves in addressing and managing a problem (Seligman, 1991). Not taking things personally is important, but can be exceedingly difficult, particularly when negative personal comments and criticisms have been levelled against them, and cannot be ignored. It is perfectly feasible to respond to these negative behaviours in an assertive way. In the above scenario the principal would have to allude to the inappropriateness of the aggressive behaviour of the teacher. However, this is more effectively done in private, and after the problem is resolved. When one reacts to negative behaviours with counter negativity, the focus shifts from the specifics of the conflict issue to the wider and more sensitive personal dimensions, which are much more emotive and difficult to recover from.

> **"**
>
> To be able to see the funny side of something embarrassing that you have said or done, instead of imagining that everyone will be thinking the worst of you, and that you will never get over it, is extremely liberating.
>
> **"**

Optimists do have a better disposition for behaving rationally in conflict situations and, if things go awry occasionally, they are more likely to have the resilience and perseverance to get things back on track. Further good news in relation to optimism emanates from the work of Carver et al., (2010). They stated that not only are optimists optimistic themselves, but that they reinforce optimism in others. Most of us are both optimistic and pessimistic, as events dictate. What we need to do is to increase our optimism so that it becomes our prevalent way of looking at events and people, particularly in conflict and adversity.

Being able to laugh, despite being in the throes of conflict, can help to put things in perspective and enable better coping and recovering.

For example, those who work to assist people who live in war-torn and poverty-stricken countries will readily admit that, if they do not have even an hour in the evenings to switch off, and have a laugh with their colleagues, they cannot sustain their efforts and maintain their energy levels in the long term.

In everyday life, laughter can cut through and diminish disappointments and even failures. Being able to laugh at yourself, however, is a real test of optimism. To be able to see the funny side of something embarrassing that you have said or done, instead of imagining that everyone will be thinking the worst of you, and that you will never get over it, is extremely liberating.

Applying Wilde's description of optimism to problem and conflict situations allows one to see the hole, but think, 'what the hell, it's a small hole in a much bigger doughnut'. True optimists do not ignore problems and challenges. They keep them in perspective, and look for ways to work through them. Why would school leaders not put the learning of optimism on their 'must do' list when, in general terms, optimists are healthier, happier and more successful and, in specific conflict management terms, they engage better with others, maintain better relationships, and use more creative strategies for resolution of difficult situations.

Finally, and more generally, adapting involves a leader being prepared to:

● modify or change their attitude to conflict and their own response to conflict situations;

● consider a range of options and new ideas in trying to solve problems;

● see the bigger picture in a potential conflict solution, rather than merely the narrower perspective of how it applies to, or impacts on, him/herself.

Adapting is also important in order for the leader to be able to recover from set-backs and, if not to bounce back, at least to step back and try again.

Adaptability goes hand in hand with flexibility in terms of the necessary attitudes and behaviours that a leader needs for managing conflict effectively and collaboratively. They are the polar opposites of intransigence and rigidity, which characterise the dominating approach to conflict, which is reflected in sentiments, either articulated or implied, such as, 'It's my way or the highway', 'They can like it or lump it', 'Just get on with it', or, the even more dismissive, 'Just get over it'. These sentiments, and the attitudes underpinning them, cause frustration and anger, and produce dysfunctional responses in conflict situations.

Key Points

- School leaders should always strive for a win-win result when trying to resolve a conflict.

- Listening, perspective taking, and adapting are the three key behaviours necessary for finding a solution to conflict.

- Listening for understanding involves actively listening to, and understanding, what each person in conflict has to say, and then checking with them to ensure that you have got it right.

- Perspective-taking involves listening to the perspective of the other person, and taking it on board in finding a solution to a conflict.

- Adapting involves being flexible and making adjustments to your feelings and needs in order to find an agreed solution to a conflict. It also involves staying positive that a solution will be found.

C. 6 Leadership Role in Finding Solutions to Conflict Situations

The entire conflict-resolution process is obviously focused on finding a solution to the problem. However, merely providing a number of steps to follow, in order to find a solution, would do a grave disservice to the many interacting dimensions that are involved in conflict-resolution. The process of finding solutions is a detailed and often a painstaking one for school leaders to undertake. However, an effective resolution process almost always involves a range of elements which are essential to achieving a sustainable solution. These elements, are underpinned by a number of key principles, two of which are outlined below.

C. 6.1 Key principles: Separate the People from the Problem

The first principle of finding effective solutions to conflict, according to Fisher and Ury (1991), is to separate the people from the problem. All school staff are familiar with this principle, but in a slightly different context. They know it, and for the most part abide by it, in dealing with difficult behaviour exhibited by students. It is always advised to depersonalise the response, for example, by labelling the behaviour as bad but never the child. Depersonalising, in the conflict context, involves associating the conflict with the issue, rather than the person. Focusing on the person often involves apportioning blame for the problem, which results in defensiveness and counter-claims from those who feel attacked. A cycle of negative, angry and increasingly personalised comments can ensue.

> **Personally, I could never understand the concept of demanding an apology. Who, in his/her right mind, could possibly want an apology that had to be demanded? One may get it, of course, but it is unlikely to be gracious or sincere.**

Personalising the conflict takes the focus off the underlying problem and leads to escalation and deterioration. It may then spiral out of control and become extremely difficult for the parties to reconcile afterwards. Demanded and often warranted apologies may not be forthcoming, leading to bitterness and further entrenchment. Personally, I could never understand the concept of demanding an apology. Who, in his/her right mind, could possibly want an apology that had to be demanded? One may get it, of course, but it is unlikely to be gracious or sincere.

Although it may be challenging and difficult in the heat of conflict , it is important for the leader to take the initiative in maintaining the focus on the conflict issue, and refraining from either resorting to, or reacting to personal comments. It is good to try to avoid the words 'always' and 'never' in your responses. 'You never take account of how your behaviour will effect others', or, 'It's always the same with you, you never listen to the opinions of others'. Certainly, a leader may have to respond to inappropriate, insensitive or rude comments but responding without attributing personal blame makes it easier for the other person to hear and heed the message. Keeping the responses courteous and short, and addressing the behaviour rather than labelling the other person, lessens the chances of further similar comments being made. The tried, tested and universally recommended 'I' messages, as opposed to the accusatory 'You' messages, are so much more effective in this regard.

Counting to ten, taking deep breaths, using mindfulness, managing emotions, or whatever it takes to stay calm and cool, are also worthwhile to prevent the conflict from further descending into a tit-for-tat feud. The depersonalising of problems is pivotal in helping to keep the relationships positive, and facilitating the parties in feeling comfortable to express their views in a more rational and dispassionate manner.

● Focus on Needs not Positions

While absolutely acknowledging the necessity and benefits of exchanging perspectives and views, it does have to be acknowledged that when conflicting parties give their perspectives, they are generally articulating their firmly-held positions on the problem. The second key principle underpinning conflict resolution involves placing a focus on interests and/or needs, rather than on positions (Fisher & Ury, 1991). It is essential that the parties move the deliberations from their differing, often polar opposite and intractable, positions to their interests/needs where, usually, there is some common ground.

This approach provides scope for increased engagement between the parties, and a better understanding of how the other person is thinking. To clarify the difference between a position and an interest/need, the former is something that you have decided on and the latter refers to the reason/s why you have so decided (Fisher & Ury, 1991). Outlining the reasons for adopting a certain position lets others know what you would like to achieve from the situation. At the same time, outlining the reasons for rejecting the other person's position informs them of your particular reservations and concerns.

A simple example would be where a principal wants a teacher to take the first class on each Monday morning, and the teacher does not want to do this. These are the positions of both and, if they are adhered to, there is no possibility of a mutually-agreed solution to the dilemma. If, on the other hand, the principal states her reasons for wanting this in terms of, for example, maintaining consistency, or preventing post-weekend absenteeism, through ensuring that the first class on Monday is one that the students are interested in, and consider important for their exams, then, already, there is more to consider. And, if the teacher states his reasons for not wanting to do this, as, for example, believing that the students are often less responsive first thing on a Monday morning, or that, on Mondays, he has a full schedule of classes and would like the first period free for preparation and corrections, then there is room for consideration of the needs of both the principal and the teacher.

Defining a problem solely in terms of positions means that at least one side must lose (Fisher & Ury, 1991). Belak, (2004) contended that positions merely provide the very limited and blinkered view of each person, on the solution they believe is needed to solve the problem. However, until the underlying needs and interests of each person are ascertained, it will not be possible to generate options for a solution, which will be mutually beneficial and agreeable (Belak, 2004). Looking for interests/needs, which are often contained in the reasons why positions are adamantly held, allows many more areas of agreement to emerge, and is a very powerful means for generating a win/win solution.

At this stage, the parties might try to elicit, from what has emerged, some common areas of agreement, no matter how small. In order to maximise the benefits from areas of agreement, it is helpful to focus on what is possible to achieve in the situation, rather than focusing on totally unrealistic options. The leader plays a key role in sensitively maintaining this realistic focus, without appearing to dismiss or disregard the suggestions of others. The emphasis also needs to be kept focused on the win-win outcome, which entails looking for a solution that allows both sides to gain.

> **"**
>
> One teacher summed it up for the others, when she suggested that as a result of buried conflict in her school, "you could cut the atmosphere with a knife".
>
> **"**

C. 6.2 Learning from Previous Conflicts

Runde and Flanagan (2012) suggested that, when endeavouring to resolve a conflict, it is advisable to consider historical approaches to similar problems in terms of their success or failure. In an effort to improve how conflicts are dealt with, and in order to learn lessons from past conflicts, it is beneficial to examine the patterns that have emerged in relation to the handling of conflicts in the school.

For example, if previous conflicts were ignored and buried, it is worth thinking about how that response impacted on the progression of the conflict, the relationships between those involved, and the atmosphere in the school generally. I asked that question, recently, of a group of teachers from a number of different schools. Not surprisingly, their accounts of the fallout from conflicts that were neither discussed nor resolved were exceedingly similar. There was a fair degree of consensus that, as a result, the atmosphere in staffrooms was tense and strained. One teacher summed it up for the others, when she suggested that as a result of buried conflict in her school, "you could cut the atmosphere with a knife". In similar situations, other teachers alluded to relationships as being either non-existent, frosty or toxic. A number of them spoke about the illusions of friendliness that appeared, as the cracks were papered over. Most of the teachers described how the unmentioned conflict constituted the elephant in the room. Although the conflict was never alluded to, frustrations abounded, and manifested in frequent arguments and disagreements about relatively minor and innocuous issues. As one of the teachers very accurately observed, "It is rarely about the photocopier, but nearly always about the elephant." Many of the teachers stated that, invariably, all the staff were aware of what was really going on, and that many of the students had picked up on the negative vibes also.

Notwithstanding the damage caused by unresolved conflict, trying to revisit long-standing problems has its dangers, and might cause an eruption of emotions and behaviours that will be very difficult to quell. Whereas my advice to new leaders is that generally they need to undo before they start to do, wiser counsel might need to be applied to long-running conflicts. A future-focus may be the better option, but with cognisance of the consequences of past failures, informing a new and better approach to resolving future conflicts. Irrespective of whether the leader feels able to revisit past conflicts or not, the main focus has to be on what is going to change and improve from now on.

C. 6.3 Finding and Implementing Agreed Solutions

In order to find an agreed solution to a current problem, and also to initiate a process of improving relationships, it is counter-productive to spend time assigning blame or trying to prove or disprove past allegations (Belak, 2004). From a moving-forward perspective, Runde and Flanagan (2012) advised that it is important not to

> "
> A celebration of the success is generally appreciated by everyone, and is an opportunity for the parties to congratulate each other and share the sense of relief and well-being that resolving a conflict brings.
> "

concentrate on one solution – rather it is necessary to consider a range and variety of options that have the potential to resolve the conflict. Brainstorming is a useful technique for doing this, and encourages inclusive participation. Leaders have many responsibilities in this process, but these do not include pushing and trying to sell their suggestions and ideas. The success of the process is contingent on continuously engaging others in the problem-solving discussion (Belak, 2004). This goes beyond simply giving others a chance to speak. It also entails giving their arguments equal weight (Kazimoto, 2013). Engaging in a genuine and collaborative problem-solving dialogue helps to improve relationships, and engender trust in the resolution process. Before a solution is finally decided on, it is necessary to ensure that everyone has been involved in it, understands the implications of it and agrees with it. If every aspect of the decision-making process is not fully clarified for everyone involved, expectations may not be fulfilled, and frustration and disillusionment may result.

Strategies for implementing the solution/s need to be decided on and agreed, and the specific logistics for implementation need to be discussed also. A timeframe for evaluating the progress of the strategies, and the evaluation methodology, also need to be discussed and agreed. In order to keep these discussions on track, it is imperative to maintain the focus on the quality of the communication to ensure that it is positive, respectful and inclusive. The leader has a responsibility to set the example by consistently modelling the most effective communication. This encourages others to mirror what they see, and what they experience.

Finding a mutually agreed solution to a conflict creates a great sense of achievement among those involved. The process is not completed, however, without an acknowledgement by the leader of the contributions of everyone in reaching the agreement, and an expression of appreciation for the commitment and effort of all those involved. A celebration of the success is generally welcomed by everyone, and is an opportunity for the parties to congratulate each other and share the sense of relief and well-being that resolving a conflict brings.

Resolving conflict is a complex and difficult task. It requires meticulous attention to the various elements of the resolution process. However, once successfully completed, the confidence and competence of everyone – especially the leader – is enhanced. The effective process of both managing and resolving conflict becomes easier and more frequently utilised, until, over time, it constitutes the norm when conflicts arise in schools.

Key Points

- Finding solutions to conflicts involves a range of complex and essential elements.

- A key principle underpinning conflict resolution involves separating the people from the problem, by concentrating of the conflict issue rather than reacting to personalities or behaviours.

- A second key principle of conflict resolution involves the participants moving from firmly held positions to what they really need from the conflict, in order to find common areas of agreement.

- Lessons can be learned from previous conflicts that were handled badly to positively influence approaches to future conflicts.

- A number of possible solutions need to be considered by all parties in order for agreement to be found.

- Strategies for implementing and evaluating the progress of solutions need to be established and agreed.

- An acknowledgement of the efforts of those involved in the resolution process, and a celebration of success, are appreciated.

C. 7. **The Conflict-Competent School**

The effective managing and resolving of individual conflicts as they arise is a vital element of a conflict-competent school. However, is it not until conflict is regarded as an inevitable and potentially positive occurrence that this approach is likely to happen. For this shift of attitude to occur, there needs to be a recognition and an acceptance that differing and conflicting beliefs, ideas and interpretations are invaluable in a school. Acknowledgement and consideration of these differing perspectives are essential for:

- functional relationships;
- informed and innovative decision making;
- inclusive and effective solutions to conflicts.

Low-level conflict occurs when differences are suppressed, and are deemed not to be discussable. Some school cultures judge the expression of conflicting perspectives to be disruptive and even threatening. In these types of cultures, staff meetings are characterised by people not saying what they really think, and not disagreeing or expressing an alternative point of view for fear of how it might be regarded or reacted to. This results in frustration and resentment, which although not often overtly expressed, can fester and worsen and escalate the conflict. The disgruntled individual or group can, and often do, engage in one or more of a variety of actions or inactions that create increased hostility and negativity.

Conflict-competent school leaders play a significant role in encouraging the open, honest, and respectful expression of differences. When these differences are articulated, they accept them in the spirit which they are expressed, consider them, and take them on board as appropriate, to inform associated decisions. They do not regard differing or conflicting perspectives as threatening, and do not feel the need to suppress them. In that environment, staff know that they can raise issues and concerns, and that there will not be any adverse consequences for them.

In open and co-operative schools, various and differing opinions and views are not only accepted, but are actively sought out. Unfortunately, in some schools, the expression of alternative or conflicting ideas is at best discouraged, and at worst not allowed. In these types of closed and defensive schools, young teachers who unwittingly make a suggestion for change or improvement can find themselves isolated and excluded as a result. When this happens, it will be a very long time before they feel safe to voice their opinion again. They learn to speak on cue and, like the remainder of the staff, keep all dissent to themselves, or for small and hushed group caucuses.

School staff invariably regard being encouraged to, and feeling able to, speak their minds, and express their views openly and honestly, as a very clear indicator of a positive/effective and safe environment. It is also one of the best indicators of effective leadership, and is the main ingredient of a conflict-competent school.

C. 7.1 **Conflict between Staff**

Conflicts between staff members, between staff and parents, and between staff and students, are commonplace in schools. The dynamics of conflicts, as discussed above, are exceedingly similar, irrespective of who is involved. However, there are nuances of differences in terms of the role of the school leader in dealing with conflicts involving the various parties.

Many school leaders ignore conflicts between staff members in the hope that they will go away. However, these conflicts have the potential to cause high levels of tension that adversely affects the school atmosphere – not just for those involved, but also for other staff members and for the students. Prolonged conflicts, in particular, contribute to a deterioration in the quality and quantity of the communication in the school and, what

> **A lack of courtesy and collegiality, and the withholding of effort and commitment, are among the more damaging consequences of unresolved conflicts between staff.**

communication there is, can be characterised by negativity, and toxicity. The disputants can become so preoccupied with the conflict, and blinkered by their sense of injustice, their anger or distress, that they lose sight of their professional responsibilities towards their colleagues, and towards their students. A lack of courtesy and collegiality, and the withholding of effort and commitment, are among the more damaging consequences of unresolved conflicts between staff.

It is the responsibility of school leaders to be vigilant in relation to inter-staff conflicts. That does not entail them being hyper-vigilant, or using a Geiger counter approach to detect any hint of an emerging conflict. Rather, they need to be judicious and strategic in deciding which conflicts merit intervention, and how and at what stage they should intervene. When conflicts have escalated without any apparent attempt to resolve them, or when they begin to impact on the work environment or the quality of educational service being provided, the leader's antenna usually registers concern that should not be ignored. Stating their concerns clearly to those in conflict is not only a legitimate option for leaders, it is also a very clear responsibility.

Prudence is advised in the language used to register concern. Using the aforementioned 'I' statements creates a much more conducive environment for those in conflict to hear and heed the concerns expressed. Examples of these include the following: 'I have noticed that there are some problems between you'; 'I am quite concerned about the situation'; 'I believe that this situation is impacting on ...'; or, 'I would like to see something done about this situation'. These types of statements alert the conflicting parties to how seriously the conflict is being taken without apportioning blame to either/any of them. Clear expressions of concern also facilitate the leader in pointing out the potential implications of the present situation.

The initial raising of concerns does not always necessitate a suggestion of an offer of help to facilitate a resolution. At this stage, it might be more appropriate to relay to the disputants the importance that is attached to finding a solution, and to invite them to work together to find one that is mutually beneficial. Using diffusing and informal language at this stage often encourages those with the problems to consider taking up the suggestions without feeling that they are putting their foot on a slippery slope. If they do consider addressing the conflict themselves, and seek the support and assistance of the leader in undertaking the task, a conflict-competent leader will be equipped to offer sound advice and guidance on the best, and most constructive and effective, approach to take.

> **Disabusing those in conflict of the notion that they are helpless in the situation can empower and foster the courage and confidence needed to enable the person to raise, and try to resolve, the conflict themselves.**

If, however, the leaders have acquired a specific conflict-coaching qualification, they will have an invaluable advantage in enabling them to equip staff members with the appropriate strategies required to attempt to resolve the conflict on their own.

Conflict-coaching is a relatively new, but very powerful, element of conflict-management. It involves a one-to-one process between the coach and the person in dispute, for the purpose of developing the latter's understanding of conflict, and his/her interaction strategies and skills in the conflict context (Jones, & Brinkert, 2008).

Training to qualify as a conflict coach is widely available, and generally uses the Cinergy model devised by Cinnie Noble, and outlined in her book, *Conflict Management Coaching: The CINERGY™ Model* (Noble, 2011). It is an excellent qualification to have when applying for the role of principal or deputy principal in a school, and for an existing leader to have in their conflict-management kit. However, it should not be used by leaders to abdicate their responsibility in relation to resolving conflict. Coaching is most appropriate when the disputant feels ready to intervene themselves, but lacks the relevant knowledge and skills, and where there is a positive attitude in the school to conflict in general, and dealing with conflict in particular. If the leader does not have a coaching qualification themselves, they can engage the services of an accredited conflict coach.

Above all else, conflict coaching should always maintain the focus on an inclusive and constructive approach to resolving conflicts, with the aim of ensuring, in as far as possible, a win-win outcome (Jones, & Brinkert, 2008). Disabusing those in conflict of the notion that they are helpless in the situation can empower them and foster the courage and confidence needed to enable them to raise, and try to resolve, the conflict themselves. The absence of a third party intervention has the distinct advantage of containing the conflict, and finding solutions with the minimum of fuss and fanfare.

For a variety of reasons, those in conflict may reject the prospect of intervening in the dispute themselves. Others may have already tried, and been unsuccessful in resolving the conflict. In these, and other, circumstances it may become abundantly clear that some form of third party intervention is required. The conflict-competent leader will be more likely to have the relevant knowledge, skills and confidence to undertake this task, and will be more likely to be accepted by the parties. Inevitably, this is not always going to be the case, and the option of engaging the services of an external professional mediator, if acceptable, is worthy of consideration in that scenario.

There is always the possibility that one or other of the disputants may refuse to engage with any intervention. It is timely, at that stage, for the school leader to assertively remind resisting staff members of their professional responsibilities in regard to resolving conflict, and more generally in relation to communicating and working with their colleagues, and contributing to a positive work environment. In the event of a continuing impasse, the school leader, while not using a sledge hammer to crack a nut, will need to escalate his/her assertiveness and allude to the inappropriateness of the behaviours being engaged in. He/she may also need to outline in some detail the effects of the continuing conflict on individuals, both staff and students, and

> **"**
>
> A principal, deputy principal, or a member of the teaching staff, by virtue of their status and authority, are in a very powerful situation when involved in a conflict with a student. It is essential that they do not abuse that power by creating a win-lose situation between them.
>
> **"**

on the school's effectiveness more generally. Whereas school leaders cannot impose a resolution option on conflicting staff, they certainly can, and must, continue to impress upon them how imperative it is that a resolution be found.

C. 7.2 Conflicts between Staff and Students

The principles of, and attitudes to, conflict resolution as outlined above also apply to conflicts between school staff and students. A principal, deputy principal, or a member of the teaching staff, by virtue of his/her status and authority, is in a very powerful situation when involved in a conflict with a student. It is essential that they do not abuse that power by creating a win-lose situation between them. Blaming the student, humiliating or embarrassing them, escalating the conflict, taking themselves too seriously, demanding an apology, and punishing the student, are all guaranteed to provoke the situation and make it worse. The person with the authority can quite easily achieve a notional win, by undermining the student and disregarding his/her point of view.

Johnson and Johnson (1995) asserted that one should never walk away with a win, not least because you will have to watch your back. Suffice it to say, students rarely forget the feeling of having been taken advantage of, and of being rendered powerless in a conflict situation with a teacher. Trust is broken, respect is lost, and both are replaced by resentment, disengagement and/or disruption. The adult in the conflict may appear to have won the battle, but they have almost certainly lost the war.

The onus is on the professionals to ensure that conflicts with students result in a win-win outcome. As previously alluded to, this is achieved by:

- diffusing the situation;
- addressing the behaviour of the students without personal comment or insult;
- listening to their perspective and giving it a fair hearing;
- being prepared to apologise if in the wrong.

It is important to remain focused on finding a mutually-beneficial solution, and to ensuring that the student is not alienated in any way. It is also vital that ill-feeling towards the student is not harboured or demonstrated in the aftermath of the conflict.

In a conflict-competent school, the use of these constructive approaches to handling conflicts with students become the norm, and the many merits of employing them are increasingly recognised and appreciated.

C. 7.3 Conflicts between Staff and Parents

A recognition, by school staff, that parents are their partners in the care and education of the students is the key to welcoming their involvement and input, and not merely their assistance and support. Where parents feel free and safe to discuss their concerns about their children, in the knowledge that they will not be met

> **"**
> Where parents feel free and safe to discuss their concerns about their children, in the knowledge that they will not be met with defensiveness, dismissal or retaliation, destructive conflicts involving, anger and frustration are much less likely to occur.
> **"**

with defensiveness, dismissal or retaliation, destructive conflicts involving, anger and frustration are much less likely to occur. When they do occasionally occur, they are much more likely to be resolved quickly and satisfactorily. Staff in a conflict-competent school will have a greater understanding of the need to:

- listen to what parents have to say;

- acknowledge their feelings;

- demonstrate that the welfare of the student is the most important consideration for them;

- outline their own perspective in a clear and calm manner;

- work with the parents to find solutions to problems.

If parents feel that their concerns are genuinely taken on board, respected, and addressed, they are more inclined to abandon a negative attitude of, 'it's you against me', and adopt the more positive attitude of, 'it's us against the problem' (McConnan & McConnan, 2008, p. 18). Adopting a collaborative, rather then a competitive, approach to resolving conflicts with parents is always the right thing to do and is, in the vast majority of cases, very much appreciated.

Key Points

- Conflict-competent schools are characterised by the valuing and expression of differences.

- Leaders have the responsibility to address conflicts between staff, because of the potential for them to cause serious disruptions in schools.

- A conflict coaching qualification enables leaders to assist staff members in trying to resolve conflicts themselves.

- School staff should always aim for a win-win solution in conflicts between themselves and their students.

- School staff have a responsibility to listen to parents, and refrain from becoming defensive when problems arise between them.

C. 8. Conclusion

Unmanaged conflict is considered to be the largest reducible cost for many organisations, including schools (McConnan & McConnan, 2008). The cost to a school cannot be measured merely in financial terms, but needs to be thought of in terms of the impact on time, energy, stress, relationships, morale, reputation, and individual and organisational effectiveness. The negative impact of unmanaged, or poorly managed, conflict is beginning to be understood more clearly. School leaders have a major responsibility to act on this understanding, and become more proactive in tackling and addressing conflict in their schools.

The inability to deal with conflict respectfully, constructively, and in a timely manner will quickly undermine not alone the leader's credibility, but also the progress of the school (Kazimoto, 2013). Addressed properly, conflict can lead to change, innovation, personal and professional growth, and many other tangible and intangible benefits. However, all these positive outcomes depend on the school leadership and how conflict is dealt with.

The importance of conflict-competence among school leaders cannot be overstated. "Those skilled at managing conflict are more likely to be considered as effective leaders, are more influential, gain respect and co-operation and increase the effectiveness of the organisation" (Kazimoto, 2013, p. 17). They also make school life much easier for students, staff, and for themselves.

Section D

Workplace Bullying in Schools

D. 1 Introduction

Bullying is widely acknowledged as a problem of significance in educational and other workplaces. Zapf and Einarsen (2005) stated that it is most prevalent in education, health and social service workplaces. However, the source of particular shock for educationalists will, undoubtedly, emerge from the considerable consensus across research and literature that workplace bullying is consistently evident in the teaching profession (Ishmael and Alemoru, 1999; Blase and Blase, 2003; O'Connell et al., 2007). A survey by the Economic and Social Research Institute (ESRI) found that the highest incidence of Workplace Bullying in Ireland occurred in the Education Sector (2007).

> **In more than 20 years of dealing with cases of workplace bullying, many of the most disturbing and horrific incidences that I have encountered have come from workplaces that are charged with providing a service to vulnerable groups.**

The fact that bullying is such a pervasive problem, in what would generally be considered as the caring professions, continues to confound many people. Yet, there is little doubt that the statistics reflect the reality of the situation. In more than 20 years of dealing with cases of workplace bullying, many of the most disturbing and horrific incidences that I have encountered have come from workplaces that are charged with providing a service to vulnerable groups. These include children, those who are ill, and those suffering from poverty, disadvantage, abuse or disability. Without adequate research having been undertaken to ascertain the reason for this, it would be inappropriate to speculate. Suffice it to say, the myth suggesting that those who bully in the workplace mainly reside in the more cut-throat, competitive world of business or politics is well and truly shattered.

Some school leaders are reluctant to accept that they are the group most often cited as being responsible for the bullying of adults in schools. They suggest that frequently *they* are the targets of this type of behaviour. I have been shocked by some of the accounts that principals and deputy principals have provided, as they outlined their bullying experiences at the hands of one or a number of staff members. Newly-appointed school leaders can be very vulnerable, particularly if negativity is already prevalent and if there are unresolved interpersonal issues in the school. They can also be vulnerable if there are unsuccessful and disgruntled applicants for the job among the staff. Difficult as it may be for leaders, especially bullied leaders, to accept, the research is quite clear that workplace bullying is most often a top-down process. This fact arguably says more about those who bully than it does about leaders. Those who bully are hell-bent on acquiring status and prominence. This may well be connected to their deep-rooted fears and insecurities and their extreme efforts to hide them from themselves and from others, by gaining power and control in their work lives. Bjorkqvist et al., (1994) asserted that those who bully at work are concerned about status and positions, are uncertain of themselves and are envious of others.

One thing is clear, those with bullying tendencies who reach high office are predominantly focused on themselves and are prepared to allow the organisation or school that they lead to disintegrate, in their efforts to maintain their control.

The research on workplace bullying also makes it clear that bullying can take place at any level of an organisation. Statistics, in relation to the situation in the USA, suggest that approximately 50% of workplace bullying is caused by co-workers (Zapf & Einarsen, 2005). The main focus of those writing about workplace bullying has been on either top-down or horizontal bullying. That is not to ignore the fact that "upwards bullying" (Branch et al., 2007) or "bottom up bullying" (Mc Kay, 2012), both of which refer to the bullying of managers by staff members, also occurs, as does the bullying of school staff by parents and students. In school terms, many would consider that the leaders in the school have all the power. Therefore, they might conclude that it would be virtually impossible for them to be bullied. This view does not take account of how much power staff members have in relation to the extent to which they provide or deny support to the leader.

School leaders who bully can make work life miserable for staff, and staff members who bully can also make work life miserable for school leaders. However, the positional power attached to the role of school leaders can make it very difficult for staff members to challenge them in relation to their bullying behaviours. School leaders who are bullied, on the other hand, are discouraged from admitting to being bullied or seeking help, because of a fear of being considered as weak or ineffective.

D. 2. The Role of School Leaders in Dealing With Workplace Bullying

The vast majority of school leaders would not and could not engage in bullying behaviours. However, their vital role in the prevention of, and response to, workplace bullying, warrants comment and attention. Leaders who ignore or by other means allow bullying to occur "are seriously impacting on the health and future viability of the organisation" (Davenport et al., 1999). They also facilitate the exodus of talented staff members who leave these toxic and counter-productive work environments (Davenport et al., 1999). Workplace bullying only thrives if the environment in the school suits it, and if it is allowed to thrive. The style of leadership and the quality of the environment in any organisation are two of the main antecedents of bullying (Hoel & Salin, 2003). It is through best practice leadership and the creation of a positive school environment, that workplace bullying in schools can be prevented.

A school leader's lack of understanding of workplace bullying and its effects, and a failure to intercede to stop the bullying of a colleague, enable the behaviours to continue and thrive. In the case of the former, unless someone has experienced bullying themselves, they may find it difficult to grasp the nasty nuances of it, or the severity of its effects. And in relation to a leader failing to intercede to stop bullying, it has to be acknowledged that without an effective policy for the prevention of bullying, and a set of

> **"**
> The placing of the destructive behaviours that constitute bullying into the school context causes particular incredulity, sadness, anger and shock for all enlightened educators.
> **"**

associated procedures and strategies for dealing with bullying problems, it is difficult for a school leader to find a forum for successful intervention. The aim of this section is to provide an overview of the main dimensions of workplace bullying, and to outline how best to deal with it.

A number of myths and misconceptions in relation to the manifestations and effects of workplace bullying still exist. However, there is an increased recognition of the abusive elements of bullying and the devastation of its effects. The placing of the destructive behaviours that constitute bullying into the school context causes particular incredulity, sadness, anger and shock for all enlightened educators. Nonetheless, it is important to examine the problem of workplace bullying in the education profession, as it serves to focus minds on the potential for devastation in the schools hosting bullying. A school's attitude and response to bullying will determine whether the school will effectively prevent or promote bullying at every level.

D. 2.1 'Bullying-Preventing' and 'Bullying-Promoting' Schools

In 'bullying-preventing' schools, through creating, maintaining and promoting a psychologically and emotionally safe environment for staff and students, bullying problems are minimised and there is effective intervention to resolve bullying when it does occur (Bluestein, 2001). These schools are characterised by reflective, enlightened and caring leadership. Priority is given to creating a sense of belonging, acceptance and safety to everyone (Bluestein, 2001). Value and importance are placed on appointing and promoting staff who demonstrate and promote emotional intelligence (EI). This type of intelligence, manifests in a person's fine-tuned and insightful self-awareness and self-management and in his/her propensity to build positive and productive relationships with others. Emotional Intelligence shapes both our understanding of ourselves and our interactions with others (Freedman et al., 1998). It also increases the ability to cope with toxic behaviours when they do occur (Lubit, 2004).

In safe school environments, the interpersonal behaviours of school leaders and staff are regarded as essential dimensions of their work and standards and norms of appropriate behaviour are articulated and expected. Problems and conflicts are taken seriously and dealt with (Ishmael & Alemoru, 1999). Effective and comprehensive policies and procedures for dealing with bullying

> **"**
> Even in the schools where anti-bullying slogans adorn the walls, if bullying is taking place among the adults there, the message that is really being communicated to students is that, "it's ok to bully here".
> **"**

and other interpersonal problems are in place, and all staff and students are made aware of their rights and responsibilities with regard to inappropriate behaviours.

One the contrary, the bullying-promoting schools are characterised by closed and dysfunctional communication, internal competitiveness, favouritism, dishonesty, power dynamics, denial, and destructive and unresolved conflicts (Kitt, 1999; Bluestein, 2001). These schools do not acknowledge bullying as a serious problem. Lip-service is paid to preventing and dealing with bullying and often there is scapegoating and further bullying of those who highlight, or complain about, bullying behaviours (Daniel, 1998). In these schools, bullying among adults thrives, and explicit or implicit messages of tolerance of bullying are communicated to students with devastating results (Kitt, 1999). Even in the schools where anti-bullying slogans adorn the walls, if bullying is taking place among the adults there, the message that is really being communicated to students is that, "it's ok to bully here".

D. 3. **Defining Workplace Bullying**

Despite an increased level of awareness and discussion in relation to all aspects of workplace bullying, there is still a lack of understanding of what bullying entails and also a reluctance to fully accept that it is a serious and destructive form of abuse. Euphemism and lack of clarity characterise many definitions of workplace bullying.

The definitions that cite various types of bullying behaviours, for example, 'offending, intimidating, insulting, demeaning, excluding' are helpful to those who feel bullied. However, specific examples of each of these types of behaviours are needed, to adequately expose the nuances of bullying (Ishmael & Alemoru, 1999; Adams, 1992). Some definitions, by citing only a small number of bullying behaviours, are excluding a significant number of other behaviours frequently experienced by those being bullied. Also, by merely naming the behaviours that constitute bullying, definitions fail to capture the "complexities of interactions" (Tehrani, 2001, p. 222) involved in those behaviours.

> **"**
> Inadequate definitions may also inhibit an understanding and acknowledgement that bullying is a proactive, albeit camouflaged, set of behaviours that targets and abuses.
> **"**

Definitions that do not capture the essence of workplace bullying increase the risk that behaviour, which does not constitute bullying, is labelled as bullying (McCarthy, 2003). Inadequate definitions may also inhibit an understanding and acknowledgement that bullying is a proactive, albeit camouflaged, set of behaviours that targets and abuses someone. It is neither a figment of the imagination nor simply a matter of perception or interpretation on the part of the target.

Inaccurate definitions may also prevent the acceptance of accounts of bullying by targets, as reflections of the reality of their experiences. Instead the accounts may be dissected and disputed. However, Leymann's (1996), description of bullying as a systematic attack goes a considerable way in explaining what bullying entails. Davenport et al., (1999) shed further light on the destructive nature of the phenomenon by calling it an "emotional assault" (p. 33), as indeed does Einarsen et al., (1999, p. 17), when they alluded to bullying as "systematic persecution" and also as "psychological drowning".

Bullying has a very distinct and unique element involving setting another person up to fail. The goal of workplace bullying is to harm and incapacitate (Keasley & Jagatic, 2003; Ishmael & Alemoru, 1999). Bullying obstructs those targeted in trying to do their jobs. It attempts to discredit their performance, competence and reputation. It aims to destroy their credibility and their relationships with others in the workplace. Bullying is a psychological brutality that produces "exploitative, unhealthy and morally unconscionable work conditions" (Hornstein, 1996, p. 23).

The Irish Government Task Force on the Prevention of Workplace Bullying was established in 1999. They reported in 2001 and defined workplace bullying as follows:

Workplace bullying is repeated inappropriate behaviour, direct or indirect, whether verbal, physical or otherwise conducted by one or more persons against another or others, at the place of work and/or in the course of employment, which could reasonably be regarded as undermining the individual's right to dignity at work An isolated incident of the behaviour described in this definition may be an affront to dignity at work but, as a once-off incident, is not considered to be bullying (Health and Safety Authority, 2001)

The definition was broadly welcomed at the time. It remains the most widely recognised and utilised definition of workplace bullying in Ireland. Over the past 10 years, it has been presented for critique and analysis at many of the training and in-service courses on workplace bullying conducted by myself and other colleagues. There has been a considerable consensus, which reflects our view that serious consideration should be given to changing the definition. The main concerns are in relation to:

- The vagueness and openness to interpretation of the definition,

- The insufficient consistency between this definition of bullying and the established definition of harassment.

The weakest element of the present definition is the suggestion that all inappropriate behaviour that undermines the individual's right to dignity at work is bullying.

The potential negative effects emanating from the use of this definition include:

- Misuse and misinterpretation of the term bullying;

- Difficulties in distinguishing bullying from other inappropriate behaviours;

- The decision by some investigators of bullying complaints to use their own criteria to tighten the definition. These criteria are unavoidably inconsistent and lead to flawed investigation findings and inadequate responses from organisations;

- Increased levels of "bullying fatigue" and complacency as a result of the use of the term bullying to describe other behaviours, and a consequent failure to understand, recognise and deal with the genuine abuse that is bullying;

- The failure to challenge acknowledged inappropriate behaviours that have been the subject of a bullying complaint, which was not upheld.

In day-to-day language, the terms 'bullying' and 'harassment' are used interchangeably, as the behaviours involved share similarities. Consequently, the definition of harassment (Equality Act, 2004) could form the basis of a new definition of bullying, with the inclusion of an additional statement, that bullying generally involves a pattern of behaviour, whereas harassment often consists of a single incident. Both

> **"**
> We suggest that Workplace Bullying would then be defined as: A pattern of unwanted behaviour which has the purpose or effect of violating a person's dignity by creating an intimidating, hostile, degrading, humiliating or offensive environment for the person (Corbett & Kitt, 2007).
> **"**

harassment and bullying are forms of discrimination, and, as such, should be not be linked exclusively to the nine protected categories, which are gender, marital status, family status, age, disability, race, sexual orientation, religious beliefs and membership of the traveller community. Everyone should be protected.

> **"**
>
> The Department of Education and Skills (DES) bears the biggest responsibility for setting and insisting on high standards of respectful behaviour from everyone who works in schools. When these standards of behaviour are considered as performance issues, they are much more difficult to dismiss and ignore.
>
> **"**

We suggest that Workplace Bullying would then be defined as: 'a pattern of unwanted behaviour, which has the purpose or effect of violating a person's dignity by creating an intimidating, hostile, degrading, humiliating or offensive environment for the person' (Corbett & Kitt, 2007).

The term 'dignity' is the appropriate one to use in the definition, although it is rather vague and requires clarification. 'Dignity at Work' policies are now part and parcel of official workplace documentation, however, the content of these policies generally provides little or no guidance on what an organisation or school is required to do to uphold the dignity of its employees.

D. 3.1 Dignity at Work

Dignity refers to the worth and value that each person has by virtue of being human. Everyone has the right to live and work with dignity. Promoting and protecting the dignity of every employee is the duty of employers and in everyday school terms, it is the responsibility of the school leader. How a person is treated determines whether their dignity is acknowledged or denied. When they are treated with equality and respect, their sense of their own worth and value is promoted. However, when they are treated in a disrespectful manner, and less favourably than others, their sense of their own worth and value is eroded. Bullying is the ultimate manifestation of disrespect and disregard and, as such, devastates a person's dignity.

In schools, ensuring that the dignity of everyone is, in as far as possible, promoted and protected is the clearest way to prevent the bullying of either staff members or students. This can only be achieved when expectations in relation to the behaviours of everyone in the school are clearly documented and communicated. A Dignity at Work policy that does what it says on the tin must outline, in no uncertain terms, the behaviours that are expected from everyone and that are considered to be appropriate, acceptable and professional. The policy must also outline in clear and unequivocal terms what workplace bullying is and how it affects the individual, the onlookers, and the school. It must also encourage those who are experiencing problems to raise the relevant issues, and it must include effective and fair procedures for dealing promptly and proactively with all interpersonal problems including bullying. Fulfilling that tall order requires the personal commitment of school leaders to uphold the dignity of everyone in the school. That commitment must also be stamped with the authority of the employer. In Ireland, The Department of Education and Skills (DES) bears the biggest responsibility for setting and insisting on high standards of respectful behaviour from everyone who works in schools. When these standards of behaviour are considered as performance issues, they are much more difficult to dismiss and ignore.

Key Points

- Workplace Bullying is prevalent in Schools.

- Despite increasing awareness of all aspects of workplace bullying, many myths and misconceptions still abound in relation to understanding what it really entails.

- Bullying is form of abuse.

- Bullying prevents victims from doing their jobs.

- Accurate defining and understanding of bullying prevents other inappropriate behaviours from being labelled and confused with bullying.

- Workplace bullying destroys workplaces.

D. 4. Workplace Bullying Tactics

There are many and various means of bullying those who are just trying to get on with their jobs at work. However, isolation and criticism are two of the most frequently-cited manifestations of workplace bullying. Occasionally, isolation may be caused accidentally and inadvertently, and criticism may be expressed constructively. Consequently, without an adequate exploration of the particular nuances and effects of isolation and criticism in the bullying context, their destructive impact can be diminished.

D. 4.1 Isolation as a Bullying Tactic

In order to understand isolation in the context of bullying, it is necessary to focus on the underlying non-verbal psychological messages of disregard and dismissal that are disseminated through the surface tactics. The simple yet evocative act of turning and walking away from someone while they are in mid-sentence, and the snubbing, ignoring or the sending to Coventry of someone, are all isolating tactics frequently used by those who bully. This is not done inadvertently, thoughtlessly or through rudeness, but rather in an attempt to discourage their target's company and contribution (Gentile, 1994) and to negate their "worth, dignity and equal human status" (Hornstein, 1996, p. 70).

The isolation of someone is often initially achieved by the suspension of verbal communication with them. The following account was provided by a teacher, in relation to a colleague in her school who absolutely refused to communicate verbally with her. "It's not just the fact that she never speaks to me that really bothers me. It's that:

- She demonstrates exaggerated friendliness to everyone else on the staff while totally blanking me;

- She looks at me with disdain, indicating to me that I have done something to deserve the silent treatment;

- When I ask her why she does not speak to me, she refuses to answer, and angrily and dismissively feigns ignorance of any such behaviour;

- She sneers and laughs when I get upset;

- Whether I ignore it, laugh it off, get annoyed or upset, the behaviour continues unabated;

- Professional issues and problems that require communication between us are not dealt with or resolved;

- Colleagues, with whom I previously had excellent relationships, are distancing themselves from me also.

There is awful tension in the school."

Those who bully do not isolate merely to exclude someone. The isolation is also a focused means of preventing that person from contributing to the organisation. They are isolated to ensure that it is virtually impossible for them to do their job. Isolating someone is a gradual and escalating process.

> **Being isolated by someone is a lonely and disempowering experience. However it is difficult, if not impossible, for the desired outcome to be achieved by one person on his/her own.**

Targets can, eventually, find themselves totally excluded and marginalised. There are many accounts of bullying in organisations, where those who are bullied find themselves, as a result of the gradual wearing down process of isolation (Ishmael & Alemoru, 1999), relegated to working alone, without any responsibility or any means of communicating.

In schools, where bullied staff members are increasingly ignored and ostracised, they can eventually resort to taking their lunch on the corridor or in their classroom, which is likely to be occupied by noisy students. It is quite shocking, when this situation arises, that it is often neither commented on by colleagues nor addressed by the school leaders. The secrecy and silence that surround bullying and its consequences, enable the behaviours to continue and thrive. In schools, those who are targeted have their responsibilities, their resources and their support system so eroded that they find themselves effectively prevented from reaching anywhere near full participation in the activities of the school. Sports enthusiasts who are being bullied, are relegated to "a nothing job" on sports day. Talented musicians, who are being bullied, are prevented from giving their services at school concerts or other performances. Others, who are generous and enthusiastic, have their offers of help and assistance flatly refused. Emphasising the ostracising effect of this typical form of rejection, Ryan and Oestreich (1991, p. 49), referred to it as "the sending off to some organisational Siberia from which there is no return."

Being isolated by someone is a lonely and disempowering experience. However it is difficult, if not impossible, for the desired outcome to be achieved by one person on his/her own. The notion that those who bully can, on their own, isolate a target is disputed (Zapf et al., 1996). They contended that while those who bully may try to orchestrate the isolation, it is a strategy that will not succeed without the involvement of others. This involvement does not necessitate others acting as accomplices, although many of them do. Denial, apathy, or disbelief that an injustice is being perpetrated, can contribute, to varying degrees, to a failure to support those isolated. The unsupportive on-lookers become either complicit in the bullying or act as inadvertent co-conspirators. Control, and fear of those who are doing the bullying also contribute to a withholding of support. By misrepresenting the target's words and actions, by publicly or privately discrediting them, and by exhibiting exaggerated and disproportionate favouritism to a selected few, those who bully engage others in willingly or unwittingly participating in the bullying. Those allied to the perpetrator exhibit no empathy or support for the target. The paucity of support triggers in targets "an inclination towards self-derogation" (Sheppard et al., 1992, p. 98), thus complicating their situation and exacerbating their suffering.

Social encounters at any level are used to express evaluations of others (Hornstein, 1996). Being excluded from conversations, social gatherings and general involvement communicates "disrespect and devaluation" (Bassman, 1992, p. 7). The deliberate isolation of a colleague demonstrates total "disregard for human relatedness" in an organisation (McCarthy et al., 1996, p. 49). It is incredibly hurtful, insensitive and cruel, and it is, without doubt, the most prevalent form of bullying in the workplace. The isolation of a staff member is particularly detrimental to the quality of the environment in a school. This is because of the importance of positive relationships in schools and because of the interdependence of everyone working in them.

D. 4.2 Criticism as a Bullying Tactic

Criticism is another frequently cited bullying behaviour. However, criticism in the context of bullying involves two particular aspects requiring exploration. Firstly, the criticisms are spurious. The innocuous and unsubstantiated incidents, which are the basis of those criticisms, are invariably "distorted, magnified and often fabricated" (Field, 1997, p. 31). Those who bully frequently scrutinise the words and actions of those they target, to try to find any small error or oversight in a frenetic attempt to discredit them. Any "grain of truth" (Middleton-Moz & Zawadski, 2002, p. 27) in this regard is exaggerated to misrepresent their intentions and actions and to portray them as incompetent and/or dishonest.

For example, Jim had been deputy principal in a city school until he was appointed as principal of a school in a rural county. Two of the teachers in that school had also applied for the position. From the beginning, he sensed that one of them, Peter, was going to make his life very difficult. The criticism began on his first day when he was accused by Peter of being patronising, after he acknowledged the experience of the staff and said he looked forward to working with them. From that day onwards, Jim was frequently forensically questioned on every suggestion he made and always in negative terms. Every new idea advanced by Jim for discussion was aggressively and summarily dismissed by Peter as ridiculous, unworkable and/or outdated. No elaboration by Peter on those criticisms was ever forthcoming. Any meeting between Jim and a parent in relation to an issue or problem was criticised by Peter, who publicly derided him and accused him of collusion or disloyalty. Attempts by Jim at clarification were discounted and sneered at. When Jim endeavoured to discuss in a rational manner the criticisms that Peter was constantly levelling at him, he was accused of trying to stifle any questioning of his power.

In an attempt to create better staff relations, Jim invited the entire staff out to lunch at the end of his first term in the school; Peter refused to attend, and accused him of trying to buy the allegiance of the staff. He also suggested to a number of the teachers that school funds would probably be used to pay for the lunch. When Jim challenged him on this, Peter accused him of being defensive and said he made no apology for ensuring that Jim was behaving ethically.

Those who have never experienced the utterly unwarranted criticism that bullying involves may find it hard to understand how challenging and difficult it is to counteract. I describe it euphemistically as slippery behaviour. In reality, it is so deceptive that one cannot get a handle on what is really going on. A bullied person can spend weeks, months or even years trying to address the bases of the criticisms without realising that they are bogus and a sham.

In relation to sham criticisms specifically, much is written on sham peer reviews in the medical profession. Those who engage in these sham reviews "frequently bring trumped-up, fabricated and totally false charges"(Huntoon, 2009, p.65), against those under review. Ambush tactics are used to try to catch out the person being reviewed and irrespective, of how they try to counter the false or grossly exaggerated accusations, there is no reprieve for them in the context of the process being rigged and the outcome being predetermined (Huntoon, 2007).

Sham dealings, a term coined by Osborne (2009), are characteristic of workplace bullying. Most people expect rational and fairly predictable behaviours from those they work with. When they are bullied, it generally takes them a considerable length of time to realise that the behaviours being exhibited towards them are

> **These actions are exceedingly difficult to credit if they have not been experienced or witnessed. They are, however, the reality of everyday work life for those being bullied.**

deceptive and designed to set them up to fail. Those who are bullied at work are often excluded from all teamwork and relegated to working on their own, only to be later unjustly criticised for being uncooperative. Some are blatantly under-resourced and subjected to arbitrary and unnecessary changes to their roles and schedules, to the extent that a deadline is missed by the smallest of margins. They are then wrongly deemed to be inefficient or incompetent.

A teacher who claimed to have been bullied by her principal, recounted how, on one occasion she left the school early with verbal permission from the principal, after receiving news of the hospitalisation of her mother. She was subsequently berated in the staffroom for setting a precedent and for taking advantage of others. Although she was certain of the details of what had actually happened, she immediately began to doubt herself.

Any small oversight or error is filed in the minds of those who bully, to be used against the target at a time when it can cause the most damage to them. These actions are exceedingly difficult to credit if they have not been experienced or witnessed. They are, however, the reality of everyday work life for those being bullied.

Criticisms that are directed at someone as an aspect of bullying are often presented in the guise of highlighting inadequacies, or shortfalls in the target's performance (Field, 1996). The bullying can then be easily legitimised as an attempt to rehabilitate the "offender" and as being for the good and improvement of the individual or the organisation. Unwarranted criticisms expressed "under the guise of monitoring job performance" (Costigan, 1998, p.31), have, among their destructive objectives, the desire to force someone out of their job or to reduce them to such a state of ill health that they will have to leave (Costigan, 1998).

In the case of Jim, the newly-appointed principal, the constant criticisms by Peter of his every action were always couched in language of concern about best practice standards. However, criticism as a bullying tactic is neither about creating awareness of professional inadequacies, nor is it about the desire to correct a flaw or failing. The goal is not to address or prevent an individual or organisational shortcoming. The criticism is unjustified and unfair and "it is abuse for the sake of abuse" (Hornstein, 1996, p. 49).

Rejection and exclusion are implicit in the use of both criticism and isolation as prevalent bullying tactics. They constitute social-evaluative threats and are especially powerful psychological stressors. They provide the potential for loss of self-esteem, social status, or social acceptance (Dickerson et al., 2004).

Key Points

- Isolation and criticism are two of the most prevalent forms of workplace bullying.
- Isolation in bullying is about proactively preventing someone from participating.
- Criticism in bullying is never about managing or correcting. It is always about undermining and destroying.
- Those who bully need the implicit or explicit support of onlookers to successfully isolate someone.
- Isolation and criticism in bullying are very damaging psycho-social stressors.

D. 4.3 Other Manifestations of Workplace Bullying

The concentration on a small number of common and recurring bullying behaviours is an important means of examining the nuances of bullying. It is however, equally important to allude to the fact that bullying involves a constellation of negative acts, such as withholding vital information and support, spreading discrediting rumours, misrepresenting the words and actions of others, unjust and unfair task allocation and organisation of timetables and schedules, preventing and restricting communication, and many other obstructive behaviours that prohibit targets from contributing their best efforts to the organisation (Mikkelsen & Einarsen, 2001; Namie & Namie, 2000).

Whereas there are obvious and visible manifestations of bullying at work, including overt aggression such as physical violence and angry verbal outbursts, they do not appear to be common in schools. Cyber-bullying is also less prevalent among adults in schools, although the content, timing and frequency of text messages and emails often constitute part of a bullying campaign.

The less obvious insidious forms of bullying are more prevalent and pervasive in schools. Indeed, bullying behaviour can be so subtle that even the targets do not realise what is happening (Beale, 2001). Initial and seemingly minor incidents, when taken out of the cumulative context, may appear trivial. This prevents the target from realising that something serious is taking place (Futterman, 2004). Those perpetrating these most manipulative of behaviours are "masters at disguising their actions, and the effect on victims is difficult to detect and to isolate" (Mann, 1996, p. 83). Turney (2003, p. 5) contended that subtle and insidious bullying "is almost impossible to detect outside the interpersonal relationships."

Karen, a young, enthusiastic and highly qualified teacher, started work on a temporary basis in a large urban school. She was introduced to the staff by the principal as Miss Jones. "She has a Master's degree in music – for all the good that will do her here", she added. There was a nervous titter in response and Karen felt slightly embarrassed. However, she mentioned later to the principal that she might be able to assist with the school choir. This offer was not taken up and the teacher who looked after the choir stopped talking to Karen. Much later Karen learned from the music teacher that the principal had said that she had asked if she could take over the choir. Although, for the following 18 months, Karen, worked with the music teacher on numerous musical events, the principal only ever mentioned the other teacher when extolling the high quality of the events.

With the money that her grandfather left her, Karen bought a new car. On the day she first drove it to school, the principal told her not to be surprised if it was autographed with a key, as people around the area did not take kindly to those with notions of themselves. Although Karen had formed excellent relationships with both the students and their parents, the principal told her that parents had concerns about her professionalism. Despite asking repeatedly, she was not given any details but was told that she should watch herself. She was frequently contacted by the principal, outside school hours, in relation to trivial issues, which were portrayed as worrying or urgent. There were numerous other examples of how she was targeted for unfavourable comment and attention, without any corroboration or elaboration on accusations provided.

Karen developed an unnatural level of vigilance. She consciously and meticulously checked and double-checked every aspect of her work in an attempt to ward off criticism. These efforts proved to be futile. Gradually, her confidence was eroded and was eventually shattered, her health deteriorated and her hair began to fall out. She described how she felt in terms of not knowing whether she was coming or going. In the staffroom on the day she was leaving the school, the other staff members wished her well and many hugged her. However, the principal did not lift her head from the newspaper. Karen may never know why she was treated in such a manner.

A central component of bullying behaviour is the ability to deeply hurt and demean, while remaining well obscured from onlookers (Adams, 1992). It is difficult to identify primarily because of its secretive nature but also because of the 'Jekyll and Hyde personality' of the perpetrator. While covertly tormenting their targets, they can overtly lavish charm and praise on

> **"**
> **Bullying is never warranted in any circumstance, but it is widely acknowledged that targets of bullying have done nothing offensive, threatening or harmful to provoke these behaviours.**
> **"**

others (Field, 1996). They also express righteous indignation and absolute denial of any wrongdoing if challenged or confronted. The psychological nature of the bullying renders it difficult to document and equally difficult to prove (Field, 1996; Adams, 1992).

Bullying is never warranted in any circumstance, but it is widely acknowledged that targets of bullying have done nothing offensive, threatening or harmful to provoke these behaviours. The behaviours result mainly from skewed and mistaken interpretations of the attitudes and behaviours of those the bullies perceive as a threat.

Susan had been teaching in the same school for over 20 years. She did not appear to meet the most basic criteria expected from teachers, which is that they must, at the very least, like children. She was constantly berating students and always in the most inappropriate of language. When, at lunch break one day, she spent the entire time deriding the behaviour and the ability of a particular student, Eileen, a relative newcomer to the staff found the tirade extremely difficult to listen to. She also taught the student in question and said that, in her opinion, he was not as bad as Susan had portrayed him. Eileen pointed out that there were mitigating home circumstances and that perhaps they should be taken into consideration in relation to his behaviour and levels of

> **"**
> **When workplace bullying occurs in schools, it has a pervasive and corrosive impact on those targeted, on on-lookers, on students and on the school generally.**
> **"**

engagement. Susan did not reply but immediately left the staffroom banging the door on the way out. That expression of an opinion by Eileen triggered a ferocious campaign of bullying which raged over the following five years. It included constantly misrepresenting her words and actions to others, spreading malicious rumours about her, her family, her relationships and her professionalism. During that time Susan never once addressed Eileen directly, but persistently denigrated and dismissed every contribution made by her. The behaviours ebbed and flowed but always peaked when something important was happening in Eileen's life. When she visited the school after the birth of her first baby, bringing the baby with her, Susan appeared very annoyed. She stood up and left the room without a glance at Eileen or the baby. At the door she turned and said "This is a professional workplace – not a crèche".

There is evidence that the simple fact of having a superior qualification, coming up with a good idea or expressing a different view point (Horstein, 1996; Namie & Namie, 1999), can be interpreted as threatening and can result in a kind of "personal retaliation" (Zapf & Einarsen, 2003, p. 170), against those wrongly perceived as threats. Workplace bullying should be considered in terms of hurtful and humiliating behaviour. It also needs to be considered in terms of the on-going and relentless nature of the bullying behaviours. Only then can a real comprehension of the adverse effects of workplace bullying on individuals and organisations be achieved.

When workplace bullying occurs in schools, it has a pervasive and corrosive impact on those targeted, on on-lookers, on students and on the school generally. Schools have a responsibility to provide a consistently high quality of educational service and this can only be achieved in an environment where healthy interpersonal behaviours are the norm (Bluestein, 2001).

Bullying is regarded as an extreme form of dysfunctional interpersonal interaction, characterised by hypocrisy, insensitivity and control on the part on the perpetrator, and by fear, confusion, frustration and incredulity on the part of the target.

It is difficult to imagine that those charged with the task of imparting knowledge and insights in an enlightened and collaborative manner could persistently deprive students of the talents and enthusiasm of colleagues. It is equally difficult to comprehend that those responsible for enabling the formation of minds and intellects could act in such a mindless and self-obsessed manner. And it is virtually impossible to fathom how those expected to promote and model the values of fairness and openness would wilfully engage in behaviours that hurt and destroy their colleagues.

A further disturbing element in relation to workplace bullying in schools is that the majority of perpetrators of these behaviours remain unchallenged and unsanctioned, while those they target are persistently subjected to humiliation, exclusion and blame (Blase & Blase, 2003). When bullying continues unimpeded, it diminishes the positivity, spontaneity, creativity, and camaraderie so essential for teaching and learning, and it destroys the "feel good factors" in our schools (Randall, 1997, p.49).

Key Points

- Bullying involves a range of destructive behaviours.
- Bullying behaviours are generally psychological, irrational and escalating.
- Bullying is difficult to document and to prove.
- Bullying is never warranted.
- It is difficult to comprehend how those responsible for the care and education of students could engage in bullying behaviours.

D. 5. Characteristics of those who Bully

Increased awareness in relation to the nature and effects of workplace bullying prompts an obvious and imponderable question. What sort of person could possibly treat another human being in that manner? Although the question cannot be definitively answered, it is encouraging that it is increasingly being asked. The focus on the perpetrators and their behaviour in terms of finding the source and cause of bullying, is a process that is slow, yet justifiable. Of course, a full understanding of all aspects of bullying is not to be found in the analysis of the characteristics and motives of the perpetrators. However it is an inevitable and necessary element of the progression towards that understanding.

Although there is still a paucity of literature and research on the characteristics and motivation of workplace bullies, some consensus is emerging. This arises from a combination of: the exploration of the shared experiences of those being bullied, the observations of objective onlookers, and the consistency evident in the behaviours and effects of bullying. Although Randall (1997) contended that there is no standard profile of the workplace bully and, as in the case of sexual harassers, there is unlikely to be a single psychological profile that would characterise all those who bully (Pryor & Fitzgerald, 2003).

> "
> **Perpetrators of bullying are adept at portraying themselves favourably to those they wish to impress.**
> "

From the many and varied listings of characteristics offered, for consideration, the following appear most prominently and frequently. In terms of the more obvious of these characteristics, it is suggested that those who bully are aggressive, angry, malicious, vindictive, self-righteous, selfish and lacking in empathy. The less obvious yet equally significant characteristics associated with those who bully are: insecurity, inadequacy, insatiability, cowardice, dishonesty, jealousy and disloyalty. A legitimate conclusion to formulate in the context of those who bully possessing all or indeed some of these characteristics is that there would be absolutely no difficulty in recognising and identifying them in the workplace.

Unfortunately this conclusion is far from the reality of the situation. Perpetrators of bullying are adept at portraying themselves favourably to those they wish to impress. Futterman (2004) asserted that bullies are not easy to spot. They are chameleon-like in their ability to camouflage their behaviours and can be superficially and opportunistically charming. They manage to ingratiate themselves to potential allies and to those in positions of power and influence. Those who are included among the favoured ones experience praise, generosity and preferential treatment. Consequently, they either refuse or fail to recognise the behaviours exhibited towards others as bullying and regard the perpetrator as being kind and caring. They become blinkered to any flaw in them. Perhaps, to see those who bully as flawed is to see the favourable regard shown to them as shallow, worthless and flawed also.

In order to build a cohort of unquestioning allies, bullying leaders frequently appoint those who are least competent. In subsequently showing favouritism to them, they are reciprocated with blind loyalty and allegiance. Others who have fallen out of favour, often for perceived disloyalty, and those who were never favoured at all, experience degradation and discrimination. When they are not blinkered by self-doubt or self-blame, they see what is happening to them as irrational, hypocritical and sadistic (Crawford, 2001). Whether in favour or out of favour, all are consciously or unconsciously, and to a greater or lesser extent, fearful around the volatility and fickleness of those who bully.

Perpetrators of workplace bullying are almost invariably aggressive (Olweus, 2003). However, the aggression is generally psychological and it more typically manifests verbally rather than physically; is passive rather than active and indirect rather than direct (Keasley & Jagatic, 2003). A "passively-aggressive bully uses secrecy, manipulation, obsessional and evasive behaviours as tactics, to get their way" (Terhani, 2003, p. 282). Leaders who bully frequently are aggressive towards anyone who is perceived as questioning, contradicting or impugning them, or their way of doing things (Zapf & Einarsen, 2003). Any differing attitude or perspective that may promote another way of seeing or doing things threatens their absolutism and undermines and jeopardises their feelings of superiority (Zapf & Einarsen, 2003). They protect and preserve their feeling of superiority by resisting with determination any real examination of any aspect of them or their behaviour.

D. 5.1 The Self-Esteem of those who Bully

Those who bully were generally thought to have low self-esteem (Hornsrein, 1996; Wright & Smye, 1996; Randall, 1997; Horn, 2002; Futterman, 2004). There is now a considerable consensus that their self-esteem may in fact be quite high, particularly in the context of their favourable views of themselves and the aggressive response to any questioning of those views (Zapf & Einarsen, 2003). This opinion is reinforced by an examination of the narcissistic behaviours of the bully. Narcissism is thought to imply a combination of high self-esteem and a disregard for others (Zapf & Einarsen, 2003). Disregard for others is a hallmark of a bully's behaviour. They have a compulsion to have their own needs met at all costs, and make constant demands for respect and consideration, while persistently denying similar treatment to others (Adams, 1992; Field, 1996). Hornstein (1996, p. 59), commented that by their self-centred, selfish behaviour they effectively treat selected others as "objects and instruments".

If indeed their self-esteem is high, it is certainly not healthy. Colvin, Block and Funder (1995) suggested that overly positive self-opinions can indicate maladjustment and delusion, rather than indicating healthy adjustment and well-being. Jordan et al., (2003), as a result of their research on those with defensive rather than secure high self-esteem, concluded that their "positive self-views mask less conscious self-doubts and feelings of inadequacy, which motivates defensive behaviours" (2003, p. 969).

Whether the self-esteem of those who bully is high and unhealthy and masks their self-doubts, or their abusive behaviours are a dysfunctional reflection of their low self-esteem, is uncertain. My own belief is that the vociferous arrogance and self-righteousness that those who bully frequently display, may serve to effectively disguise their low self-esteem and cause them to present as having the opposite. The fact that their self-appraisals are "heavily dependent on external validation" is an indicator of their own lack of confidence (Zapf & Einarsen, 2003, p. 168). The aggressive and territorial reaction to any negative evaluation is an indicator of the fragility and instability of the self-assessment of those who bully. Middleton-Moz & Zawadski (2002, pp. 125-126) asserted that, "because of their deep-seated feelings of worthlessness, they are terrified of being proven 'wrong.'"

D. 5.2 The Inadequacies and Insecurities of those who Bully

While there is a dearth of insight into the motivation of those who bully, there tends to be a general acceptance in the literature on workplace bullying that the behaviours are reflective of their inherent inadequacies and insecurities. Bullies fearing exposure, have learnt to defend themselves, by deception and distraction (Middleton-Moz & Zawadski, 2002). They diminish the fine qualities of others in order to deflect attention from their own inadequacies (Hornstein, 1996). They are empowered by de-emphasising the "strengths, abilities, competencies, intelligence and integrity of others" (Mann, 1996, p. 83).

> **"**
> **Personal illness or tragedy failed to elicit either empathy or compassion from the perpetrators, but rather seemed to be a signal to escalate and redouble the abusive behaviour.**
> **"**

The worst excesses of their behaviour can be seen by those targeted and by certain onlookers, but remain unseen by the perpetrators, indicating, in terms of the Johari Window model of analysis of the various selves, that they have a very considerable blind self (Luft & Ingham, 1961).

Consequently, whereas bullying behaviours follow a systematic pattern and appear to have been meticulously planned, they may, in the context of the bully's inability to see themselves or their behaviours for what they are, be conducted unconsciously. In this context, I suggest that many of their behaviours are unconsciously strategic.

Those who bully are consistently described as being insensitive. Field (1996, p. 66) described their insensitivity as "perhaps the bullies' worst trait." Showing no consideration for the feelings of those they hurt and humiliate, they appear impervious to the effects of their behaviour (Field, 1996). Hornstein (1996, p. 36) described bullying bosses who display grossly insensitive behaviour as "dehumanizers". Finding it difficult to understand their callousness, Hornstein (1996, p. 37), further suggested that, "they self-administer a kind of emotional anaesthesia that diminishes their awareness of harm done". All of the participants in my study (Kitt, 1999) agreed that those who abused them displayed gross insensitivity to their feelings. To a greater or lesser extent, they were all cruel and hurtful. Personal illness or tragedy failed to elicit either empathy or compassion from the perpetrators, but rather seemed to be a signal to escalate and redouble the abusive behaviour.

An examination of the characteristics of those perpetrating the bullying behaviours is a vital component in exposing bullying in all its ugliness and in dispelling the myths and misconceptions propagated by those fearing, and fighting against this exposition. However, a focus on the personality of those who bully, in terms of labelling them as psychopathic or evil, is to exclude many others who also bully. While not discounting the psychopathic behaviours of many of those who bully, in terms of the absence of remorse, or empathy, and the lack of insight into their behaviour (Babiak & Hare, 2006), the categorisation and labelling of them is ill-advised as it may lead to witch-hunting.

When the teachers who participated in my study (Kitt, 1999) depicted those who were deemed responsible for bullying them, they concentrated more on their behaviours and on the interpretations of their behaviours rather than on their personalities. They portrayed those who bullied them as being incapable of listening to, or accepting, any alternative point of view. They appeared to be threatened by any question or suggestion that was perceived as criticising or challenging their opinions or their methodology. All of those who were responsible for the bullying displayed gross inadequacies in their ability to communicate in an open manner and build healthy relationships with others. Deficiencies in social competencies, particularly those that are necessary for close relationships, are linked to behaviours that offend and humiliate others (Hudson & Ward, 2000).

The principals who were deemed responsible for bullying were perceived to lack vision and initiative. According to those targeted, they reneged on their responsibilities, distrusted competence, and put their own positions before the welfare of the school and the students. When organisations are subjected to power-hunger and ego-needs, the organisation and its people are jeopardised (Davenport et al., 1999). Bullying leaders or managers are what Kelly (1988) labelled as 'destructive achievers'. They have filtered upwards into positions of power that become increasingly impenetrable. They take credit for others' achievements, stifle discussion and resist change and innovation. They allow staff relations to disintegrate, and perhaps the saddest of all the behaviours of school leaders who bully is that they deprive the students of the talents and competence of those they target.

School leaders who bully are very much in the minority. However, the damage that those bullying leaders cause far outweighs their number. Schools with bullying leaders slowly but surely deteriorate and disintegrate. Competent staff members leave and student numbers decrease. Yet even in the context of those obvious effects, it does not register with those who bully that they

> **"**
> **Serial and unrelenting bullies appear to have no capacity to reflect critically on their actions or, indeed more generally, have little or no inclination or ability to introspect analytically.**
> **"**

are in any way to blame for what is happening to their school. Rather, they display intransigence in their continuous abuse of others. They are uncompromising and unforgiving. They are in denial about their wrongdoing, and despite the toxic atmosphere in the schools, are dishonest in their attempts to give the impression that normality prevails. They are also extremely litigious, and take grave offence and seek legal redress in relation to any accusation made against them. It is little wonder that those who are bullied despair and feel powerless and helpless in terms of affecting any change in their situation.

Serial and unrelenting bullies appear to have no capacity to reflect critically on their actions or, indeed more generally, have little or no inclination or ability to introspect analytically. Consequently, they either fail to acknowledge their behaviour or fail to interpret their behaviour as inappropriate. Where there is an acknowledgement by the perpetrators of the different and less favourable treatment meted out by them to others, it is perceived by them as being necessary, even obligatory and always justified.

Key Points

- Those who bully share many obvious and less obvious personality characteristics.

- Behaviours perpetrated by those who bully are exceedingly similar irrespective of the environment.

- There are mixed views in relation to whether those who bully have high and unhealthy self-esteem or low self-esteem disguised as being the opposite.

- Those who bully are to a greater or lesser extent in denial about their behaviour.

- Most leaders who bully have been promoted beyond their competence and despite the damage they cause, try to give the impression that everything is alright.

D. 6 Being Bullied

There is one prevailing, albeit diminishing, myth, which is that those targeted for bullying share to some extent characteristics and attitudes that render them naturally vulnerable to being bullied. Leymann (1996, p. 172) suggested that concentrating on personalities to explain bullying behaviour is a "fundamental attribution error". If there is a typical profile of a bullied victim in the workplace, and if it includes suggested attributes such as being submissive, anxious, sensitive, passive or insecure, then the majority of those who have been bullied are excluded.

There is also a school of thought suggesting that certain characteristics contribute to individuals becoming 'provocative victims' (Randall, 1997; Hoel et al., 2000). The term was first used by Olweus (1978), when referring to a group of targets of school bullying who behaved in ways that caused irritation or exasperation to either fellow students and/or teachers. He further alluded to those students in terms of their social exclusion or isolation. It is not difficult to conjure up a picture of people who could be considered as having annoying traits or behaving in an annoying manner. However, the labelling of those who are considered to be annoying as 'provocative victims' can be problematic. Although not stated or intended by any of the writers who use this term, it could be interpreted that those who are labelled as provocative victims are in some way the authors of their own destiny in relation to being bullied.

One of the indicators of bullying is that those who are picked on are a source of annoyance to those who pick on them. The list of so called annoying characteristics is, however, extremely extensive (Wilkie, 1996). Those who bully can be annoyed by someone who talks too much or talks too little, is confident and outgoing or shy and introverted, is fat or thin, or is in any way different from the norm. Those who bully can get really annoyed with others just because they mind their own business, get on with their lives and are contented and happy. Bullying is frequently initiated by envy or jealousy in relation to a possession, a position or an attribute of

> **"**
> **Anyone can be targeted. However, the problems arise when those, for their own reasons, select and abuse others.**
> **"**

another. It is impossible to guard against bullying, specifically because one cannot predict what will provoke it. Anyone can be targeted. However, the problems arise when those, for their own reasons, select and abuse others.

Those who are picked on are never to blame for the abuse committed by others who have chosen to act in an abusive manner. "They are the recipients of harm and not its agent" (Hornstein, 1996, p. 117). Predecessors have suffered at the hands of their tormentor, as will successors (Field, 1996).

A special needs assistant, who really loved her job, felt she had to leave the school as a result of being persistently undermined and excluded by a teacher colleague. She had received absolutely no support from other members of staff or the school leaders when she made an informal complaint about the behaviours, and ultimately felt that she had no option but to resign. Subsequently, she learned that there had been two others, who had also left their jobs in the school citing the behaviour of the same teacher as the reason.

Targets unfortunately just happen to be in the wrong place at the wrong time. It may be worth adding "with the wrong person" to the above, in order to complete the bullying conditions. Interestingly, it is observed that there are similar risks of being bullied at all organisational status levels (Hoel et al., 2001). Bullies will pick on others just because they don't like the look of them, or the way they walk, or the way they pray (Middleton-Moz & Zawadski, 2002).

D. 6.1 Personality Changes as a Result of Workplace Bullying

The notion that the personality characteristics of the target contribute to the bullying is widely disputed. However, there is considerable consensus that personalities change as a result of bullying. Previously confident and assertive people who are bullied often become insecure and submissive. Wright and Smye (1996, p. 22) suggested that bullying "makes us doubt ourselves, sometimes even doubt our sanity."

Those who participated in my study reflected the views of the many others whom I have spoken to over the years. They all described how, to varying degrees, their personalities altered as a result of bullying. Those who had previously been communicative, open, confident and trusting with colleagues became introverted, withdrawn, suspicious and fearful. Many spoke about experiencing intense feelings of sadness and also alluded to being occasionally uncontrollably tearful. As the preoccupation and obsession with the abuse increased, vigilance and defensiveness also increased. The participants in my study also cited anger, moodiness, volatility, intolerance of noise, inability to engage with normal conversations or with social activities as consequences of being bullied (Kitt, 1999).

When bullying begins with the initial impression by the target that something is wrong, the impression is often triggered by a distinct feeling of being intensely disliked. The way they avoid making eye contact, or the way they shake your hand can provide a gut feeling that something is amiss long before anything tangible surfaces (Middleton-Moz & Zawadski, 2001). The feeling of being intensely disliked at a first encounter with someone is disconcerting and confusing. The very tenuous and intangible source of this feeling provides little assistance in understanding or contextualising the subsequent abusive behaviours when they occur. As more tangible manifestations of distaste and disapproval are unveiled, a sense of bewilderment and disbelief begins to creep up on the unsuspecting target. Further encounters often find the target presenting as unusually tentative, nervous, and even deferential. If encounters take place in public and involve increasing and subtle hostility or reprimands, targets can become totally inhibited in expressing themselves and may stutter and stammer. This results in acute embarrassment and humiliation that is aggravated by the failure of the perpetrator to interject and redeem the situation or alleviate the embarrassment. Being made to feel foolish or being shamed is ranked in psychological and anxiety tests as having a most powerful, destructive and long-lasting impact (Wright & Smye, 1996).

If the bullying continues and progresses, it takes a "spellbinding hold" of the target (Cavaiola & Lavender, 2000, p. 69). Middleton-Moz and Zawadski (2002) suggested that a dance begins between the bully and the target which can last a very long time: "Bullies lead and targets wittingly or unwittingly follow" (p. 124). Competent, confident people act in an uncharacteristically incompetent and uncertain manner. They often begin to feel stupid and worthless (Wright & Smye, 1996). With an escalation of the bullying comes an erosion of their personal position (Crawford, 1992), and they feel completely devalued and demoralised (Randall, 1997; Crawford, 1992).

Targets of bullying often express uncharacteristic frustration and anger aggravated by the incredulity of what is happening to them, and also by the blatant injustice of the behaviour perpetrated against them. This anger, if channelled appropriately into a well-thought-out strategy to challenge the bullying, may serve a useful and productive purpose. However, it usually festers internally until levels of exasperation or a particularly hurtful incident causes the anger to explode as an outburst of distress or rage. Field (1996, p. 142) suggested that targets of bullying who have previously exhibited a "robust and well-balanced mental state" may, as a result of bullying, display "bizarre, irrational and erratic behaviour" (Field, 1996, p. 142). Adams (1992) asserted, that an angry outburst in this context generally fails to produce a sense of off-loading or release, and invariably produces feelings of shame and guilt. Those being bullied lose sight of the provocation contributing to the outburst, blame themselves and often attempt to apologise and make amends for their reaction. A rejection of their apology leads to further humiliation and confusion as the cycle of abuse continues. On-lookers also fail to link these explosions or outbursts to the bullying that is being experienced, but rather judge the person to be volatile and paranoid.

With reference to the case of Eileen and Susan, Eileen returned to school after her maternity leave and on her first day back, Susan made a number of sneering and nasty comments under her breath in relation to Eileen's return. Eileen shouted at Susan and told her she was not going to put up with this behaviour any longer. She then left the staffroom and went to her classroom. No-one followed her and she felt totally isolated and alone. When her anger subsided, she was left with an overpowering feeling that she had let herself down. She had a strong urge to return to the staffroom and to apologise, but she was confused and embarrassed and could not muster either the strength or the energy to do it. When she heard that Susan had reacted to her outburst by stating to the entire staff that it was the first time she had seen post-natal depression in action, and that no-one had challenged her on the comment, Eileen felt that the school was no place for her.

She began the process of finding a position in another school. The fact that she had spared herself the humiliating effects of offering Susan a grovelling and unwarranted apology served to hasten her recovery from the bullying ordeal.

Those who are being bullied are frequently perceived as trouble makers. However, when changes in their demeanour and emotional reactions occur, they can be regarded as time-bombs waiting to explode and can present an excuse for getting rid of them (Field, 1996).

> **However, without a more general understanding and intolerance of bullying, the climate of acceptability persists and the frustration and suffering of those affected is exacerbated and prolonged.**

D. 6.2 Reactions of those who are Bullied at Work

A target's ordeal is intensified by his/her inability, or the inability of others, to recognise the problem for what it is. Blase and Blase (2003) suggested that many of those targeted do not know how to react to the problem because they frequently do not know what the problem is. Adams (1992) claimed that their personal survival depends on them recognising what is happening to them while they are still only slightly affected. With increasing discussion and the highlighting of bullying in literature and in the media, those targeted have an improved chance of identifying and labelling the irrational behaviours perpetrated against them. However, without a more general understanding and intolerance of bullying, the climate of acceptability persists and the frustration and suffering of those affected is exacerbated and prolonged.

When those being bullied accurately and honestly tell their stories, they are frequently disbelieved. Their viewpoint on the problem, should they have the ability to articulate it, may not be accepted by their colleagues or management. A sense that they are disbelieved, or regarded as being over-sensitive, paranoid or in some way to blame, creates a feeling of helplessness and causes disappointment and disillusionment. Their concerns about being disbelieved are justified in the company of those who regard accounts of bullying as being solely "in the eye of the beholder" (Hornstein, 1996, p.76). The 'beholder's eye' theory has been questioned and disputed by Michela et al., (1992), and is further discredited in the context of reports of bullying being frequently corroborated by others who were similarly treated, and by the accounts of multiple targets of bullying by the same perpetrator, exhibiting similar levels and types of effects (Hornstein, 1996).

While many of those who are bullied, for a variety of reasons, never discuss their experiences, others have a compulsive urge and need to share them with others. The overwhelming, almost uncontrollable, desire to tell their story (Field, 1996) is reflective of their obsession with the bullying. They think about it to the extent that it is their last thought before sleep and their first thought on awakening. They obsess with trying to rationalise the behaviour, with the injustice and unfairness of it, and with their own reactions and responses to it. They obsess particularly in the absence of established and effective mechanisms for dealing with bullying (Bassman, 1992).

The denial, obstruction and further victimisation by the organisation of those raising a concern or making a complaint are as shocking and devastating as the offending bullying behaviours. Those being bullied are robbed of their credibility, their professional integrity and their reputation (Davenport et al., 2000). Their isolation and helplessness increases and suspicion and fear become their constant companions.

Fear of making the situation worse silences protest or challenge. Fear of being regarded as a whistle-blower or a troublemaker stifles the quest for justice. Fear of further intimidation pushes the target into relinquishing autonomy, and "forfeiting self-direction for self-protection" (Hornstein, 1996, p. 79). An overwhelming and inexplicable fear is evoked in the person being bullied by the mere presence of the perpetrator. Their voice, their footsteps, or the sight of their car in the car park can induce this fear. The fear can be so intense that it constitutes psycho-terror which, as McCarthy (2004, p. 81) pointed out, is the result of "repeated psychological abrasions experienced over months or years".

Intense fear causes a paralysis of rational thought, action and reaction in those being bullied. The fear instilled in them, as a result of being "bludgeoned, belittled and betrayed" (Hornstein, 1996, p. 79), compels them to advance with extreme caution, rendering them either as inconspicuous or as compliant as possible in an attempt to avoid further unfavourable attention.

Many of those bullied in schools have talked about their experience in terms of being intimidated into employing "as little independent judgement and discretion as possible" (Hornstein, 1996, p. 80). They become disgusted with their own disempowerment and failure to effect a change in their situation. Bassman (1992) maintained that when they become self-critical and acquire feelings of incompetence, they lose control not only in their workplace, but also in their personal lives. Field (1996) suggested that those who are bullied carry the effects home with them, often causing unhappiness and stress to the family. Some of the targets of bullying in my study described their moods at home as being uncharacteristically irritable, snappy and contrary. They experienced pangs of guilt when there were accusations from their spouses or children of them being constantly in bad humour (Kitt, 1999).

D. 6.3 Effects of Workplace Bullying on those who are Targeted

Bullying has a wide range of adverse and debilitating effects on individuals. The magnitude of the psychological and physiological symptoms found in targets of bullying is an indication of the impact of bullying on health and well-being (Tehrani, 2003). Effects of bullying are listed under the various headings of physical, psychological, behavioural, emotional, psychosomatic, and social. (Field, 1996; Adams, 1992; Leymann, 1996). Field (1996) grouped the more common of these effects under the umbrella term of negative stress. He described negative stress as an "almost cancerous condition which eats away at self-worth, self-image, self-esteem and self-confidence" (Field, 1996, p. 123). Despite some variations in interpretation of the effects of workplace bullying, the literature presented an overwhelming consensus that those targeted become deeply and profoundly affected on a daily basis. They feel sick, hurt and trapped.

Many of those who are being bullied despair of getting any alleviation in their situation. Some blame themselves for causing or escalating the bullying behaviours. Through manipulation and control, a number of those who are bullied accept as fact the lies and distortions told by those who bully them and often believe that they are deserving of the treatment meted out to them. In these and other extreme cases, bullying may result in suicide (Hornstein, 1996; Randall, 1997; Leymann, 1996).

Bullying makes working life a misery for those who have been targeted and the effects, irrespective of how they manifest, are completely unacceptable. In the case of the five participants in my study the failure of colleagues to give any indication that they were aware of their suffering, combined with the paucity of tangible support, and validation of their abuse, aggravated their sense of total isolation and loneliness (Kitt, 1999).

Key Points

- Anyone can be targeted for bullying.

- There is no specific profile of those who are bullied.

- Those who are bullied have a deep sense of injustice, powerlessness and incredulity in relation to what is happening to them.

- Organisations frequently aggravate the suffering of those who are bullied by their inadequate, ineffective and/or inappropriate handling of the problem.

- Targets of bullying in the workplace are profoundly affected by bullying.

- In extreme cases bullying causes those who have been bullied to commit suicide.

D. 7. Organisational Culture and Organisational Effects of Workplace Bullying

Whether a hostile and toxic organisational culture leads to increased bullying or whether bullying behaviours are responsible for causing the culture to become hostile and toxic is a matter for continuing debate (Glomb, 2001). However, there are two undisputed organisational constants in relation to workplace bullying. Job-satisfaction and morale are adversely affected and stress levels are increased (Mann, 1996; Randall, 1997; Rayner et al., 2002). In terms of the latter, interpersonal stressors have a greater impact on individuals than impersonal stressors. When someone has done something to hurt you and that involves malice, cruelty or indifference, it adds to the severity of the experience (Norris et al., 2002). The effects of the stress-hormone, cortisol, can be three times greater for interpersonal stressors and can last 50% longer than with impersonal stressors (Dickson & Kemeny, 2004). Because of the severity and on-going nature of workplace bullying, it constitutes an extreme form of interpersonal stressor.

The financial cost of bullying in organisations, while not fully appreciated, is immeasurable. One has to combine the figures for absenteeism, turnover and productivity costs and that is merely the tip of the ice-berg. Ismhael and Alemoru (1999) described organisational effects of bullying in terms of both tangible and intangible costs. The tangible costs include absence and sickness, time-loss, stress, recruiting and retraining, tribunal proceedings, and loss of public image. The equally damaging intangible psychological and social costs include, among others, the breakdown in relations, the withholding of discretional effort, the lapses in concentration, confidence, commitment and creativity, and the presence of festering and lingering resentment (Ismhael & Alemoru, 1999). One can only imagine the impact of these psychological costs on schools. The resulting effects include a gradual deterioration in the quality of service, an erosion of the school's reputation, and an increasingly negative and stressful work environment for staff and students (McCarthy, 2004).

I have spoken to numerous teachers and other staff members who have been bullied in their schools. Whereas the advice often given to them by family and friends is that they should not give those who are bullying them the satisfaction of quitting their jobs, many of them, for health reasons, have ignored this advice and resigned. A number of those have left permanent positions, while others have moved to schools that were much further away from their homes. Irrespective of the losses incurred and the inconvenience caused to them, there was a fairly consistent view among them that they had made the right decision. They all alluded to the peace of mind that they now experienced, by virtue of just being able to get on with the job.

> **"**
> I always advise the graduating student teachers that I work with, to make sure that they do a good reconnaissance to assess the quality of the work environment and the interpersonal dynamics in a school before they take a job there.
> **"**

One young teacher, who had been bullied by the principal in her school, questioned whether she had made the right decision in staying in the school until she secured another job. She felt that those extra months spent there had nearly killed her. Happy and secure in her new teaching post, she talked in terms of getting her life back and getting herself back also. She was not alone in keeping the details of her ordeal from her former colleagues. She did not know who to trust and she did not know if she would be believed, as on the surface everyone seemed friendly and collegial. However, no one ever questioned or disagreed with the principal. There had also been an unusually high turnover of staff in the school over the years. Those starting out in a new job do not expect to be bullied. In that context, I always advise the graduating student teachers that I work with, to make sure that they do a good reconnaissance to assess the quality of the work environment and the interpersonal dynamics in a school before they take a job there. Workplace bullying thrives in organisations that are characterised by secrecy, denial, aggressive management, mistrust, disrespect and favouritism (Ishmael & Alemoru, 1999; Adams, 1992; Wright & Smye, 1996; Namie & Namie, 2000). Who would want to work in a school that ticked any or all of those boxes?

D. 7.1 Workplaces in which Bullying can Thrive

Bullying is an extreme form of negative social interaction that has a corresponding negative influence on an individual's resources and fulfilment at work (Vartia, 1996). Those who participated in my study (Kitt, 1999), described staff interactions in their schools as consisting of a concoction of superficial statements and flippant conversations that avoided any real or purposeful discussion. Obvious problems and discontent were unmentioned. There was no real consultation or collegiality in relation to professional matters and definitely no sharing of ideas (Kitt, 1999). Those who dismiss human relations in the workplace as peripheral to effectiveness are oblivious to the view that far from being irrelevant to good business they are part of its foundation (Hornstein, 1996).

How employees feel about each other, how they interact with each other and how well they work together, determines whether the workplace will be an abusive or a sustaining one (Wright & Smye, 1996). They put it succinctly when they stated, "employees who have to protect themselves in abusive workplaces have little time, or mental energy for inspiration" (1996, p. 183). They absent themselves from decision-making, and risk-taking (Mann, 1996; Ryan & Oestreich, 1991). They are definitely not working to their potential (Mann, 1996). Targets of bullying describe

> **"**
> **Unfortunately, schools, where workplace bullying exists, are as frightening and dangerous as any other workplace.**
> **"**

their work environments as stressful, obstructive and overwhelmingly tense at one level, and as frightening and dangerous at another more serious level. Many of those who work in functional schools might find it almost impossible to contemplate a school environment where these conditions apply. Unfortunately, schools, where workplace bullying exists, are as frightening and dangerous as any other workplace. Middleton-Moz and Zawadski (2002), equated these workplaces to abusive homes, where employees behave like scarred children. They cower and hide in their offices or classrooms instead of under the bed.

Lack of understanding of the effects of bullying on a workplace may explain some incidences of tolerance of the behaviours. However, a more likely explanation is that through the bullying-promoting attitudes that characterise their organisational culture, workplaces normalise and legitimise bullying. The attitudes that value power and dominance over tolerance and caring are hallmarks of these organisations (Geffner et al., 2001). In particular, leaders and managers who demonstrate total disrespect for their staff effectively give permission to themselves and others to bully.

A workplace culture that tolerates or accepts bullying creates a huge disincentive to those who are bullied to confront the problem and effectively allows the bullying to continue. Bullying is further facilitated in an environment where secrecy and denial prevail. Resch & Schubinski (1996) suggested that, as with the problem of alcoholism, many workplaces, including schools prefer to ignore bullying, by denying the existence of the problem. The fact that bullying is endemic in some workplaces is revealed by the difficulties in convincing managers that it exists at all (Ironside & Seifert, 2003). A denial of the problem ensures that it becomes "an undiscussable" (Ryan & Oestreich, 1991, p.36). In silent organisations where problems are "undiscussables", they tend to stay underground, festering and taking a huge toll on communication, morale and effectiveness (Ryan & Oestreich, 1991, p.36). Those who are being bullied, and onlookers also, are silenced in a climate where a "kill the messenger mentality is rampant" (Wright & Smye, 1996, p.138). Perpetrators benefit when they are part of the organisation's defence team fighting to prevent others from speaking out.

Increasingly, schools have become aware of the workplace bullying phenomenon and have added anti-workplace bullying policies to their suite of anti-bullying initiatives. However, the vast majority of those with concerns about workplace bullying in schools that I have spoken to have found that even when policies and procedures are in place, they are very difficult to engage with in terms of support or assistance in trying to resolve problems. Informal procedures are neither well thought-out nor actionable. There was a general feeling that the only real option available is to lodge a formal complaint. Among those who had taken that course of action, the consensus was that the ensuing investigation was at best painful, protracted and unsatisfactory and, at worst, a total sham.

Justice is frequently denied to those who are targeted and they are left with only two feasible options. They can keep their heads down, endure the abuse and watch helplessly as their spirits become totally broken, or they can leave. As previously mentioned, many who leave and move to a safe and functional working environment are relieved, comforted and positive about their decision. Others, unfortunately, bear a lifetime "legacy of defeat" (Adams, 1992, p. 113). Irrespective of whether they stay or go, the downward spiral in organisations and schools that continue to host bullying is inevitable.

Key Points

- Workplace bullying adversely affects workplaces including schools.
- Workplace bullying thrives in organisations that do not value people.
- Good interpersonal relations are central to organisational effectiveness and prevention of bullying.
- Workplaces that host bullying are toxic and stressful.
- Aggressive workplaces frequently allow and condone bullying.
- Many organisations including schools are in denial about their bullying problems.
- In abusive organisations, there are two options for those being bullied. They can endure it or leave.
- Schools that host bullying at any level are on a downward trajectory.

D. 8. The Dynamic of Workplace Bullying

Bullying is essentially an interpersonal interactive process. It is a dynamic created by the behaviours involved in the interaction. Negative behaviours produce a response from the recipient and a process of escalation begins (Tehrani, 2001). Any change in the interaction changes that dynamic. In this context, those who feel bullied are often strongly advised to intervene and challenge their alleged abuser. Those issuing such advice may be partially or totally ignorant of the fears and obstacles precluding individuals from taking that suggested action (Kitt, 1999).

The process of challenging or confronting, which is often a typical aspect of an anti-bullying policy in workplaces, is particularly difficult for those suffering from the trauma associated with bullying. They may know well what they should say or do, they may have rehearsed over and over again what they want to say, but unfortunately when the time comes to follow through on their intentions, they simply freeze (McKay & Fratzl, 2011). The control that is quickly gained by those who bully, combined with an increasing power-imbalance between them and those they target, can stun the latter into silence and inaction. They believe that challenging will affect little or no improvement in their treatment and may actually make matters worse (Beale, 2001). They also have a justifiable dread of challenging the person responsible for the bullying, as it may further provoke them and project them into defensiveness, distortion, and counterclaims.

In some schools, it is deemed helpful to bring a bullied student together with the student accused of bullying, in an attempt to sort out the problem. It is important to be aware of the potential dangers in this approach. It is very rarely an effective intervention. It can escalate the problem and can exacerbate the suffering of the student who is being bullied. Those who bully can lie and be very convincing. They often use tears and false counter-claims to gain the support of those facilitating the meeting. The demeaned and disempowered target can sound uncertain and unconvincing by comparison.

One of the biggest problems in dealing with bullying among students is that the targets are terrified of letting anyone know what is happening to them. The terror is caused by their belief that any intervention will make their situation worse. The main criterion that a teacher or school leader must fulfil before they can intervene in any bullying situation is that they have a full understanding of all aspects of bullying. Treading warily, maintaining confidentially, and making sure that the targeted student is consulted and supported at every step of a resolution process provide the only hope of the process being successful.

D. 8.1 The Difficulties in Challenging Workplace Bullying

Those who feel bullied at work are disinclined to challenge in an organisation that ignores or dismisses bullying. And they are totally disempowered in an organisation that rewards and promotes those who perpetrate bullying. They may take on board the view that intervening is the key to stopping bullying behaviours and that fighting back offers the only possibility of a solution to their problems (Adams, 1992; Middleton-Moz & Zawadski, 2002,). They may master the appropriate skills for intervention. They may even find the inner resources and strengths necessary to intervene (Davenport et al., 1999). However, without an enlightened and supportive work environment they rarely undertake the challenge. A further deterrent to challenging bullying behaviours comes in the form of Post-Traumatic Stress Disorder (PTSD), which affects many of those being bullied. As bullying involves an on-going series of negative actions, PTSD can be experienced while the bullying is still taking place. It manifests, for example, in the re-experiencing of the bullying incidences through rumination in the waking hours and/or through nightmares in the sleeping hours. It can also manifest in the compulsive need to avoid contact with the people or places that are associated with, or provide reminders of the bullying. It is hardly surprising that those experiencing PTSD would find it extremely difficult, if not impossible, to engage with and challenge the person whom they deem responsible for their ordeal.

D. 8.2 Why Dealing with Workplace Bullying is so Difficult

As previously stated, workplace bullying is an extreme form of social stressor. It causes targets to be traumatised and it detrimentally affects their health and well-being (D'Cruz & Noronha, 2010). Bullying attacks the three core needs for well-being that everyone has. These needs include:

- Competence – the need to feel capable and effective;

- Relatedness – the need to feel accepted by, connected to and involved with others;

- Autonomy – the need to have a degree of control over one's own actions and behaviours.

These needs are universal, innate and psychological. They are essential for human thriving (Ryan, 1995).

> **"**
> The main aim of bullying is to create a feeling of worthlessness in those being targeted. This is achieved by eroding their sense of competence, relatedness and autonomy.
> **"**

The main aim of bullying is to create a feeling of worthlessness in those being targeted. This is achieved by eroding their sense of competence, relatedness and autonomy. For example, the tactic of excessive, unwarranted criticism deprives those targeted of their need to feel competent at work. The tactic of ignoring and excluding them attacks their need for inclusion and acceptance and the tactic of controlling every aspect of their work attacks the need for autonomy. Satisfying basic psychological needs is as essential for an individual's functioning, as water, minerals and sunshine are for plants to thrive (Ryan 1995).

Key Points

- Bullying is a dynamic between those who bully and those who are targeted.

- Challenging bullying is much more difficult than generally understood.

- Bullying is very difficult to deal with because it attacks and erodes the three core needs for well-being.

D. 9 Dealing with Workplace Bullying

Those who have never experienced bullying can find it very difficult to understand why those, who have been bullied, become so badly affected by it. Even when they observe the bullying of a colleague, they can firmly believe that there is no way they would allow bullying to happen to them. When that message is communicated to those who are being bullied, they become more convinced that their failure to deal with what is happening to them is because of some inadequacy in their personality. The ability to cope with a serious stressor, such as bullying, is not a reflection of the strength or weakness of an individual's personality but rather is contingent on a number of factors. These factors include:

- the nature of the problem;

- the appraisal of the problem;

- the personal and social resources available to the individual in dealing with the problem (Lazarus & Folkman, 1984).

These elements are interdependent and determine the types of coping strategies applied to bullying problems. Coping in this context does not refer to finding ways to tolerate or put up with the bullying. Rather, it refers to coping in the psychological sense, which is defined as "constantly changing cognitive and behavioral efforts to manage specific external and internal demands that are appraised as taxing or exceeding the resources of the person" (Lazarus & Folkman, 1984, p. 14).

D. 9.1 The Nature of Workplace Bullying as the Problem

Despite differences in the understandings and interpretations of the various dimensions of workplace bullying, there are very few detractors from the view that it is an extremely serious, destructive and damaging type of behaviour. There is also a fairly widespread realisation that workplace bullying is perpetrated in a sneaky and insidious manner and often by those who portray themselves, outside the bullying relationship, as charming and caring. Those who bully are frequently successful in terms of promotion at work. They surround themselves with sycophants who see no wrong in them or their behaviour, and they are relentless and ruthless in their campaign to destroy those they target.

I think it is safe to conclude that in terms of severity, workplace bullying ranks with the very worst of stressors. It is not easy for anyone to cope with bullying. While the pessimism in this assessment may be discouraging for those in bullying situations, it should serve to reassure them that their difficulties in dealing with bullying are justified in the context of the summary of the phenomenon as provided above. The nature of the problem is just one of the factors influencing an individual's coping strategies. The person's appraisal of the bullying problem can be changed to positively affect coping and their personal and social resources can be maximised and utilised to that end also.

D. 9.2 The Appraisal of the Problem

An individual's appraisal of bullying is determined by whether they believe anything can be done to change the situation or not (Lazarus, 1993). During the early stages of workplace bullying, individuals may not fully appreciate what is happening and they may endeavour to deal with the situation by, for example:

- Approaching the perpetrator to try to ascertain what the cause of the problem is so that a solution can be found;

- Taking criticisms on board, despite reservations about their validity, and trying to make improvements to performance;

- Trying to ignore what is happening and focusing on getting on with their work;

- Continuing to behave in a courteous and friendly manner to the perpetrator despite the inappropriate behaviour;

- Trying to convince themselves that they are just imagining it.

Some may also discuss the situation with others as a support mechanism, while others may remain silent and try to be self-reliant.

As bullying is an insidious and escalating behaviour, it generally does not respond to rational and constructive actions. Eventually those who are bullied come to believe that there is nothing they can say or do to resolve the situation. They become convinced that there will be no cessation of the bullying behaviours and no positive outcome to their situation. This negative appraisal pushes them towards panic, despair and helplessness. They regard their situation as being absolute. They also view it through the three categories of learned helplessness, which are described as, personal , permanent and pervasive (Seligman, 2004). For example, those who are bullied can interpret the behaviours as:

- personal (it is somehow my fault / there is something wrong with me);

- permanent (this is going to last forever);

- pervasive (this problem is controlling every aspect of my life).

If they continue to think in those absolute terms, the bullying will take over every aspect of their lives. However, if they can change their thinking, explore the beliefs that underpin their sense of helplessness and challenge each of them, they may be able to change the way they behave in the bullying situation. Consequently, they can change the dynamics of the bullying. The following diagram offers some examples of helpless thinking, and some suggestions for more helpful alternatives.

Helpless Thinking	Helpful Thinking
This must be my fault; there must be something wrong with me.	Anyone can be targeted. Bullying behaviour says much more about the perpetrator than it does about me.
Others would be able to do something about this situation, but not me.	Bullying is irrational and dysfunctional behaviour and it would be difficult for anyone to deal with it. I have as good a chance of dealing with it as anyone else.
This situation is never going to change.	Bullying is totally unacceptable. It is unfair and unjust and I am determined to find a solution that will improve my life.
This problem is controlling every aspect of my life.	I still retain control of some aspects of my life.

D. 9.3 Personal Resources

The personal resources of the individual constitute another dimension of coping. Some personal resources such as attitudes, behavioural styles and skills are built up over the years. They may have served the individual well in dealing with other stressful and difficult situations. However, it is likely that they have changed or become depleted in terms of dealing with bullying.

Bullying causes confusion and many of those targeted begin to believe that they deserve what is happening to them. This attitude may have been alien to them in other difficult circumstances where they would have been able to challenge affronts and defend themselves. Replenishing and utilising personal resources can provide strength of mind and can change the bullying dynamic. Words may not be possible to articulate, but the formation of an attitude in the mind that says, "this behaviour is not ok with me" can lead to a person radiating a more resilient demeanour.

The skill of assertiveness is a personal resource that is effective in challenging bullying (Ismhael & Alemoru, 1999). Responding assertively to bullying behaviour may not change the underlying attitude of the perpetrator. However, as it does not reinforce the behaviour by producing the desired/expected passive and fearful response, it is likely to change subsequent behaviour in some way.

Assertive thinking enables those who are targeted to have an understanding of their legitimate right not to be subjected to bullying behaviours. It further facilitates the use of powerful and appropriate language that articulates the unacceptability of the behaviour. Assertive language describes the offending behaviour, states the effects of the behaviour and requests a cessation or change of behaviour. The language used is clear, unambiguous, and contains no personal attack or attribution of blame. Those challenging are merely asking that their rights to be respected. The request does not in any way infringe on the rights of the perpetrator (Namie & Namie, 1999).

Challenging bullying behaviours can have an extremely empowering effect. And despite the fact that those who bully may ridicule or ignore the challenge, it gives those who feel able to do it, a sense of breaking the control that bullying involves. In this context, challenging or confronting the behaviour sends a strong message to the perpetrator that their behaviour has been identified as inappropriate and will not be tolerated. Using learned, approved and practised strategies is thought to be the most effective means of affecting a change in the dynamic of bullying (Namie & Namie, 1999; Namie & Namie, 2000; Crawford, 2001). Namie and Namie (2003) offered encouragement to those who feel able to challenge bullying behaviour by suggesting that failing to confront costs more than the worst imagined consequences of confronting. They also suggested that in evaluating the risk involved in challenging or confronting, one might consider it in terms of the guaranteed misery of continuing bullying, versus the chance for peace of mind that challenging could offer (Namie & Namie, 2003). Bandura (1997) recalled the old Chinese proverb which stated that, 'You cannot prevent the birds of worry and care from flying over your head, but you can stop them from building a nest in your hair'.

He alluded to this wise saying to suggest that a person can exercise some control over his/her situation. It may assist those who feel helpless in bullying situations to build the self-belief necessary to overcome them.

Those, who for a variety of reasons cannot and do not challenge bullying behaviours, often find it more difficult to recover from bullying. Their recovery is impeded by longer-term intrusive negative thoughts in relation to having in some way allowed the bullying to continue (Namie & Namie, 2000). A sense of helplessness or lack of control over a situation has been shown to magnify the impact of social-evaluative stressors and to delay recovery significantly (Dickerson et al., 2004).

> **"**
> **When they get a sense of support from those around them who understand what is happening to them and what they are going through, it can make the difference in relation to whether they survive bullying and get their equilibrium back or not.**
> **"**

The most effective method for improving the personal resources of individuals in bullying situations is to:

● Gain a full understanding of the dynamic of bullying;

● Identify their own role in that dynamic;

● Find alternative ways of responding to the behaviour of the bully.

Helpful personal resources, such as increased energy levels, acquisition of information or distraction, can also be worked on as positive coping strategies.

D. 9.4 Social Resources

Social resources refer to the support that is available to the individual from others. These resources are absolutely vital to a person's ability to cope with bullying. The support offered from either family, friends, colleagues or the organisation can, at times, be unhelpful and misguided. However, it is critical that those who are bullied recognise the importance of social support and actively seek it from those they trust. When they get a sense of support from those around them who understand what is happening to them and what they are going through, it can make the difference in relation to whether they survive bullying and get their equilibrium back or not. It can also have a significant impact on their health and well-being and on the quality of their coping strategies.

Social support can take a number of different forms, ranging from the empathic smile or word to full scale helpful intervention. Schwarzer (1998) described social support as instrumental, tangible, informational and emotional. In the bullying context, instrumental support would include for example, a supportive person getting involved and suggesting problem solving strategies Tangible support would involve, for example, someone spending time with the targeted person, sitting beside them in the staffroom or refuting something derogatory that had been said about them. Informational support would entail, for example, providing the target of bullying with relevant research or media articles, or offering informed advice to them. Finally, emotional support is invaluable whether it involves providing reassurance, empathy, acceptance, friendship or love.

Effective social support is appropriate and informed, reflecting the needs of the individuals who are seeking it. These needs include:

● Being listened to and heard;

● Acknowledgement of their perspective and their feelings;

● Getting the information that they need.

Lack of appropriate support frequently results from a lack of understanding of the nuances of bullying, a failure to realise the extent of its effects, and a misguided concept of how best to deal with the problem.

In addition, fearful, distressed or angry targets of bullying, frequently, and understandably, engage in excessive attempts to convince others of the veracity of their situation. This behaviour manifests as repeated and persistent recounting of incidents and an almost exclusive focus in their workplaces and at home on what is happening to them. Unfortunately, this obsessive behaviour can alienate others and reduce the likelihood of support being forthcoming.

> **"**
> However, it is important for them to know that secrecy is the greatest ally that those who bully have, as it allows them to continue to bully unimpeded.
> **"**

On the other hand, social support is often denied to those who do not discuss or divulge to anyone, the essence or the details of their situation. Those who are being bullied can be terrified of opening a can of worms in disclosing details of what they are experiencing. However, it is important for them to know that secrecy is the greatest ally that those who bully have, as it allows them to continue to bully unimpeded. Romain (1997) suggested that when bullying is brought out into the open, the bully is no longer in control. In a workplace that adopts a positive approach to dealing with bullying, those who are bullied can and do play a more proactive role in seeking and accepting support from others

When organisations, including schools, provide support to those with concerns about bullying, there is a huge incentive for them to use effective problem-solving coping strategies in dealing with it. In Ireland, schools and other workplaces are obliged to provide the services of an appropriately trained and resourced contact person to those with concerns about bullying (Code of Practice on the Prevention of Workplace Bullying, 2007). A key component of the role of contact officers is to provide emotional as well as practical support. This source of social support is not available in the majority of schools in Ireland. There were some stringent efforts made, prior to the recent recession to comply with this and other elements of the

Code (Code of Practice on the Prevention of Workplace Bullying, 2007). However, during the recession, when issues of reduced salary and job insecurity were uppermost in people's minds, the focus on bullying-prevention receded to an almost non-existent level. In such an environment, those who had bullying tendencies could more easily bully with relative impunity and those being bullied would feel that they could do very little about it in a climate of "aren't

> **However, during the recession when issues of reduced salary and job insecurity were uppermost in people's minds, the focus on bullying prevention receded to an almost non-existent level.**

you lucky to have a job" attitude. The pieces are being picked up now, but there is a lot of catching up to do and a considerable number of legal cases in the pipeline. Interestingly, in all of the bullying cases that I have provided reports for over the past number of years, those taking the cases were adamant that they would never have chosen the legal route, if genuine alternative avenues for resolution had been available to them. Schools that bury their heads in the sand in relation to workplace bullying or the bullying of students do nothing to offer those alternatives.

Whether those who are bullied feel able or unable to use effective coping strategies to deal with bullying behaviours, they should never be held responsible for stopping the bullying. This responsibility rests primarily and definitively with the organisation (Ishmael & Alemoru, 1999; Crawford, 2001).

Key Points

- Coping with bullying involves a number of interdependent elements.
- Whether the target believes that anything can be done to alleviate bullying or not determines the coping strategies they use.
- Targets can change the way they appraise their bullying situation.
- An individual's attitudes and behaviours can be changed and improved to help them cope more effectively with bullying.
- The support received from others plays a major role in how those targeted deal with bullying.
- Organisational support is vital to enable targets to deal with bullying.

D. 10. Organisational Responses to Workplace Bullying

Organisations, including schools, are to varying degrees either bullying-promoting or bullying-preventing. The degree to which bullying is prevented or promoted is directly related to the prevailing attitudes of those who manage and those who work in schools. That is not to exempt employers, including, in the case of schools, the Department of Education and Skills, from their overall responsibility in relation to providing psychologically safe work environments for their employees. However, the day-to-day conditions of employees in terms of how they are treated and whether their dignity is protected or not are the responsibility of the management and the staff.

The attitudes and behaviours of school leaders in particular, not only determine the prevalence of bullying but also the effectiveness of the response to bullying problems when they occur. The effects of workplace bullying on individuals have been well documented in this section. Increasingly, the organisational effects are acknowledged as being pervasive, infectious and crippling (Randall, 1997). Yet, organisational responses to the problem are very far from being adequate or effective. Responses to bullying in workplaces fall generally into four categories, which are referred to as, dismissive, minimum compliance, reactive and proactive responses (Corbett & Kitt, 2006). Each level of response is influenced and determined by a commensurate set of underpinning attitudes and beliefs, and manifests in associated behaviours.

> **In schools adopting a dismissive response to bullying, there is an unquestioning tolerance of bullying and it can flourish with impunity, as a result.**

D. 10.1 Dismissive Response to Workplace Bullying

Organisations that adopt a dismissive response to bullying share, to some extent, the following attitudes and beliefs. In those workplaces, it is generally considered that bullying is an inevitable part of working life and that very little can be done to prevent or stop it. It is also regarded in dismissive terms as merely being a current talking point (flavour of the month), and it is believed that if ignored it will go away, in a 'least said soonest mended' attitude. Employees rarely complain about bullying in workplaces with a dismissive attitude as the subject is neither talked about nor taken seriously. Like many other inappropriate behaviours, it may even be regarded as normal in workplaces. Those who do complain of being bullied are regarded as being weak, timid, oversensitive and /or paranoid. They are, at best, considered to be nuisances, and, at worst, troublemakers who need to be silenced.

Many of those who report bullying are further isolated and often suffer reprisals. There is a strong belief in dismissive workplaces that whereas some leaders or managers may bully, they get the job done. This attitude is less prevalent in schools, although schools that adopt a dismissive attitude to bullying often share the belief of other like-minded organisations, that those who complain of bullying should "either put up, shut up or get out" (Corbett & Kitt, 2006). In schools adopting a dismissive response to bullying, there is an unquestioning tolerance of bullying and it can flourish, as a result.

D. 10.2 Minimum Compliance Response to Workplace Bullying

In organisations and schools that adopt a minimum compliance response to workplace bullying, there is an awareness of having to be seen to be addressing the problem. However, the bare minimum is done to fulfill basic legal responsibilities and to cover their backs. Minimum compliance organisations usually comply with the requirement for having an anti-bullying policy, but it is generally not custom made and can often consist of cut-and-pasted extracts from policy templates. In these organisations, there is neither the interest in nor the inclination to make genuine and sustainable attempts to prevent and deal effectively with bullying.

> **...it is likely that a significant number of schools and colleges in Ireland fall into the minimum compliance category in terms of their response to this serious problem.**

Complaints of bullying and not the bullying itself are regarded as being the cause of problems.

Those seeking advice and support with bullying issues find that they are not available and often their concerns are shared with the person whose behaviour is in question. When this happens, the ordeal of the person with the concern is considerably worsened. Those who do make a complaint are encouraged to put it in writing, thereby propelling them to a formal approach and an investigation. Even when informal procedures are contained in anti-bullying policies, they are neither adequate nor resourced. Schools with a minimum compliance response to bullying can give the impression that they are dealing with it, but those who try to access or use their procedures find that they are totally inadequate and effectively worsen their situation. Because the response to bullying is a sham in terms of dealing with problems and because there are very few if any consequences for those engaging in bullying behaviours, there is a high tolerance of bullying in these workplaces.

In speaking to a number of individuals who have been bullied in schools, many of them are adamant that the worst excesses of their suffering were associated with how they were treated after they drew attention to their situation by telling those in authority. Because of this view, and because of the perceived hands-off approach of the Department of Education and Skills in relation to ensuring that there is a consistently effective response to workplace bullying, it is likely that a significant number of schools and colleges in Ireland fall into the minimum compliance category in terms of their response to this serious problem.

D. 10.3 Reactive Response to Workplace Bullying

A reactive response to bullying is underpinned by the belief that bullying is a serious problem and that it needs to be addressed. The main focus is on having policies and procedures and indeed sanctions in place. However, bullying problems are dealt with on an individual case-by-case basis and without reference to the workplace context. The organisation's role in dealing with bullying is taken seriously but their role in the prevention of bullying is not. Those who feel they are being bullied can report it usually without fear of reprisal or ridicule. They generally do get a fair hearing and depending on the effectiveness of all aspects of the anti-bullying policy and procedures, their situations can be rectified. However, because there is a tendency to focus exclusively on resolving individual cases of bullying, there is often a strict code of secrecy and silence attached to this type of reactive response.

The need for confidentiality is wholly justified whereas the demand for secrecy can be suspect. The secrecy and silence that surrounds the bullying of adults and children in schools prevents an examination of the behaviours and practices that may have contributed to the bullying problem. In these circumstances, although individual cases of bullying may be dealt with, bullying problems may well continue to occur.

D. 10.4 Proactive Response to Workplace Bullying

Organisations including schools that respond proactively to bullying are in an exclusive and enviable position. They have an understanding that:

- Bullying is a destructive and devastating form of abuse with serious individual and organisational effects;
- The culture and climate of the organisation can prevent or promote bullying;

- Bullying does not thrive in an organisation with a positive/effective work environment.

Standards of acceptable and professional behaviours are outlined in these types of workplaces and there is an expectation that they will be complied with. Breeches of these standards are consistently challenged and addressed.

In schools with a proactive response to bullying, the focus is consistently on preventing problems. There is a realisation that creating a bullying-free environment will have beneficial effects on the quality of the experiences of both students and staff members and on their general well-being. There is a recognition and appreciation of the myriad responsibilities that are attached to providing a high-quality educational service to all students, in a respectful and fair manner, and associated competency requirements inform the selection and promotion of school leaders and staff members. There is a zero tolerance of bullying. However, if bullying does occur, it is openly discussed and addressed. Information, support and training are available to enable those with concerns to deal effectively with them.

In a school that adopts a proactive response to bullying, there is an anti-bullying policy to deal specifically with workplace bullying. This policy is not a stand alone document but is part of a more comprehensive Dignity at Work programme. The policy is essential to assist those in dealing with workplace bullying problems.

Schools with a proactive approach, put considerable time and effort into compiling a customised policy document that meets the specific needs of the school. An effective policy recognises that an informal process is the best means of resolving issues. Therefore, that approach is promoted and supported, in order for it to be perceived as a positive and viable option for those with concerns. It is also essential that school leaders are:

- genuinely interested in addressing inappropriate behaviour informally;
- clear on their role in an informal process;
- competent to carry out their role.

Support and mentoring are available to them and on-going training is provided.

It is the prerogative of anyone to make a formal complaint. However, this option is often taken because of the perceived lack of any real alternatives. Workplaces have a responsibility to deal effectively with formal complaints when they do occur. In schools adopting a proactive approach, the processing of formal complaints is characterised by:

- objectivity and fairness;
- efficient management;
- open and honest communication.

Realistic time-frames are set and adhered to, in as far as possible.

When a complaints process has concluded, there are frequently residual problems for those who have been involved and who have to continue to work together. Irrespective of the outcome of a complaint, the resulting impact on individuals and their work environment must be monitored and managed.

In management terms, proactive organisations place an equal focus on the task and on the people. They recognise that high standards of performance can only be consistently achieved through the constant valuing of all staff members. In a school that is proactive in its response to bullying, problems are generally prevented and there is a very strong message emanating from leaders and staff members, that "it is not ok to bully here".

Reflective Questions:

- In terms of the four organisational responses to workplace bullying, how would you describe the response to bullying in your school?

- How does this response impact on bullying problems in your school?

- What needs to be done in the short, medium and long term to improve the response to bullying in your school?

Key Points

- There are four main responses to workplace bullying in organisations. They are the dismissive, minimal compliance, reactive and proactive responses.

- The dismissive response is reflective of an organisation that does not understand, care about or deal with workplace bullying.

- The minimal compliance response is all about complying with legal requirements and ensuring that the organisation is protected if a claim of bullying is made.

- The reactive response reflects a view that bullying is inappropriate and has to be dealt with. However, there is no focus on the work environment in terms of preventing it.

- The proactive response is the most effective response in terms of providing a psychologically safe environment for everyone, preventing workplace bullying and dealing with problems that arise in an efficient and fair manner.

D. 11. Conclusion

The examination of the various elements of workplace bullying in this section is intended to provide an understanding of the phenomenon as a link to possible avenues of prevention and minimisation of bullying problems. All workplaces, including schools, have a responsibility to ensure that the health and safety of every employee is protected and maintained. They have a further responsibility to ensure that obstacles are not placed in the way of employees, to prevent them reaching their potential and contributing their best efforts to the organisation (Turney, 2003).

A psychologically-safe working environment is, determined by the degree to which the dignity, self-esteem and confidence of those who work there remain intact at the end of the working day.

Schools that provide a psychologically safe work environment consistently attract, motivate and retain staff. There is a greater commitment from staff members, a higher quality of work, less absenteeism and less stress, and there is a much lower turnover of staff (Ismahel & Alemoru, 1999). In this type of safe school, leaders are constantly reflecting on and managing their behaviours, relationships and emotions as they strive to maintain a high-quality work environment for everyone.

It is a basic human right for everyone to feel safe at work and to be spared the oppression and humiliation of bullying. We have come some way towards understanding and accepting this fact but there are still considerable obstacles to overcome to ensure that this human right is universally recognised and is afforded to all employees. In this regard, schools should be up there setting an exemplary example.

This section on Workplace Bullying in Schools has been based on a chapter that I previously wrote for an International Handbook It has been amended and updated for this book. Permission to use the previous chapter entitled "Facing up to Workplace Bullying in the context of Schools and Teaching", which appeared in De Souza, M., Francis, L., O'Higgins-Norman, J. & Scott, D. (Eds.) (2009) International Handbook of Education for Spirituality, Care and Wellbeing, was kindly granted by the publishers Springer Academic Publishers: Dordrecht, Netherlands.

Section E

School Leadership...
Getting it Right

E. 1. Introduction

I have had the privilege of working, for many years, with student teachers as they are about to embark on their new careers. They are quite surprised when I allude to the job of teaching as one of the most important jobs in the world. There is no other job – I propose – with the exception of the unpaid job of parenting – where a person has the power to shape the lives of those they work with on a daily basis? How often have we heard famous writers, artists, musicians, and other successful people give credit to former teachers for their inspiration, and for the influence that they have had on their achievements. The student teachers themselves are able to recall, with clarity, the teachers who have encouraged and supported them, in both primary and secondary schools. They can articulate precisely how this validation has impacted on their lives to date. The confidence and self-belief instilled in students, by a teacher's simple but powerful words, and acts of kindness, can help to sustain them through the many challenges that they will encounter in life. On the contrary, the negative experiences that students have had, with teachers who humiliated, embarrassed or intimidated them, can undoubtedly leave an indelible mark on their memory, and have a serious impact of their self-esteem and confidence.

Individual teachers are responsible for how they behave towards their students. However, the school leaders have the overall responsibility to ensure that the quality of teaching and learning is consistently high, and that their own behaviours, and the behaviours of individual staff members, are consistently professional, respectful and fair. That is a very tall order, and yet it is at the core of what constitutes an effective school.

> **"**
> **Excellence in schools is, thankfully, more widely and correctly associated with school leaders and staff members working collaboratively, to facilitate every student in reaching their personal potential.**
> **"**

One of the main considerations in the purchasing of a property in the UK is its proximity to an 'excellent school'. I often wondered what criteria are used to determine that a school is deemed to be excellent. From speaking to a number of UK colleagues, I surmise that some of these highly-prized schools are extremely competitive. They attract students from similar backgrounds, and appeal to parents of similar social status. We are very fortunate, in this country, that there are very few schools that rely on these criteria for their badge of excellence.

Those select few, however, are favoured by parents who perhaps attach a disproportionate priority to ensuring that their children attend, what they consider to be, the right type of school, where they will meet the right type of people, and ultimately get the right type of job.

Excellence in schools is, thankfully, more widely and correctly associated with school leaders and staff members working collaboratively, to facilitate all students in reaching their personal potential. This is achieved through maximising their learning, while enhancing their confidence and self-esteem. Developing students' empathy and their sense of justice is also a priority in excellent schools. It is little wonder, therefore, that teaching is regarded as a very important and influential job. However, as the effectiveness and success of the teachers are contingent on the leadership in the school: the job of a school leader is also hugely influential.

There has been significant research to indicate that school leaders, particularly school principals, are the driving force in achieving the standards of excellence in schools. The findings of Gurr and Drysdale (2007), cited a principal's personal traits, work behaviour, beliefs and values, as contributing to the quality of teaching and learning, and student outcomes. It is also suggested that the work that a school leader puts into creating and promoting a positive school environment impacts on student achievement and inspires trust among students and teachers (Leithwood et al., 2004).

E. 2. The Effective School...
The Role of the School Leader

School leaders have, in their hands, the power to make or break a school. It takes time and sustained effort to 'make a school'. It only takes a short time to break it. An inadequate leader can wreak havoc in a school. This can be done by both the sins of commission, as well as the sins of omission (Francis & Woodcock, 1990). Leading an effective school is an onerous responsibility. However, it is a responsibility that brings with it an opportunity for school leaders to get it right, and to be truly successful. It can also provide the school leader with a sense of satisfaction and fulfilment. That is what Maslow (1954), in terms of his famous hierarchy of needs, would call having the supreme need of self-actualisation well and truly met. Self-actualisation is attained when one's personal and professional potential is reached. A leader's potential can never be realised however, without gaining, and maintaining, the engagement and commitment of others.

E. 2.1 Building a School Community

As previously stated, high-quality relationships between school leaders and their staff have a significant influence on the effectiveness of a school. These relationships do not happen by chance. They have to be developed over a period of time. This is a key part of a school leader's role. A school is not a formal organisation; rather, it is a community of people, inextricably linked and bonded together by the task of caring for, and teaching, the students. This responsibility

> **"**
> A diversity of personalities and characteristics is what makes a staffroom, or a classroom, interesting and unique. However, there must be a sense of unity and common purpose among staff in order for a community to be created.
> **"**

dictates that all of the relationships in schools are required to be of a higher quality than those in more formal organisations. Relational-satisfaction is essential in schools, because of the interdependence of those who work and study there.

Sergiovanni has written extensively on the merits of developing schools as communities. He defined a school community in terms of the shared values and beliefs that are necessary for creating strong connections in schools. Close collegial relationships help to transform individuals from a collection of 'I's' into a collective 'We' (Sergiovanni, 1994). This does not mean that staff should become clones of each other, or sacrifice their individuality or their idiosyncrasies. A diversity of personalities and characteristics is what makes a staffroom, or a classroom, interesting and unique. However, there must be a sense of unity and common purpose among staff in order for a community to be created.

E. 2.2 Establishing a Shared Vision

Gaining the commitment of all staff members to a shared vision is essential for building the type of relationships necessary to implement it. The content and wording of the vision statement should not be the brainchild of the leader. It has to be the product of long discussions, and agreement among all the staff in relation to what the school's priorities are. However, the facilitation of the discussion on having a shared vision, and the initiation of the process of agreeing on it, are the responsibility of the school leader. Leaders have to be able to sell the powerful and convincing message about the interdependent nature of the roles in schools, and the associated responsibilities for all staff, in order for buy-in to a shared vision and purpose to take place.

Staff members are also more likely to contribute to finding a shared vision if it reflects core ethical values, such as trustworthiness, respect, responsibility, fairness, caring and citizenship. They are also more likely to give positive consideration to shared goals if they reflect best practice approaches to teaching and learning. Furthermore, dissenters find it much more difficult to opt out of their responsibilities in relation to a shared vision when it is based on solid values, and on effective teaching and learning. However, in order for a shared vision to have credibility and relevance, it has to be presented in language that is clear and accessible.

● Vision and Mission Statements

I have observed, on numerous occasions, the adorning of school entrances with highly-polished plaques outlining the vision and mission of the school. Many of these statements are clearly reflective of the identity of the particular school, and warrant their place of honour. Unfortunately, this is not always the case. The language used in some of these statements would be considered as 'flowery', but might be more accurately described as abstract and generalised. Some schools combine vision and mission statements – which is understandable, because of the links between what is aspired to in a school, (vision), and how those aspirations will be realised, (mission). Vision and mission statements are essential to give the school a sense of direction and purpose. The articulation of a thoughtful school vision will incorporate the language of hope and dreams, in relation to future goals. The vision will also include ambitious and challenging targets. However, they must be attainable and achievable. Time is needed for agreement to be reached on a vision statement, so that it reflects genuinely held aspirations for the identity of the school into the future.

A mission statement, as I understand it, outlines in clear and tangible terms what the school needs to do to achieve the stated goals. Many vision and mission statements can sound very profound on first reading. However, they can be quite ambiguous and open to a number of interpretations. The following statements provide some examples: 'We believe in and will uphold the integrity of every child'; 'We will strive to be an inclusive school, dedicated to innovation, creativity and excellence in teaching and learning'; 'In this school, we prioritise the social, emotional, physical, and intellectual development of each student in our care'; or, 'In this school, we support the development of the whole child'.

While there are laudable sentiments included in these statements, the words used are unlikely to evoke a clear picture of what specifically, the school would like to provide for the students. If lofty and inaccessible language is included in a vision or mission statement, it will be very difficult for a school leader to get staff to engage with and commit to it. Some staff members may regard it as mere window-dressing, and simply ignore it. The brasso-shone plaques, bearing grandiose aspirations, can seem particularly incongruous in a school where two members of staff have had a disagreement, and have not spoken to each other for months, or where a teacher of many years' experience, who labels himself a consummate professional, has consistently refused to update his teaching methods.

● Choosing Image-Based Language

Vision and mission statements incorporating language that is accessible and practical have a much better chance of being activated in a team effort. Murphy and Clark (2016) recommended that these statements be couched in image-based language that can be realistically envisaged by everyone. For example, the following vision statements, while aspirational, are clear and accessible:

- we envisage that every child will feel safe coming into this school;

- that all of our students will develop a love of learning;

- that all of our students will experience kindness and caring in this school.

The following mission statements are clear and practical:

- We, in this school, will establish how best, each student learns, and teachers will use a range of teaching methods to cater for the differences in learning styles.

- Those working in this school will give recognition to each child for their achievements, but will not pit students against each other to create winners and losers.

- We, the staff at ..., will not shout at or embarrass our students and cause them to be fearful or upset.

- In this school, we will demonstrate to students and parents that they are our partners, by listening to them and taking on board what they have to say, without acting in a defensive or superior manner.

- We will be vigilant and watch out for changes in students' demeanour or behaviour to ensure that they are not being excluded or bullied.

- In each classroom we will have a system in place to ensure that all students get a chance to answer questions, and contribute to class discussions.

These sentiments provide an indication of what image-based language involves and also outline the standards of behaviour that can be expected in the school.

Communicating a vision and a mission in tangible terms is a prerequisite for a common understanding by staff, students and parents of what can be expected

> **Communicating a vision and a mission in tangible terms is a prerequisite for a common understanding by staff, students and parents of what can be expected from a school.**

from a school. It is also essential in order for those expectations to be met. However, the values underpinning a shared vision and mission must also be clear. This does not necessitate or require that a proliferation of value words be part of a vision or mission statement, but rather that the essence of it is guided by the espoused values of the school. In the image-based statements cited above, the values of fairness, responsibility, caring, empathy and equality can be easily identified.

When a shared vision and purpose has been established and agreed by a school's staff, there is a more unified context to enable the realisation of that vision and purpose. However, the commitment of staff members cannot be taken for granted. How the school leader communicates on a daily basis and the communication climate that is created as a result, will determine to a large extent the level and quality of that commitment.

Reflective questions

1. What process was used to compile the vision/mission statements in your school?

2. How do these statements impact on the school on a day to day basis?

3. Do you need to revisit or update your vision/mission statements? Why?

E. 2.3 Creating a Positive Communication Climate

Communication is not merely the sharing of information, opinions and ideas. It is a relationship-building activity that begins with a first interaction or encounter. As soon as two people start to communicate, an initial impression of each other is formed, and an almost instant aura or tone is created between them. Tone, in this context, does not refer to the tone of a voice, but rather the social tone. For example, when a receptionist in a hotel is attentive and friendly, a good impression is formed – not merely about the person but also the hotel. A good aura or social tone is created, and guests begin to look forward to their stay. If, on the contrary, the receptionist is offhand and preoccupied, an immediate impression can be formed that not only is the person disinterested and rude, but that a mistake has been made in booking that particular hotel. A negative aura is quickly created that can impact negatively upon their stay.

The aura or tone that is created as a result of both verbal and non-verbal communication is generally referred to as the 'communication climate'. A parent's angry reaction to a child's spilled milk can expose the communication climate in that home. A manager's public dismissal of a suggestion by a staff member highlights the type of communication climate in that company. A teacher's measured response to a student's outburst is a clear indicator of the communication climate in that classroom.

In workplaces, generally, positive communication climates influence the attitude of employees, in relation to the:

- effort they put in;

- support they provide to colleagues;

- introduction of change and improvements.

In schools, as in other workplaces, the way the leader communicates is one of the key factors in determining the quality of the communication climate. That communication climate influences, for the better or worse, "how we feel, how hard we work, how innovative we are, what we want to accomplish, and how we seem to fit into the organisation" (Pace, 1983, p. 125).

Key Points

- School leaders are in a very influential position in relation to securing the commitment of staff and ensuring the success of the school.

- The establishment of a shared vision in a school, that is reflective of core values and best practice approaches to teaching and learning, requires a consultative and participative approach.

- The quality of the school leader's communication is a key determinant in the quality of the communication climate in a school.

School leaders are never going to get it right all of the time. There will always be mistakes and misjudgements. However, in order for them to do a consistently good job and get it right most of the time, they need to focus on:

- communicating and behaving in ways that bring others with them;

- continuously reflecting on and evaluating their performance;

- consistently demonstrating that they do not take themselves too seriously.

E. 3. Effective Communication

When leaders communicate effectively, they do not merely contribute to a climate that is positive and healthy; they also make life considerably easier for themselves, by bringing others with them. Communication is a very complex process that involves much more than just talking. The much disputed statistic – that only 7% of all communication is verbal, with the remainder divided between body language at 55%, and tone of voice at 38% – is worth alluding to for one specific reason. It facilitates an appreciation that communication involves a number of different means. Messages are often transmitted to others without a word being said.

When a student carries a lunch tray over to a table in the canteen, and the group already sitting there immediately becomes silent, the message that the student is not welcome to join them is received and felt. When two teachers suspend verbal communication with each other for a period of time, they communicate a very strong message to others that something is wrong between them. Perfectly ordinary and everyday words can take on a very different meaning according to the tone of voice used. 'I'm just fine', spoken in a certain tone, can indicate that a person is anything but fine. 'Hello', spoken in a certain tone, can infer to someone that they have said something stupid. 'Great, that's just what we needed', can indicate a blaming of someone for an error or mistake, and 'Whatever', spoken in a certain tone, can indicate that the person couldn't care less about what the other person has just said.

While effective communicators are conscious of their body language and their tone of voice, the main focus must be on the words they use. In advance of examining the various categories of words that constitute good and bad communication, it is worth alluding to a number of phrases that can be extremely annoying. The phrase 'With all due respect' causes annoyance, as it usually prefaces total disrespect. The phrase 'No offence, but' is very often followed by an insult. 'In my humble opinion' is a phrase rarely, if ever, used by anyone with an ounce of humility. And, 'You're missing the point' is about as condescending as it gets. 'Calm down', 'Chill out', 'Keep your hair on', or 'It's not the end of the world' are guaranteed to have an escalating rather than a diffusing effect on a person's anger or anxiety.

Acquiring the skill of effective communication involves continuous reflection and learning. Those who are poor communicators usually:

- give very little thought to how they communicate;
- have very little knowledge of what good communication looks like;
- regard themselves as good communicators.

One only has to listen to certain news programmes on the radio, to hear extremely aggressive and rude language being used by some presenters in interviews that induce discomfort or anger. The so-called guests are often treated with total disrespect, and even contempt. The interviewee's replies are regularly focused on surviving the obstacle course, rather than on imparting relevant information. A negative and defensive communication climate is created, and whereas some people enjoy that confrontational approach, the average listener is generally the loser. Those who work in the media like those who work in schools are in positions of power and influence. They have a responsibility to communicate in a respectful manner. Meryl Streep in her eloquent speech at the Golden Globe Awards Ceremony (2017), suggested that when the instinct to humiliate is modelled by someone powerful, it gives permission for others to do the same. One would like to think that reporters, who show no empathy when interviewing those who have been personally affected by tragedy, would be given assignments better suited to their communication style. And it is a pity that sports commentators who deride professional and dedicated sportspeople as 'worthless', 'useless' or a 'waste of space' would not realise how insensitive, inappropriate and humilitating these comments are.

One can only presume, because of the consistency of their behaviours, that these presenters/reporters do not give much consideration to how they communicate, that they are not aware of what good communication is, and that they consider themselves to be doing a good job of communicating.

As previously discussed, schools are communities and not merely organisations. The relationships, therefore, are required to be close and caring. School leaders have a responsibility to communicate effectively with everyone in the school. Their role does not allow for aggressive or rude behaviours, nor does it tolerate insensitivity. And, without doubt, there is no place in a school leader's repertoire of behaviours for derogatory, insulting or hurtful comments.

E. 3.1 Types of Communication

Jack Gibb's ubiquitous communication theory was formulated after his long observation of group dynamics in the workplace. Although dating back to the 1960s, his published work has informed a huge body of communication literature and textbooks ever since. Gibb's (1961) theory of supportive and defensive communication provides an insight into very specific communication behaviours that influence workplace relationships.

He identified six types of supportive communication, and the six polar-opposite types of defensive communication, which respectively influence the communication climate for the better or the worse. A supportive climate has an atmosphere that is open and trusting and encourages people to engage, while the defensive climate is stressful and discourages people from engaging. Gibb's model provides an excellent framework for the examination, by leaders, of their own prevailing style of communicating, and of the consequences of how they communicate for the levels of engagement of their staff.

The six supportive communication types, and their defensive counterparts, have been adapted slightly to include:

Supportive Communication	Defensive Communication
Descriptive	Judgemental
Assisting	Controlling
Transparent	Manipulative
Empathic	Apathetic
Equitable	Superior
Open-minded	Dogmatic

A general description of each of the six supportive and defensive communication types is provided below. School-based scenarios are also cited, with suggested supportive and defensive responses, under each of the six headings.

"Descriptive" communication is clear and honest, and does not contain interpretations or evaluations. "Judgemental" communication, on the other hand, passes judgement on another person, or on what they have said or done.

SCENARIO 1:
A member of staff has made a suggestion at a staff meeting. The school leader does not think it will work.

Descriptive response:
"For the following reasons, I have some concerns that your idea may not work."

Judgemental response:
"That idea hasn't a hope in hell of working."

SCENARIO 2:
A principal observes a teacher shouting at a student in a busy corridor.

Descriptive response:
"When you shout at a student, it can cause upset and hurt and it is something that we, as a staff, have decided is unacceptable."

Judgemental response:
"What was all the shouting about? You really let yourself down in front of everyone."

SCENARIO 3:

A teacher did not attend an important staff meeting, where various roles for a forthcoming 'Open-day' were allocated.

Descriptive response:
"Because you were absent from the staff meeting, others had to take on extra work. What was the reason for your absence?"

Judgemental response:
"You didn't bother to come to the staff meeting yesterday, and the rest of the staff members were saddled with all the work."

"Assisting" communication involves working with others to solve problems and get things done, whereas "controlling" communication involves dictating what should be done, or insisting on getting your own way.

SCENARIO 1:

A teacher suggests an alternative to the current daily assembly for all students.

Assisting response:
"That is certainly worth considering. Would you do a little more research on it, and we can have a good discussion at the next staff meeting?"

Controlling response:
"Things are fine as they are, and I am happy with them."

SCENARIO 2:

A teacher, who was unsuccessful in an interview for a post of responsibility, is unhappy with the decision.

Assisting response:
"I know that you are disappointed with the result of the interview. Would it be helpful to go through the selection process with you?"

Controlling response:
"The decision was made fair and square, so just get over it."

SCENARIO 3:

A teacher comes to the office of the principal, crying, after an encounter with a student.

Assisting response:
"I can see that you are very upset. We can sit down and have a chat after class if that helps."

Controlling response:
"I'm far too busy to be dealing with this kind of thing. You'll just have to learn not to let things get to you."

"Transparent" communication is open, honest and direct, and people know where they stand. "Manipulative" communication implies hidden agendas and insincerity at best, and deceit at worst. Those on the receiving end of manipulative behaviours feel confused and misled.

SCENARIO 1:

A parent speaks to a teacher, to express her concern that her child was upset by the teacher shouting at him.

Transparent response:
"I was angry and I did shout at him and I'm sorry about that. It was a very busy day yesterday with preparations for the exams, and he was talking and laughing during class."

Manipulative response:
"If only he would do what he was told, I wouldn't have to get annoyed with him."

SCENARIO 2:

The principal missed the deadline for submitting a form that a teacher who was applying for a career break, had completed.

Transparent response:
"I completely forget to forward your application form. I will get on to the Department immediately, to explain what happened."

Manipulative response:
"Your application was late. It's a pity that you did not hand it to me rather than just leaving it on my desk."

SCENARIO 3:

A school leader cracked a joke with a teacher in the staffroom. The following day the teacher did not respond to a greeting by him.

Transparent response:
"I notice that you did not answer me, when I spoke to you this morning. I hope I did not offend you yesterday."

Manipulative response:
"Don't tell me you are sulking. Can you not take a joke?"

"Empathic" communication indicates a concern for others and their feelings, whereas "apathetic" communication displays a lack of interest, or caring for others.

SCENARIO 1:
A colleague has interrupted a teacher three times while she was trying to make a point at a planning meeting. The teacher has come to the principal's office to talk about what happened.

Empathic response:
"I can see why you are angry. I would be too, if that happened to me."

Apathetic response:
"What do you expect me to do about it?"

SCENARIO 2:
A music teacher is seeking funding from the school leader for a proposed trip to a classical recital by a world famous artist.

Empathic response:
"I know you are passionate about your subject and I will do everything I can to find funding for your trip."

Apathetic response:
"We can't be spending money willy-nilly."

SCENARIO 3:
A teacher complains that she is exhausted.

Empathic response:
"You have had a very busy day. Try to take a little break when you can."

Apathetic response:
"We're all busy, you're no exception."

"Equitable" communication implies that everyone is deserving of equal treatment, irrespective of their role or ability. "Superior" communication involves looking down on others, and treating them as inferior.

SCENARIO 1:
The school leader is informing the entire staff of a forthcoming presentation on creating a positive work environment.

Equality response:
"I would like all the staff to attend the presentation on a positive work environment, as it applies to everyone."

Superiority response:
"There is a presentation on a positive work environment taking place tomorrow. Only the teaching staff need attend."

SCENARIO 2:

A teacher brings a student to the principal's office to report his alleged misdemeanour. He tells the student to be quiet when the student tries to tell his side of the story.

Equality response:
"I acknowledge your account of what happened. However, I would like to hear what the student has to say also."

Superiority response:
"How dare you interrupt the teacher when he is speaking?"

SCENARIO 3:

A teacher, who has specialised in teaching children with special needs, has made a suggestion for a change of approach.

Equality response:
"I appreciate your knowledge and expertise in the area and will be happy to go with your suggestion, once you have agreed it with the other special needs teachers."

Superiority response:
"I'm a lot longer at this job than you. I think I know what's best for the school."

"Open-minded" communication is indicative of a willingness to be flexible and open to changes and new possibilities. "Dogmatic" behaviours indicate rigidity in thinking, and an unwillingness to see an alternative point of view or to compromise.

SCENARIO 1:

A staff member proposes setting up a student council.

Open-minded response:
"I think the idea of a student council might present some problems. However, I am certainly willing to support you in setting it up if other staff members see merit in it, and we can assess the progress after six months."

Dogmatic response:
"Those student councils are nothing but trouble, there is no way I am having one in my school."

SCENARIO 2:

The deputy-principal tells the principal that he thinks she could have handled a certain issue better.

Open-minded response:
"Thank you for that feedback. Can you be specific on what, exactly, you think I did wrong?"

Dogmatic response:
"What I said about that issue I meant and I'll thank you not to undermine me."

SCENARIO 3:
A new printer is required and the principal is considering one.

Open-minded response:	Dogmatic response:
"I really like this new printer and it is very good value for money. Would you all have a look at it to see if it meets your needs before I make the purchase?"	"I have made a decision on the new printer. It's good value and it serves our needs. I don't want to hear any complaints about it."

Everyone, at various times and in various circumstances, engages in supportive as well as defensive communication. It is difficult for leaders, or indeed anyone, to objectively assess their own communication standards in the context of the full range of behaviours that are included in Gibb's work. However, if the examples provided above can be identified by school leaders as being part of their communication profile, it is a very useful step in establishing which of their behaviours need to be retained, and which ones need to be changed.

Key Points

- In order for school leaders to be effective in their communication, they need to engage in continuous reflection on every aspect of how they communicate.

- Poor communicators are generally not aware of what effective communication is.

- Gibb's theory of supportive and defensive communication provides a framework for leaders to examine the effectiveness or ineffectiveness of their communication.

For leaders to gain further insight into what constitutes effective communication, an examination of the three main communication styles, and the behaviours that characterise each of them, may also be a useful exercise.

E. 3.2 Communication Styles

Passive communication, aggressive communication, and assertive communication are the three principle communication styles. The manifestations and effects of passive and aggressive communication are generally well understood. This claim cannot be made in relation to assertive communication. When the latter is mentioned, it conjures up aggression in the minds of many –

> **"**
> Apart from its general effectiveness, the main benefit that assertive communication has is that it includes a variety of manifestations that enable a person to communicate appropriately in a variety of situations.
> **"**

particularly those who admire people who can, 'give as good as they get', or, 'tell others what they think of them in no uncertain terms'. The word assertive is often wrongly used, to describe aggressive behaviours.

● Passive Communication

Passive communication involves failing to stand up for your rights, or doing so in such a way that others can easily disregard them. It also involves expressing your opinions, feelings and needs in "apologetic or self-effacing" (Michel & Fursland, 2008 p. 2) ways. This can give the impression that they are less important than the needs of others. When a person persistently uses passive communication, they can find it very difficult to refuse to accede to a request or a demand. Consequently, they are regularly prevailed upon to do more than their fair share. This can result in feelings of being used and abused, and can cause anger and resentment.

● Aggressive Communication

Aggressive communication, on the other hand, involves standing up for your own rights in a way that disregards or violates the rights of other people. It also involves the expression of your own needs and opinions in controlling and selfish ways. Aggressive people may feel powerful at times, but they create fear and resentment in those around them. They are usually neither liked nor trusted.

● Assertive Communication

An understanding of assertive communication incorporates a recognition, and an appreciation of, its effectiveness as a style of communication. Apart from its general effectiveness, the main benefit that assertive communication has is that it includes a variety of manifestations that enable a person to communicate appropriately in a variety of situations.

> **"**
> **Assertiveness has an important additional benefit in that, when you communicate assertively, there is a significantly greater chance of having your own needs understood by others, and met.**
> **"**

Assertive communication, as the most effective and appropriate style of communicating, involves expressing oneself in an open and direct manner, that does not undermine others. It also involves the honest expression of opinions, feelings and needs. The ability to communicate thoughts and feelings appropriately prevents resentment from building up in either party to the communication. Those who have experienced the benefits of using and being on the receiving end of assertive communication, usually become exponents of the practice.

Assertive communication is positive, and focuses on preserving good relationships with others. It is instrumental in initiating and maintaining socially-supportive relationships that contribute to emotional well-being (Eskin, 2003). Those who communicate assertively are generally able to stand up for their own rights, without violating the rights of others. Assertiveness also assists people in getting their message across in difficult situations, without being left with a residue of anxiety or stress. Being able to walk away from an interaction, without a sense of having said something embarrassing or stupid, prevents rumination and worry, and provides a peace of mind that is addictive. Assertiveness has an important additional benefit in that, when you communicate assertively, there is a significantly greater chance of having your own needs understood by others, and met.

Leaders who are assertive communicators are more consistent in their behaviours towards others. Unlike aggressive communicators, they will be less volatile and, unlike passive communicators, they will be less indecisive. Assertive communication is arguably the most important skill that a leader can have.

● Becoming Assertive

It is important for everyone to master assertiveness, in order to have their needs met in everyday situations. It is quite surprising how many people find it really difficult to ask for something that they are perfectly entitled to. For instance, it would appear like a very simple task to ask a shop assistant to exchange a previously purchased item. Yet so many people have problems using a basic assertive statement, such as 'I would like to exchange this item please'. Rather, they provide a context and an explanation for the request. If only those who have a tendency to provide their life story as an accompaniment to a simple request could realise that busy staff in shops, restaurants or elsewhere, would much prefer if customers simply asked for something that is their right.

It is also very difficult for some people to honestly express how they feel about something. For example, in a restaurant, after having a meal that was unsatisfactory or sampling wine that they did not like, they may tell the waiter that everything was fine.

Politeness is always an element of assertiveness. However, embellishment or a fear of expressing your true feelings is not.

E. 3.3 Types of Assertiveness

Michel & Fursland (2008) listed six types of assertiveness as:

- Basic;
- Empathic;
- Responsive;
- Discrepancy;
- Negative feeling;
- Consequence.

Different situations merit different types of assertiveness. A description and examples of each of the six types of assertiveness are included below and have been adapted from Michel & Fursland (2008).

● Basic Assertiveness

Basic assertiveness usually involves a simple statement, outlining what a person wants or does not want. The following examples which demonstrate basic assertiveness, can save time and energy, and get a message across clearly and succinctly:

- "I need to have a word with you, as soon as class is finished."
- "Please, do not read the paper, while I am speaking about an issue that affects the entire staff."

Basic assertiveness is also a very powerful instrument when used regularly, to give acknowledgement or show appreciation. These opportunities should never be missed by a leader. For instance, simple and basic statements, such as:

- "Thank you very much for completing that task so quickly."
- "Well done that was a really good presentation.",

do not take much time or effort, yet they have a very positive impact on relationships.

● Empathic Assertiveness

Empathic assertiveness demonstrates an appreciation of the situation of others, while, at the same time, expressing one's own needs and getting things done. It is very important for leaders in getting their message across, that they maintain good relationships with others. For example, "I can see that you are very busy at the moment. When you get a chance, I would like to discuss something with you". This statement indicates that a request, rather than a demand is being made.

● Responsive Assertiveness

Responsive assertiveness is effective in avoiding misinterpretation. It seeks to clarify what someone has just said. For example, "You have expressed reservations about the new approach. Can you elaborate on what problems you envisage with it?" This statement encourages a specific, rather than a general, response. Responsive assertiveness is particularly helpful in keeping communicating channels open, in the context of the negativity of others.

● Discrepancy Assertiveness

Discrepancy assertiveness is appropriate when emphasising what has been previously agreed, and what still needs to happen (Michel & Fursland, 2008). For example, "When we spoke last week you agreed to complete your written report by the end of the week. It is important that I have it before the meeting tomorrow". This statement provides a gentle but firm reminder of what has been agreed, and is not yet done.

● Negative Feeling Assertiveness

Negative feeling assertiveness is effective in pointing out, in a calm and controlled way, the consequences of another person's action and the negative affect that their behaviour is having on you (Michel & Fursland, 2008). For example, "When you remain in the staffroom after lunch break is over, your class is not supervised. I feel quite anxious and concerned about this. I would like you to return to your class as soon as lunch break is over". This statement may be difficult to deliver. However, it is honest, fair and warranted in the circumstances.

● Consequence Assertiveness

Consequence assertiveness informs others of the consequences of not changing their behaviour. It is appropriate when repeated reminders have been ignored. It should, generally, only be used as a last resort. For example, "Three times this week, you have been fighting in the school yard. If it happens again, I will call your parents, even though I would prefer not to have to do this". In this statement, the consequences of the continued behaviour are clearly signalled, while still providing the student with a chance to improve.

All the above types of assertiveness are designed to keep communication channels open, and bring others with you. When leaders practice assertive communication, they signal that they are strong yet fair. They send a message that they will not allow others to take advantage of them, nor will they take advantage of anyone else. In order for school leaders to become truly assertive, they need to have an understanding of what is fair and reasonable for them to expect in their relationships and their communication with others. They also need to be clear that whatever rights they claim for themselves, they must extend the same rights to others. Small changes, made to the ways that leaders presently communicate, can significantly improve how others perceive them and respond to them.

E. 4. The Psychological Contract

Reciprocity is at the heart of communication, as it is at the heart of relationships. In order for school leaders to foster good communication and engagement with their staff, there has to be give and take in the relationship.

The expectation of reciprocity is the foundation of the psychological contract that exists between parties in various relationships. A psychological contract is neither written nor formalised, but is very firmly formed in the minds of the parties involved in relationships. It refers to the set of expectations that each party has, in relation to what they should contribute to

> **A good psychological contract bears no resemblance to a rigid tit-for-tat arrangement, where the parties are constantly fighting about who does what and when.**

the relationship, and what they should receive in return. Those in relationships, whether they are between friends, partners, spouses, family members, colleagues, or manager/leader and employees, have expectations in relation to their input and the input of the other party to the relationship. Argyris (1960) was the first to introduce the concept of a psychological contract. Since then, many writers have contributed to the development of the concept, in particular Rousseau (1989), whose influential article has informed much of the subsequent thinking on the concept.

The quality of the psychological contract, which is frequently neither articulated nor negotiated, is dependent on its balance and fairness. A good psychological contract bears no resemblance to a rigid tit-for-tat arrangement, where the parties are constantly fighting about who does what and when. Rather, it is an understanding that, in the context of the overall relationship, there will be a balance between what is given, and what is received.

There are times in any relationship when one party needs a disproportionate level of help and support that will not be immediately reciprocated. However, where there is a healthy psychological contract, there is an understanding on the part of the supportive party that, should they need help and support in the future, it will be forthcoming. There is a distinct paucity of research into the importance and benefits of the psychological contract in relationships other than those in the workplace. However, the work of Rousseau (1989); Guest (1998); Coyle-Shapiro (2000) and many others, has focused on workplace settings.

E. 4.1 The Psychological Contract (PC) Between a School Leader and a Member of Staff

A formal contract, that is agreed and signed when a new member of staff is appointed, usually refers to tangibles, such as job description and remuneration. This explicit agreement forms the tip of the iceberg in terms of the expectations of both employer and employee. It is in the psychological contract, that the majority of the expectations are held. This is an implicit agreement, the content of which generally remains undiscussed. Despite this fact, the elements of the contract are crystal clear in the minds of the both the employer and the employee. These elements also constitute the largest part of the metaphorical iceberg, which remains hidden below the water.

In schools where the employer is distanced from the workplace, the school leader is perceived as representing the organisation. In that scenario, the psychological contract is considered to be between the individual staff member and the leader. So, what sort of undocumented expectations do staff members in a school have in relation to their contributions, and what they will receive in return?

When teaching on a leadership and management course, I invariably include a module on the psychological contract in schools. The post-graduate students, all of whom are teachers, are asked to draw up their own contract based on what they believe they contribute to the school, and what they would like to receive in return. The contributions cited are many and varied, and include skills, knowledge, expertise, personality traits and attitudes, among other things. Interestingly, when it comes to what they expect in return, there is a higher degree of similarity in stated expectations. Pay is mentioned, but mainly in the context of fairness. Respect, support, appreciation, autonomy, job satisfaction and professional development opportunities are repeatedly mentioned as essential. While specifically in relation to the behaviours of the leader, they consistently state that they expect the leader to be competent, trustworthy, caring, open, fair, consistent and loyal.

The teachers on the course are then asked to state whether they perceive their psychological contract to be fulfilled or breached, and to outline the consequences of that assessment for themselves and for the school. It is hardly surprising that those who perceive their psychological contract to have been breached are clear and definitive in that assessment. Furthermore, they are definitive on how exactly it was breached, and what the consequences were. Obviously, the breaching or violating of an individual's psychological contract indicates that their specific expectations have not been met. However, there has also been, over the years, a considerable consensus among the teachers in relation to the consequences of a breached contract. The majority have cited a diminution of their motivation and their job-satisfaction. They also alluded to a loss of trust in the leader. The latter is mainly associated with a perception of having been unfairly treated.

Guest, (1998) suggested that, in broad terms, a violated psychological contract results in negative attitudes and behaviours. These behaviours can be unintentional or intentional (Rosen et al., 2009). Staff members who feel that their contributions go unreciprocated can be angry and resentful. This can manifest in constant disagreeing and complaining, which makes life very difficult for a leader trying to get agreement and co-operation. Coyle-Shapiro (2000) goes further, by suggesting that a breached contract can result in destructive deviant behaviours. When behaviours threaten the well-being of the organisation or its members, they are considered to be deviant (Robinson & Bennett, 1995). Passive negligence, such as the withholding of effort and commitment or active destruction, such as sabotage, harassment or bullying, are among the manifestations of deviant behaviours.

The literature is very clear on the implications of a fulfilled or breached psychological contract. The PC governs the ongoing employment relationship, which in schools is the relationship between the school leader and the individual staff member. In general terms, if the PC is breached then that relationship deteriorates and, if the PC is fulfilled, it grows and thrives. When staff members perceive that their PC is fulfilled, and that there is a fair exchange between what they give and what they get in return, their work outcomes improve (Organ,1988). Collegiality, flexibility, job-satisfaction and well-being are also potential positive outcomes of a fulfilled psychological contract.

School leaders play two vital roles in the fulfilment of the PC between themselves and individual staff members. Firstly, as each member of staff will have their own idiosyncratic notion of what they are expected to contribute to the school, this individual perspective must be contextualised in, and informed by, what the school expects from them. The leader has a responsibility to articulate and clarify these expectations.

Secondly, school leaders have a responsibility to ensure that their contributions adhere to the standards that the staff would expect, in order for them to reciprocate. I am firmly of the view that, as in more intimate and personal relationships, the expectations of reciprocity, and the details of what is expected from both parties, should be openly discussed at the commencement of the relationship, and checked periodically for compliance. This exercise would help to ascertain how the relationship is going, and what needs to be changed and improved. In the meantime, it is helpful for school leaders to know that if there is reciprocation in their relationships with their staff, the quality of both parties work life will be significantly enhanced.

E. 4.2 Organisational Citizenship Behaviour (OCB)

Organisational Citizenship Behaviour (OCB) generally refers to the extra time and commitment that employees give to promote and enhance the work and welfare of an organisation. It is the discretionary effort, that is not formally included in their job description, and for which there is no specific remuneration. Organ defined OCB, "as a readiness to contribute beyond literal contractual obligations" (1988, p. 22). Bassman (1992) suggested that discretionary effort is a gift that can only be given freely. It cannot be forced or coerced. She further proposed that, "employees do not owe their managers discretionary effort any more than they owe them respect – both have to be earned" (Bassman, 1992, p. 47). However, it is widely believed that OCB is the life blood of every organisation, including schools.

Schools could not survive without the OCB that numerous staff members engage in on a daily basis. Making an exclusive association between OCB and extra-curricular activities, such as sport, art, music, dance etc., does not do justice to the array of other planned and spontaneous actions that constitute OCB in schools.

These include:

- helping and supporting students outside class time;
- supporting and mentoring new teachers;
- assisting and providing information and resources to substitute teachers;
- helping out colleagues with work overload;
- contributing positively to staff meetings;
- serving on committees and boards;
- actively engaging in professional development courses;
- organising social events;
- acquiring expertise in new areas.

The willingness of staff members to give above and beyond the call of duty is essential to the effectiveness of a school, and dramatically reduces the pressures on school leaders. Podsakoff et al., (2000) linked OCB to altruism, among other attributes. However, it is the premise of many OCB theorists that the continued engagement in the discretionary behaviours that constitute OCB is related to how staff perceive they are treated by the organisation. In schools, the incidence and prevalence of OCB is contingent on the leader's treatment of his/her staff. OCB, with all its benefits, is directly related to the fulfilment of the Psychological Contract (PC) between the individual staff member and the school leader.

> **"**
> **Many people sail through life without ever questioning the way that they do things, or how what they say and do impacts on others. Consequently, they remain ignorant of the flaws and failings in how they relate to others, and of the possibilities that there could be a better way to behave in relationships.**
> **"**

E. 4.3 Reflective Practice for School Leaders

In order for school leaders to be able to assess how they are doing, and whether they are effective or not, they need to constantly reflect on their practice and behaviour. Many people sail through life without ever questioning the way that they do things, or how what they say and do impacts on others. Consequently, they remain ignorant of the flaws and failings in how they relate to others, and of the possibilities that there could be a better way to behave in relationships. When things go wrong, they invariably look to the other party to apportion fault or blame.

Being open to thinking about your own role in a problem or disagreement is an essential first step towards reflecting, more generally, on everyday interactions and behaviours. Reflective Practice involves engaging in a continuous cycle of self-observation and self-evaluation of how one behaves in various situations. The purpose of the reflection is to facilitate a better understanding of one's actions and reactions, in an effort to reinforce or refine one's behaviours as appropriate (Cunningham, 2001).

The following quotes are insightful in understanding the need for reflective practice. Albert Einstein suggested that an indication of insanity is, "to keep doing the same things but expect a different result," and Jackie 'Moms' Mabley, a renowned American comedienne, stated wisely that: "If you always do what you always did, then you'll always get what you always got." In order for reflective practice to take place, I suggest that for every two steps of doing, there is a need to stop and ask yourself, 'How am I doing?' Thus begins the process of Reflective Practice.

● Becoming a Reflective Practitioner

Only those who entertain the notion that there is room for improvement in how they do things will engage in the level of reflection necessary to deconstruct long-held habits, and to examine why they do what they do (Silvermann & Cazassa, 2000). Schon (1983), whose research underpins much of what is written about Reflective Practice, suggested that it involves both reflecting in action, as well as reflecting on action. In other words, the reflecting takes place while something is being done, through self-observation, and also after it has been done, through evaluating how it went.

A starting point for school leaders, who are novice reflective practitioners, is to examine everyday encounters and interactions to ascertain whether they went well or not. In either case, reflecting on one's words and actions can help to establish which behaviours worked and should be repeated, and which ones did not work and should be scrapped or changed. It is worth remembering that, even if behaviours appear to be working well, they should be periodically scrutinised and evaluated, so that complacency does not set in. As previously alluded to in this book, one must never wait for things to be broken to begin the process of fixing them.

If leaders are unused to making self-assessments, then they would benefit from having the assistance of an objective person to help with the reflective process. That person, if permitted and encouraged, will often spot and make known to leaders the nuances of how they have handled events or situations. It is then up to the leaders to develop insights into those assessments, by analysing the behaviours used, and the outcomes of the events. When leaders do not have the benefit of a critical friend to help them to reflect on how they are doing, they need to assume the perspective of an external observer in order to make an objective evaluation of their behaviour (Imel, 1992).

Busy and overworked school leaders may be protesting at this stage that they simply do not have the time to engage in reflection. Suffice it to say, if they do not reflect on how they are doing, they may:

- continue to get things wrong without being aware of it;

- become complacent about how they are doing things;

- miss golden opportunities to change and improve;

- encourage the wrath of those offended by their actions or inactions;

- engender disrespect in the majority of the onlookers.

> **"**
>
> Leaders who reflect on their actions and behaviours are regarded as being thoughtful and sensitive to others. They have a better chance of getting things right, and bringing others with them.
>
> **"**

Reflective Practice is part and parcel of learning and professional development. It enables leaders to use insights from past experiences to inform and improve future ones. Leaders who reflect on their actions and behaviours are regarded as being thoughtful and sensitive to others. They have a better chance of getting things right, and bringing others with them.

Key Points

- Assertive communication is the most effective style of communication, and enables leaders to get their message across, while at the same time maintaining , in as far as possible, their relationships with others.

- The six different types of assertiveness provide a range of responses that are appropriate in a variety of situations.

- Reciprocity is central to good communication and relationships. The Psychological Contract is an unwritten, and often undiscussed, understanding between the school leader and an individual staff member that relates to their expectations of reciprocity.

- Organisational citizenship behaviour refers to the discretionary effort provided by staff. It is essential to the functioning of the school, and is contingent on staff feeling that they are valued and appreciated.

- Reflective Practice is a process of evaluating one's progress, and is essential for leaders to identify their strengths and areas in need of improvement.

E. 5. The Role of Humility in School Leadership... not taking yourself too seriously

Humility is a characteristic not often associated with leadership in the minds of many, including leaders themselves. However, it is a characteristic that, when fully understood, in a contemporary context, can be seen to have a very positive influence on the quality of leadership. Humility, as an historic characteristic, was often associated with meekness or weakness. Being humble, in biblical terms, often denoted lowliness and poverty.

Many researchers and scholars have focused on the importance of humility in leadership. It is credited with contributing to an array of benefits and advantages in the workplace. There is absolutely no comparison between having a degree of humility, and being weak or passive. Whereas those with low confidence are perceived as being indecisive and insecure (Oyer, 2015), the lack of confidence is not considered to be an aspect of humility.

Humility in leadership is associated with strength of character and self-confidence. It is also synonymous with honesty and integrity (Oyer, 2015). Humility is not merely the absence of negative traits such as arrogance and narcissism, but the presence of a number of positive traits. Owens et al., (2013) alluded to humility in terms of three positive traits:

- self-awareness: through accurately assessing one's strengths and weakness;

- teachability: in terms of being willing to learn from others;

- appreciation: with regard to recognising the strengths and accomplishments of others.

In the many schools that I have visited over the years, I have encountered many excellent school leaders, who are endowed with the gift of humility. What they appear to have in common is that, they do not take themselves too seriously, and are generally referred to as being 'down to earth'. They are consistently informal and respectful in their demeanour and their approach to others. They treat everyone equally, and are neither deferential to those with power and influence, nor arrogant and dismissive towards anyone else.

> "
> Leaders with humility know their strengths, and know their weaknesses also. Whereas they are alert to what they know, they also know that they do not know everything. They are unassuming and keep their abilities and achievements in perspective. They do not feel the need to seek recognition or praise for their accomplishments, and they do not let success go to their heads.
> "

E. 5.1 Accurately Assessing one's Strengths and Weaknesses

Leaders with humility know their strengths, and know their weaknesses also. Whereas they are alert to what they know, they also know that they do not know everything. They are unassuming and keep their abilities and achievements in perspective. They do not feel the need to seek recognition or praise for their accomplishments, and they do not let success go to their heads. Consequently, they are considered to have a low self-focus. The low self-focus assessment is captured in Blanchard and Johnson's book, *The One Minute Manager*, (1982), when they stated that those with humility do not think less of themselves – they just think less about themselves.

However, it is important not to portray leaders with humility as having no self-focus or as being totally selfless. Whereas they are not overly or exclusively focused on themselves, they are, nonetheless, ambitious and interested in pursuing their career opportunities. The difference between them, and leaders with a more self-centred and selfish attitude, is that they seek promotion to positions of authority with a dual

> **"**
> **Leaders without a modicum of humility have a tendency to be self-centred and selfish. Their profile includes self-promotion at every opportunity and, in school leadership terms, they frequently refer to 'my school', or, 'my staff'.**
> **"**

purpose. They are focused, primarily, on what they can bring to the position. Understandably though, they are also focused on what the position can bring to them. This is a healthy and fair-minded attitude.

Leaders without a modicum of humility have a tendency to be self-centred and selfish. Their profile includes self-promotion at every opportunity and, in school leadership terms, they frequently refer to 'my school', or, 'my staff'. They place themselves centre stage in school successes. They dominate and star in 'front of house' appearances, at school performances by students. They engage in PR exercises designed to highlight their own standing and contribution. Through exaggerating their own capabilities, they refuse to acknowledge their mistakes or failures. It is often difficult for outsiders to see the self-promotion that underpins the carefully crafted and perfectly articulated speeches made by self-centred school leaders at graduations, open days, or parent meetings. However, staff members are always painfully aware when school leaders give disproportionate credit to themselves.

Relationships with leaders who overestimate either their importance or contribution are tinged with distrust and fear. Unfortunately, they make the job of leadership primarily about themselves, and what is in it for them.

E. 5.2 Being Willing to Learn from Others

Leaders with humility do not see themselves as being better than, or superior to, others. They realise that they do not have all the answers, and seek out and actively encourage others to voice their opinions and views. They also acknowledge their limitations and actively enlist the ideas and advice of others. They are happy to change their course of action, if the suggestions of others prove more viable.

In O'Toole's 1995 book, entitled *Leading Change*, the author alluded to four illustrious American presidents (Washinton, Jefferson, Lincoln and Roosevelt), whom he referred to as the Rushmoreans, with reference to the giant carvings of their heads into the side of Mount Rushmore. The carvings, however, are not their claim to fame. Rather, it is their leadership style that singles them out as special. In relation to taking on board and reflecting the values and suggestions of others, O'Toole (1995) stated that all four Rushmoreans listened to their advisors, and encouraged a range of diverse opinions from them. All ideas were tested, all sides of the arguments were explored, and a full range of opinion was sought.

It takes self-assuredness, self-confidence, and a good sprinkling of humility for those in positions of power to behave in this modest manner. O'Toole further surmised that, if any of the Rushmoreans had lacked self-confidence and had surrounded themselves with, "worshipping sycophants who posed no threat to them intellectually, their administrations would have been mediocre." (O'Toole, 1995, p. 30)

Leaders who lack humility tend to make decisions unilaterally, and do not listen to or consult with others. They seem to find it very difficult to take advice, are resistant to feedback, and can be defensive in the face of even minor criticism. They often have illusions about their own indispensability, as they second guess the decisions and actions of others. When things go wrong they tend to adopt an 'I told you so' attitude, as they remonstrate generally, or single out and scapegoat one unlucky individual.

> **If only those who retain the focus on themselves, in the context of successes, could realise that there is always enough credit to go around, and that the more credit you give to others, the more credit you get for yourself.**

E. 5.3 Recognising the Strengths and Accomplishments of Others

Leaders with humility revel in, and celebrate, the achievements and accomplishments of others. Humility and self-confidence prevent them from feeling threatened by the successes of others, as they readily and willingly give due credit. They are parsimonious in taking credit for themselves, while they regularly elucidate on the achievements of others.

School leaders, who are willing to relinquish or share the lime light, enable and facilitate others to shine. In the process, they gain admiration and appreciation. They have, what Covey (1989) so eloquently described as, an "Abundance Mentality". (1989, p. 219) They know that there is plenty of limelight for everyone. If only those who retain the focus on themselves, in the context of successes, could realise that there is always enough credit to go around, and that the more credit you give to others, the more credit you get for yourself.

E. 5.4 Narcissism and Arrogance

There is no place for narcissism or arrogance in school leadership. Narcissism, according to Bennis (2004), is the opposite of humility. Morris et al., (2005) agreed, citing self-promotion and an inflated sense of self-worth as characteristics of narcissism. Those who have an exaggerated sense of their own importance only have to be given a shiny button on their uniform, or an extra stripe on their sleeve, for them to take on notions of grandeur and superiority. Arrogance is a close relation of narcissism. Arrogant behaviours are also intended to exaggerate a person's sense of superiority. However, there is an additional dimension to arrogance, in that it frequently involves the undermining of others (Johnson et al., 2010). Arrogant leaders show off their knowledge, and directly or by inference purport to be more knowledgeable than others. Also, they regard any questioning of them, or their decisions, as an undermining of their authority, and find ways and means of getting the perceived perpetrators back.

Most current school leaders will not identify with narcissism or arrogance, with reference to their own behaviours. Some would instinctively feel that they would never get away with that type of behaviour, while many more would instinctively know that behaving in an arrogant manner would be totally alien to them. While effective school leaders are at pains to distance themselves from arrogance, it has to be said that arrogance in leadership, generally, appears to be on the increase. In a 2012 article entitled *Arrogance: A formula for leadership failure,* Silverman et al., stated that, "arrogance has run amok lately". This comment was based on four years of research that Silverman and a number of colleagues had conducted into arrogance in the workplace. Interestingly, but not surprisingly, they also stated that arrogant behaviour is typically not associated with actual superior performance or knowledge (Silverman et al., 2012). It is associated with a lack of agreeableness in a person, which negatively impacts on their relationships with others.

Arrogant behaviour is further related to the cultivation of a toxic social environment that impacts negatively on the well-being of everyone in the school. One would really like to believe that arrogance is not prevalent among school leaders. However, a number of studies have focused on the dark-side of school leadership. In particular, the work of Blase and Blase (2006), and Brooks (2006) set out in very clear terms how the arrogant behaviours of school leaders are manifested. Silverman et al., (2012) reported that the empirical findings in relation to the pitfalls of arrogance, show that arrogant behaviours at work have detrimental consequences, and that when arrogance is replaced by humility, there are many benefits for leaders and also for the organisation.

E. 5.5 The Benefits of Humility

Doty and Gerdes (2000) suggested that "humility transcends context to permeate every action of the leader" (p. 89). Indicators of humility in school leaders are found in their everyday attitudes and actions. For example, they generally take their lunch with everyone else in the staffroom. They do not segregate 'important' visitors from the staff, and provide them with expensive lunches in the office. They do not talk down to anyone. They do not show favouritism to, or discriminate against, anyone in the school community based on status or ability. A core element of humility is the value that leaders place not merely on themselves but on everyone else as well (Morris et al., 2005). This stems from the deeply held belief in the equal dignity of everyone, that those with humility hold dear (Grenberg, 2005).

Because they do not get carried away with themselves, or adopt a pretentious disposition, leaders with humility build solid relationships and alliances and "inspire camaraderie and esprit de corps" (Doty & Gerdes, 2000, p. 90). Also, because leaders with humility admit when they are mistaken or wrong, and take the blame when it is warranted, they enhance the support and commitment of others (Owens & Hekman, 2012). Humility and the

> **"**
>
> **Leaders with humility do not make a song and dance about everything. They just want to get on with the job. This attitude is very far removed from that of celebrity type leaders, who think that they are great, and require constant reminders of their greatness.**
>
> **"**

ability to admit to an error are considered by Gutrie and Venkatesh (2012), as being two of the most important qualities of truly creative leaders. Leaders with humility do not make a song and dance about everything. They just want to get on with the job. This attitude is very far removed from that of celebrity type leaders, who think that they are great, and require constant reminders of their greatness.

The real question for leaders is, how do you know whether you have humility or not? The chances are, if you think you have it, you probably do not, and if you do have it, you probably do not realise that you have it. Humility is unamenable to self-reporting, because those who tick yes to the attributes of humility may be automatically disqualifying themselves. Whereas humility resides in the person, it is primarily perceived by others (Argandona, 2015).

There is no formula for leaders in acquiring a modicum of humility. There is, however, a guiding principle, which is a realisation that the quality of their leadership is dependent on their own skills and commitment, combined with the skills and commitment of the whole team. Once this principle is accepted, the other elements of humility – which involve the utilisation, acknowledgement and appreciation, of the skills of others – will follow.

Key Points

- Humility is a characteristic not traditionally associated with leaders. It is, however, widely credited with contributing significantly to effective and successful leadership.

- The humility of school leaders is reflective of their confidence and assuredness, and involves the ability to identify their strengths and weaknesses, accept the input of others, and provide recognition generously.

- Narcissism and arrogance in leaders is easily identified by others, and is detrimental to the school environment and the well-being of staff.

- Leaders with humility do not take themselves too seriously. They get on with the job and bring others with them.

E. 6. Conclusion

The job of a school leader has more than its fair share of trials and tribulations. It can be made more or less difficult, depending on the attitudes and behaviours of the individual leader. Those who consistently use effective communication to evoke in others a sense of being included, respected, and appreciated, bring their staff with them. Those who consistently reflect on how they do things gain a level of self-awareness that encourages them to learn new and better ways of doing things. Having the desire and inclination to learn and change, rather than, "assuming away any need for learning because they already know everything they need to know" (Senge, 1999, p. 419), is what distinguishes leaders with humility from those with arrogance. Doty and Gerdes (2000) expressed the opinion that humility in leadership is uncommon. However, they suggested that when authentic humility is applied to relationships, mutual trust develops, and an environment is created in which great things can be achieved.

Beating a squash ball against a wall used to be considered a good way for leaders to release and relieve the stress and worries of work. The focus, of late, is on preventing problems through engaging in leadership behaviours that incorporate best practice, and that are successful in engaging the staff. Leadership behaviours are now, more than ever, considered as performance issues, and not as optional extras. It is through their behaviours that school leaders can be effective, care for, and get the best out of others and, in the process, care for and get the best out of themselves.

Bibliography

Adams, A., (1992) *Bullying at work: How to confront and overcome it.* London: Virago Press

Albrecht, K. (2006) *Social intelligence: The new science of success.* San Francisco: Jossey-Bass

Argandona, A. J. (2015) Humility in management. *Journal of Business Ethics,* **132**(1), pp. 63-71

Argyris, C. (1960) *Understanding organizational behavior.* Homewood, IL: Dorsey Press

Arnaud, A., & Sekerka, L. (2010) Positively ethical: The establishment of innovation in support of sustainability. International *Journal of Sustainable Strategic Management*, **2**(2), pp. 121-137. doi: 10.1504/IJSSM.2010.032556

Ashley, G., & Reiter-Palmon, R. (2012) Self-awareness and the evolution of leaders: The need for a better measure of self-awareness. *Journal of Behavioral and Applied Management*, **14**, pp. 2-17

Babiak, P. & Hare, R.D. (2006) *Snakes in suits: When psychopaths go to work.* New York: Harper/Collins

Bandura, A. (1986) *Social foundations of thought and action: A social cognitive theory.* Englewood Cliffs, NJ: Prentice-Hall, Inc.

Bandura, A. (1997) *Self-Efficacy: The exercise of control.* New York: Freeman

Bandura, A. (2000) Cultivate Self-Efficacy For Personal And Organizational Effectiveness, In E.A. Locke (ed.), *The blackwell handbook of principles of organizational behavior.* Malden, MA: Oxford University Press, pp.120-136

Barsade, S. G. & O'Neill, O. A. (2016) Manage your emotional culture. *Harvard Business Review*, **94**(1), pp. 58-66

Barsade, S.G. (2002) The ripple effect: Emotional contagion and its influence on group behavior. *Administrative Science Quarterly*, **47**(4), pp. 644-675

Bartolome, F. (1989) Nobody trusts the boss completely-now what? *Harvard Business Review* **67**(2), pp.135-42

Bassman, E. (1992) *Abuse in the workplace: Management remedies and bottom line impact.* Westport, CT: Quorum Books

Baumeister, R. F., & Leary, M. R. (1995) The need to belong: Desire for interpersonal attachments as a fundamental human motivation. *Psychological Bulletin*, **117**(3), pp.497-529. doi: 10.1037/0033-2909.117.3.497

Baumeister, R. F., Smart, L., & Boden, J.M. (1996) Relation of threatened egotism to violence and aggression: The dark side of high self-esteem. *Psychological Review*, **103**(1), pp. 5-33

Beale, D. (2001) Monitoring bullying in the workplace. In Tehrani, N. (ed.), *Building a culture of respect: Managing bullying at work.* London: Taylor & Francis, pp. 77-94

Beck, J. S. (1995) *Cognitive therapy: Basics and beyond.* New York: Guilford

Belak, T. (2004) How to handle difficult behavior in the workplace. http://www.mediate.com/articles/belak4.cfm

Bennis, W. & Nanus, B. (1997) Leaders: The strategies for taking charge. New York: Harper & Row

Bennis, W. (2004) The seven ages of the leader. *Harvard Business Review*, **82**(1), pp. 46-53

Berkovich, I., & Eyal, O. (2015) Educational leaders and emotions: An international review of empirical evidence 1992-2012. *Review of Educational Research*, **85**(1), pp. 129-167

Bjorkqvist, K., Osterman, K. and Hjelt-Back, M. (1994) Aggression among university employees. *Aggressive Behavior*, **20**, pp. 173-84

Blake, R.R., & Mouton, J.S. (1982) Theory and Research for Developing a Science of Leadership. *Journal of Applied Behavioural Science*, **18**, pp. 275-291

Blanchard, K. H., & Johnson, S. (1982) *The one minute manager*. New York: Morrow

Blase, J., & Blase, J. (2003) *Breaking the Silence: Overcoming the problem of principal mistreatment of teachers*. Thousand Oaks, CA: Corwin Press, Inc.

Blase, J., & Blase, J. (2006) Teacher perspectives of principal mistreatment. *Education Administration Quarterly*, **38**(5), 671-727

Block, J.H. & Block, J. (1980) The Role of ego-control and egoresiliency in the organization of behavior. In W. A. Collins (ed.), *Minnesota symposia on child psychology, Vol. 13*. Hillsdale, NJ: Erlbaum, pp. 39-101

Bluestein, J. (2001) *Creating emotionally safe schools: A guide for educators and parents*. Deerfield Beach, FL: Health Communications

Bonanno, G.A. (2004) Loss, trauma, and human resilience: Have we underestimated the human capacity to thrive after extremely aversive events? *American Psychologist*. **59**(1), pp. 20-28

Boyatzis, R.E. & Oosten, E. V. (2002) Developing emotionally intelligent organizations. In Roderick Millar (ed.), *International Executive Development Programmes, 7th Edition*. London: Kogan Page Publishers

Branch, S., Ramsey, S. and Barker, M. (2007) Managers in the firing line: contributing factors to workplace bullying by staff—an interview study. *Journal of Management and Organization*, **13**, pp. 264-282

Brennan, J., & Mac Ruairc, G. (2011) Taking it personally: Examining patterns of emotional practice in leading primary schools. *International Journal of Leadership in Education*, **14**(2), pp. 129-150 doi: 10.1080/13603124.2010.536261

Brooks, J. S. (2006) *Leading with smoke and mirrors. In The dark side of school reform: Teaching in the space between reality and utopia*. Lanham, MD: Rowman & Littlefield, pp. 129-145

Brunetti, G.J. (2006) Resilience under fire: Perspectives on the work of experienced, inner city high school teachers in the United States. *Teaching and Teacher Education* **22**(7), pp. 812-825

Bryant, F. B., Chadwick, E. D., & Kluwe, K. (2011) Understanding the processes that regulate positive emotional experience: Unsolved problems and future directions for theory and research on savoring. *International Journal of Wellbeing*, **1**, pp.107-126. doi:10.5502/ijw.v1i1.18

Bryk, A.S. & Schneider, B.L. (2003) Trust in schools: A core resource for school reform. *Educational Leadership*, **60**(6), pp. 40-44

Burns, D. (1980) *Feeling good*. New York: Morrow

Carver, C. S., Scheier, M. F., & Segerstrom, S. C. (2010) Optimism. *Clinical Psychology Review*, **30**, pp.879–889

Caviola, A. & Lavender, N. (2000) *Toxic coworkers*. Oakland CA: New Harbinger Publications, Inc.

Chang, M. (2009) An appraisal perspective of teacher burnout: Examining the emotional work of teachers. *Educational Psychology Review*, **21**(3) p.p 193-218 doi:10.1007/s10648-009-9106-y

Colvin, R., Block, J., Funder, D. (1995) Overly positive self-evaluations and personality: Negative implications for mental health. *Journal of Personality and Social Psychology*, **68**(6), pp. 1152-1162

Cooley, C. H., (1902) *Human Nature and the Social Order*. New York: Scribner

Corbett, S. & Kitt, J. (2006) Paper presented to 3rd Annual Occupational Health and Safety Summit, Dublin: Unpublished

Corbett, S. & Kitt, J. (2007) Submission made to the Health and Safety Authority, Ireland, for the proposed revision of the Code of Practice on the Prevention of Workplace Bullying, Dublin: Unpublished

Costigan, L. (1998) *Bullying and harassment in the workplace*. Dublin: Columba Press

Côté, S., Gyurak, A., & Levenson, R. W. (2010) The ability to regulate emotion is associated with greater well-being, income, and socioeconomic status. *Emotion*, **10**(6), pp. 923-933. doi: 10.1037/a0021156

Covey, S.R. (1989) *The seven habits of highly effective people*. London: Simon & Schuster

Coyle-Shapiro, J. A. (2000) *Psychological contracts: What is the measurement trade-offs and are they worth it?* Paper presented at the Academy of Management Meeting, Toronto,Canada

Craft, A. (2007) Possibility thinking in the early years and primary classroom In T, Ai-Girl (ed.) *Creativity: A handbook for teachers*. Singapore: World Scientific Publishing, pp. 231-250

Crawford, M. (2007) Rationality and emotion in primary school leadership: An exploration of key themes, *Educational Review*, **59**(1), pp. 87-98

Crawford, M. (2009) *Getting to the heart of leadership*. London: Sage

Crawford, N. (2001) Organizational responses to workplace bullying in Tehrani, N., (Ed.), (2001) *Building a Culture of Respect, Managing Bullying at Work*, London: Taylor and Francis

Cunningham, J. B. (2001) *Researching organizational values and beliefs: The Echo Approach*. London: Quorum Books

D'Cruz, P., & Noronha, E. (2010) Employee Dilemmas in the Indian ITES-BPO Sector. In J. Messenger and N. Ghosheh (eds.), *Remote work and global sourcing*, Basingstoke: Palgrave Macmillan, pp. 60-100

Dana, D. (2005) *Managing differences: how to build better relationships at work*. Prairie Village, KS: MTI Publications

Dana, D. (2006) Managing differences: How to build better relationships at work and home (4th ed.) Prairie Village, KS: MTI Publications

Daniel, A. (1998) *Scapegoats for professions*. London: Gordon and Breach

Davenport, N., Schwartz, R., & Elliot, G. (1999) *Mobbing, emotional abuse in the workplace*. Iowa, U.S.A: Civil Society Publishing

Deal, T. & Key, M. (1998) Corporate celebration, play, purpose and profit at work, San Francisco, CA: Barrett-Kolhler Publishers Inc.

Deci, E. L., & Ryan, R. M. (1987) The support of autonomy and the control of behavior. *Journal of Personality and Social Psychology*, **53**(6), pp. 1024-1037

De Souza, M., Frances, L., O'Higgins-Norman, J. Scott, D. (Eds.) (2009). *International Handbook of Education for Spirituality Care & Wellbeing*, Dordrecht, Netherlands: Springer Academic Publishers

Deutsch, R.; Gawronski, B.; Strack, F. (2006) At the boundaries of automaticity: Negation as reflective operation. *Journal of Personality and Social Psychology*, **91**(3), pp. 385-405. doi:10.1037/0022-3514.91.3.385

Dickerson, S. S., Gruenewald, T. L., & Kemeny, M. E. (2004) When the social self is threatened: Shame, physiology, and health. *Journal of Personality*, **72** (6), pp. 1191-1216

Doty, J., & Gerdes, D. (2000) Humility as a leadership attribute. *Military Review,* **80**(5), pp. 89-90

Drucker, P.F. (2005) Managing oneself. *Harvard Business Review*, **83**(5), pp. 100-109

Economic & Social Research Institute (ESRI) (2007) *Bullying in the workplace: Survey reports, 2007. Report to the Department of Enterprise, Trade and Employment*. Dublin: ESRI

Einarsen, S., Matthiesen, S. B. and Mikkelsen, E.G. (1999) Does time heal all wounds? Long-term health effects of exposure to bullying at work. Bergen: University of Bergen

Einarsen, S., Hoel, H., Zapt, D. & Cooper, C. (Eds.), (2003) Bullying and Emotional Abuse in the Workplace, London: Taylor and Francis

Eskin, M. (2003) Self-reported assertiveness in Swedish and Turkish adolescents: A cross-cultural comparison. *Scandinavian Journal of. Psychology*, **44**, pp. 7-12

Everand, B., & Morris,G. (1990) (2nd Ed.), *Effective School Management*, London: Paul Chapman

Field, T. (1996) *Bully in sight: How to predict, resist, challenge and combat workplace bullying.* Oxfordshire: Success Unlimited

Fisher, R., Ury, W., & Patton, B. (1991) Getting to yes: Negotiating agreement without giving in. 2nd ed New York: Penguin Books

Francis, D., & Woodcock, M. (1990) *Unblocking organizational values.* Glenview, IL: Scott, Foresman

Fredrickson, B. L., & Losada, M. F. (2005) Positive affect and the complex dynamics of human flourishing. *American Psychologist*, **60**(7), pp. 678-686. doi: 10.1037/0003-066X.60.7.678

Fredrickson, B.L, (2001) The Role of Positive Emotions in Positive Psychology: The broaden and build theory of positive emotions. *American Psychologist*, 56(3): pp. 218-226

Fredrickson, B.L. (2003) Positive Emotions and Upward Spirals in Organizations. In Cameron, K., Dutton, J. & Quinn, R. (eds) *Positive Organizational Scholarship: Foundations of a New Discipline.* San Francisco: BerrettKoehler, pp. 163-175

Freedman, J. (2015) What's the difference between an emotion, a feeling, and mood? [ONLINE] Available at: http://www. 6seconds.org/2015/01/02/ emotion-feeling-mood/. [Accessed 18 October 2016]

Freedman, J. M., Jensen, A. L., Rideout, M. C. & Freedman, P. E. (1998) Handle with care: Emotionally intelligent activity book. In Bluestein. J. (2001) Creating emotionally safe schools: A guide for educators and parents. Florida: Health Communications Inc.

Fussell, S. R. (2002) The verbal communication of emotion: Introduction and overview. In S. R. Fussell, Ed.,*The verbal communication of emotion: Interdisciplinary perspectives.* Mahwah, NJ: Lawrence Erlbaum Associates. pp 1-22

Futterman,S. (2004) *When you work for a bully.* New Jersey: Croce Publishing Group

Galinsky, A. D., Magee, J. C., Inesi, M. E., & Gruenfeld, D. H. (2006) Power and perspectives not taken. *Psychological Science*, **17**, pp.1068-1074

Gardner, W. L., Avolio, B. J., Luthans, F., May, D. R., & Walumba, F. O. (2005) Can you see the real me? A self-based model of authentic leader and follower development. *The Leadership Quarterly*, **16**(3), pp. 343-372

Geffner, R., Loring, M., and Young, C. (2001) Bullying behaviour: Current issues, research, and interventions. New York: The Haworth Press, Inc.

Gentile, N. (ed.), (1994) Differences that work: Organisational excellence through diversity. Boston, MA: The Harvard Business School Publishing Corporation

George, J.M. (2000) Emotions and leadership: The role of emotional intelligence. *Human Relations*, **53**(8), pp. 1027-1055

Gibb, J. R. (1961) Defensive communication. *Journal of Communication*, 11, pp. 141-148. doi:10.1111/j. 1460-2466.1961.tb00344.x

Gibson, S. & Dembo, M. (1984) Teacher efficacy: A construct validation. *Journal of Educational Psychology*, **76**(4), pp. 569-582

Glasser, W. (1998) Choice theory: A new psychology of personal freedom. New York, NY: Harper

Glomb, T. (2001) Workplace aggression: Antecedents, behavioural components and consequences. In Einarsen, S., Hoel, H., Zapt, D. and Cooper, C. (eds.) *Bullying and emotional abuse in the workplace.* London: Taylor and Francis

Goleman, D. (1995) Emotional intelligence: Why it can matter more than IQ for character, health and lifelong achievement. New York: Bantam

Goleman, D. (1998) Working with emotional intelligence. New York: Bantam

Goleman, D. (2000). An EI-based theory of performance. In D. Goleman, & C. Cherniss (eds.), *The Emotionally Intelligent Workplace: How to Select for, Measure, and Improve Emotional Intelligence in Individuals, Groups, and Organizations.* San Francisco, CA: Jossey-Bass.

Goleman, D., Boyatzis, R. E., & McKee, A. (2002). *Primal leadership: Realizing the power of emotional intelligence.* Boston, Mass: Harvard Business School

Grandey, A. (2000) Emotion regulation in the workplace: A new way to conceptualize emotional labor. *Journal of Occupational Health Psychology,***5**(1), pp. 95-110

Grenberg, J. M. (2005) *Kant and the ethics of humility: A story of dependence, corruption and virtue.* Cambridge, MA: Cambridge University Press

Gross, J. J. (2007) *Handbook of emotion regulation.* New York, NY: Guilford Press

Gross, J.J. (1998) The emerging field of emotion regulation: an integrative review. *Review of General Psychology* **2** (3), pp. 271-299

Gross, J.J., & Munoz, R.F. (1995) Emotion regulation and mental health. *Clinical Psychology: Science and Practice,* **2**(2), pp. 151-164. doi:10.1111/j.1468-2850.1995.tb00036.x

Gross, J.J., (2002), Emotion regulation: Affective, cognitive, and social consequences. *Psychophysiology,* **39**(3) pp. 281-291

Grover, S., Hasel, M., Manville, C., & Serrano, A. C. (2014) Follower reactions to leader trust violations: A grounded theory of violation types, likelihood of recovery, and recovery process. *European Management Journal,* **32**(5): pp. 689-702

Gruenewald, T. L., Kemeny, M. E., Aziz, N., & Fahey, J. L. (2004) Acute threat to the social self: Shame, social self-esteem, and cortisol activity. *Psychosomatic Medicine,* **66**, pp. 915-924

Gu, Q. & Day, C. (2007) Teachers resilience: A necessary condition for effectiveness. *Teaching and Teacher Education* **23**(8), pp. 1302-1316

Guest, D. E. (1998), Is the psychological contract worth taking seriously? *Journal of Organizational Behavior,* 19(51), pp. 649-664

Gurr, D., & Drysdale, L. (2007). Models of successful principal leadership: Victorian case studies. In K. Leithwood & C. Day (Eds.), *Successful school leadership in times of change* Toronto: Springer, pp. 39-58

Guthrie, D. & Venkatesh, S. (2012) Creative leadership: Humility and being wrong. Retrieved from http://www.forbes.com/sites/dougguthrie/2012/06/01/creative-leadership-humility-and-beingwrong/

Hargreaves, A. (1998) The emotional practice of teaching. *Teaching and Teacher Education,* **14**(8) pp.835-854

Hartley, C.A., & Phelps, E.A. (2010) Changing fear: the neurocircuitry of emotion regulation. *Neuropsychopharmacology,* **35**(1), pp.136-46

Health and Safety Authority (2007) *Code of practice for employers and employees for the prevention and resolution of bullying at work.* Dublin: HSA

Health and Safety Authority. (2001) *Dignity at work: the challenge of workplace bullying. Report of the task force on the prevention of workplace bullying.* Dublin: Stationery Office

Heatherton, T., & Vohs, K.D. (2000) Interpersonal evaluations following threats to self: Role of self-esteem. *Journal of Personality and Social Psychology,* **78**, pp. 725-736

Hill, K (1991) *An ecological approach to creativity: Trait and environment influences in the college classroom.* Unpublished Ph.D. dissertation. Brandeis University. Waltham, MA

Hoel, H. and Salin, D. (2003) 'Organisational antecedents of workplace bullying' in S. Einarsen, H., Hoel, D., Zapf and C. Cooper (Eds). *Bullying and emotional abuse in the workplace: International perspectives in research and practice.* London: Taylor & Francis

Hoel. H., Coyne, L., Seigne, E., & Randall, P. (2000) Predicting workplace victim status from personality. *European Journal of Work an Organisational Psychology,* **9**(3), pp. 335-349

Horn, S. (2002) *Take the bully by the horns*, New York: St. Martins Press

Hornstein, H. (1996) *Brutal bosses and their prey: How to identify and overcome abuse in the workplace*. New York: The Berkeley Publishing Group

Hudson, S. M., & Ward, T. (2000) Interpersonal competency in sex offenders. Behavior Modification, **24**(4), pp. 494-527

Humphrey, R. H. (2002): The many faces of emotional leadership. *Leadership Quarterly*, **13**(5), pp. 493-504

Huntoon, L. (2007) Editorial: The psychology of sham peer review. *Journal of American Physicians and Surgeons*. **12**(1), pp. 3-4

Imel, S. (1992) *Reflective practice in adult education*. ERIC Digest No. 122 (Columbus, Ohio, ERIC Clearinghouse on Adult Career and Vocational Education

Ironside, M., & Seifert, R. (2003) Tackling bullying in the workplace: The collective dimension. In Einarsen, S., Hoel, H., Zapt, D. and Cooper, C. (eds.), *Bullying and emotional abuse in the workplace*. London: Taylor and Francis

Ishmael, A., & Alemoru, B. (1999) *Harassment, bullying and violence at work*. London: The Industrial Society

Jackall, R. (1983) Moral Mazes: Bureaucracy and Managerial Work. *Harvard Business Review*, **61**(5), pp. 118-130

Jennings, P. A., & Greenberg, M. T. (2009) The prosocial classroom: Teacher social and emotional competence in relation to student and classroom outcomes. *Review of Educational Research*, **79**, pp. 491-525

Johnson, D. W. (2003) Social interdependence: The interrelationships among theory, research, and practice. *American Psychologist*, **58**(11), pp.931-945

Johnson, D.W., & Johnson, R.T. (1995) Why violence prevention programs don't work and what does. *Educational Leadership*, **52**(5), pp. 63-68

Johnson, R. E., Silverman, S. B., Shymsunder, A., Swee, H., Rodopman, O. B., Bauer, J., & Chao, E. (2010) Acting superior but actually inferior?:Correlates and consequences of workplace arrogance. *Human Performance*, **23**, pp. 403-427

Jones, T., & Brinkert, R. (2008) *Conflict coaching: Conflict management strategies and skills for the individual.* Thousand Oaks, CA: Sage

Jordan, C. H., Spencer, S. J., Zanna, M. P., Hoshino-Browne, E., & Correll, J. (2003). Secure and defensive high self-esteem. *Journal of Personality and Social Psychology*, **85**(5), pp. 969-978

Jordan, D., & Le Metais, J. (1999) Developing emotional intelligence in the classroom. *Set No. 1.* New Zealand Council for Educational Research and the Australian Council for Educational Research

Jordan, J. (2006) Relational resilience in girls. In Goldstein, S. & Brooks, R. (eds.) *Handbook of Resilience in Children*, New York: Springer

Jordan, P.J., & Troth, A.C. (2002) Emotional intelligence and conflict resolution: Implications for human resource development. *Advances in Developing Human Resources.* **4**(1), pp. 62-79. doi:10.1177/1523422302004001005

Kador, J. (2009) Effective apology: Mending fences, building bridges, and restoring trust. San Francisco: Berrett-Koehler Publishers

Kanter, Rosabeth M. (1979) *Men and Women of the Corporation*. New York: Basic Books

Kaplan, S., Bradley-Geist, J.C., Ahmad, A., Anderson, A., Hargrove, A.K., & Lindsey, A. (2014), A test of two positive psychology interventions to increase employee well-being. *Journal of Business and Psychology*, **29**(3), pp. 367-380

Kazimoto, P. (2013) Analysis of conflict management and leadership for organizational change. *International Journal of Research in Social Sciences*, **3**(1), pp. 16-25

Keashly, L., & Jagatic, K. (2003) By any other name: American perspectives on workplace bullying. In Einarsen, S., Hoel, H., Zapt, D. and Cooper, C. (eds.), *Bullying and emotional abuse in the workplace*. London: Taylor and Francis

Kelly, C. (1988) *The Destructive Achiever: Power and ethics in the American corporation*. New York: Addison-Wesley Publishing Co.

Kitt, J. (1999) Workplace bullying in primary schools: A case study. Unpublished Thesis, Dublin: Trinity College

Kitt, J. (2009) ' Facing up to workplace bullying in the context of schools and teaching'. In De Souza, M., Francis, L., O'Higgins-Norman, J. & Scott, D. (Eds.) (2009) *International Handbook of Education for Spirituality, Care and Wellbeing.* Dordrecht, Netherlands: Springer Academic Publishers.

Kohl, Herbert R. (1998) *The discipline of hope*, New York, NY: Simon & Schuster

Lazányi, K. (2009) The Role of Leaders' Emotions. *APSTRACT* **3**(3), pp. 103-109

Lazare, A. (2004) *On apology.* New York: Oxford University Press

Lazarus R.S. (1993) From psychological stress to the emotions: A history of changing outlooks. *Annual Review of Psychology*, **44**, pp. 1-21

Lazarus, R. S., & Folkman, S. (1984) *Stress, appraisal, and coping.* New York: Springer Pub. Co.

Leary, M. R., & Baumeister, R. F. (2000) The nature and function of self-esteem: Sociometer theory. In M. P. Zanna (ed.), *Advances in experimental social psychology* San Diego, CA: Academic Press, pp1-62

Lee, K.L (2008) An examination between the relationships of conflict management styles and employees' satisfaction, *International Journal of Business and Management*, **3**(9), pp. 11-25

Leithwood, K., Jantzi, D., Earl, L., & Fullan, M. (2004) Strategic leadership for large-scale reform: The case of England's national literacy and numeracy strategy. *School Leadership and Management*, **24**(1), pp. 57-79 doi: 10.1080/1363243042000172822

Leithwood, K., Jantzi, D., Earl, L., Watson, N., Levin, B., & Fullan, M. (2004). Strategic leadership for large-scale reform: The case of England's national literacy and numeracy strategies. *Journal of School Leadership and Management*, **24**(1), pp. 57-80

Leymann, H. (1996) The content and development of mobbing at work. *European Journal of Work and Organisational Psychology*, **5**(2), pp. 165-184

Locke, E. A. (2005) Why emotional intelligence is an invalid concept. *Journal of Organizational Behavior*, **26**, pp. 425-431

Luft, J. and Ingham, H. (1955). The Johari Window: a graphic model for interpersonal relations, *Proceedings of the western training laboratory group development,* Los Angeles. University of California, Los Angeles.

Luft, J., & Ingham, H. (1961) The Johari window: A graphic model for interpersonal relations. *Human Relations Training News*, **5**(1), pp. 6-7

Luibit, R. (2004) *Coping with toxic managers, subordinates and other difficult people.* New Jersey: Prentice Hall

Luthans, F., Avolio, B.J., Avey, J.B. & Norman, S.M. (2007) Positive Psychological Capital: Measurement and Relationship with Performance and Satisfaction. *Personnel Psychology*, **60**: pp. 541-572

Luthans, F., Luthans, K. W., & Luthans, B. C. (2004) Positive psychological capital: Beyond human and social capital. *Business Horizons*, **47**(1), pp. 45-50

Mann, R. (1996) Psychological Abuse in the Workplace. In McCarthy, P., Sheehan, M. & W. Wilkie (eds.), *Bullying: From backyard to boardroom.* New South Wales: Millennium Books

Maslow, A. H. (1954) *Motivation and personality.* New York: Harper

Mayer J.D. (2000) Emotion, intelligence, emotional intelligence. In Forgas J.P. (ed.) *The Handbook of Affect and Social Cognition*, Mahwah, NJ: Erlbaum, pp. 410-431

Mayer, J.D. & Salovey, P. (1997) What is emotional intelligence: Implications for educators. In P. Salovey and D. Sluyter (eds.) *Emotional development, emotional literacy, and emotional intelligence.* New York: Basic Books. pp. 3-31

Mayer, R., Davis, J., & Schoorman, F. (1995) An Integrative Model of Organizational Trust. *The Academy of Management Review*, **20**(3), pp. 709-734

McCarthy, P. (1996) When the mask slips: Inappropriate coercion in organisations undergoing restructuring. In McCarthy, P., Sheehan, M. & W. Wilkie (eds.), *Bullying: From backyard to boardroom*. New South Wales: Millennium Books

McCarthy, P. (2003) Bullying at work: A postmodern experience. In Einarsen, S., Hoel, H., Zapt, D. and Cooper, C. (eds.), *Bullying and emotional abuse in the workplace*. London: Taylor and Francis

McCarthy, P. (2004) Occupational violence, psycho- terror and terrorism. In McCarthy, P., and Mayhew, C. (eds.), *Safeguarding the organisation against violence and bullying: An International Perspective*. New York: Palgrave Macmillan

McCarthy, P., Sheehan, M. & Wilkie W. (1996) *Bullying: From backyard to boardroom*. New South Wales: Millennium Books

McConnon, S. & McConnon, M. (2008) *Managing conflict in the workplace*. Oxford, U.K.: Howtobooks

McCormick, M.J. (2001) Self-efficacy and leadership effectiveness: Applying social cognitive theory to leadership. *Journal of Leadership Studies*, **8**(1), pp. 22-33

McKay, R. B. (2012) When I knew it was time to leave: Bottom-up workplace bullying. *International Journal of Economics and Management Sciences*, **2**(3), pp. 25-34

McKay, R. and Fratzl, J., (2011) A cause of failure in addressing workplace bullying: Trauma and the employee. *International Journal of Business and Social Science*, **2**(7), pp. 13-27

Michel, F. & Fursland, A. (2008) Module 4, Hot to Behave More Assertively. In Michel, F. (2008) Assert Yourself! Perth, Western Australia: Centre for Clinical Interventions.

Michel, F. & Fursland, A. (2008) Module 2, How to Recognise Assertive Behaviour. In Nichel, F. (2008) Assert Yourself! Perth, Western Australia: Centre for Clinical Interventions.

Michel, F. (2008) *Assert yourself!* Perth, Western Australia: Centre for Clinical Interventions

Michela, J., Flint, D. H., & Lynch, A. (1992). Disrespectful supervisory behaviour as social-environmental stressor at work. Paper presented at American Psychological Association NIOST Work Stress Conference. In H. Hornstein (ed.) *Brutal bosses and their prey: How to identify and overcome abuse in the workplace*. New York: Riverside Books

Middleton – Moz, J. & Zawadski, M., L. (2002) *Bullies from playground to the boardroom: Strategies for survival*. Deerfield Beach, Florida: Health Communications Incorporated

Moberg, P. (2001) Linking conflict strategy to the five-factor Model: theoretical and empirical foundations. *International Journal of Conflict Management*, **12**(1), pp. 47-68. doi:10.1108/eb022849

Moore, B. (2009) Emotional Intelligence For School Administrators: A Priority For School Reform? *American Secondary Education*, **37**(3), pp. 20-28

Morris, J. A., Brotheridge, C.-M., & Urbanski, J. C. (2005) Bringing humility to leadership: Antecedents and consequences of leader humility. *Human Relations*, **58**(10), pp. 1323-1350

Muchinsky, P. M. (2000) Emotions in the workplace: The neglect of organizational behavior. *Journal of Organizational Behavior*, **21**.pp. 801-805

Murphy, C., & Clark, J.R. (2016) Picture this: How the language of leaders drives performance. *Organizational Dynamics*, **45** (2) pp. 139-146 doi: 10.1016/j.orgdyn.2016.02.008

Namie, G. & Namie, R. (1999) *Bullyproof yourself at work*. California: DoubleDoc Press

Namie, G. & Namie, R. (2000) *The bully at work: What you can do to stop the hurt and reclaim your dignity on the job*. Illinois: Sourcebooks Inc.

Newman, M.G., Przeworski, A., Consoli, A.J. & Taylor CB. (2014) A randomized controlled trial of ecological momentary intervention plus brief group therapy for generalized anxiety disorder. *Psychotherapy (Chic)*; **51**(2), pp 198-206

Noble, C. (2011) *Conflict Management Coaching: The CINERGY™ Model*. Toronto, ON: CINERGY Coaching

Norris, F. H., Friedman, M.J., Watson, P. J., Byrne, C.M., Diaz, E., & Kaniasty, K. (2002) 60,000 disaster victims speak: Part I. An empirical review of the empirical literature, 1981-2001. *Psychiatry*, **65**(3), pp.207-239

O Connell, P., Calvert, E., & Watson, D. (2007) *Bullying in the workplace: Survey reports.* Dublin: The Economic and Social Research Institute

O Connor, E. (2004) Leadership and Emotions: An exploratory study into the emotional dimension of the role of the post-primary school principal in Ireland. *Educate*, **4**(1), pp.46-59

O Toole, J. (1995) *Leading change: Overcoming the ideology of comfort and the tyranny of custom.* San Francisco, CA: Jossey-Bass

Olweus, D. (1978) *Aggression in the schools: Bullies and whipping boys.* Oxford, England: Hemisphere

Olweus,D. (2003) Bully/victim problems in schools: basic facts and an effective intervention programme. In Einarsen, S., Hoel, H., Zapt, D. & Cooper, C. (eds.), *Bullying and emotional abuse in the workplace.* London: Taylor and Francis. pp. 62-68

Organ, D. W. (1988) *Organizational citizenship behavior: The good soldier syndrome.* USA, D.C. Heath and Company

Osbourne, D. (2009) Pathways into bullying. In B. Martin (ed.), *Educational Integrity: Creating an Inclusive Approach.* Proceedings of the 4th Asia Pacific Conference on Educational Integrity (4APCEI), APFEI, Wollongong, pp. 1-61

Owens, B. P., Hekman, D. R. (2012) Modeling how to grow: An inductive examination of humble leader behaviors, contingencies, and outcomes. *Academy of Management Journal*, **55**(4), pp. 787-818

Owens, B. P.; Johnson, M. D. & Mitchell, T. R. (2013) Expressed Humility in Organizations: Implications for Performance, Teams, and Leadership. *Organization Science,* **24** (5), pp. 1517-1538

Oyer, B. (2015) Teacher perceptions of principals' confidence, humility, and effectiveness implications for educational leadership. *Journal of School Leadership.* **25**(4), pp. 684-719

Pace, R.W. (1983) *Organizational communication.* Englewood Cliffs, N.J.: Prentice-Hall

Perrone, V. (1991) *A Letter to Teachers.* San Francisco, CA: Jossey-Bass

Pipher, M. (1994) *Reviving Ophelia.* New York: Ballantine Books

Podsakoff, P.M., MacKenzie, S.B., Paine, J.B., Bachrach, D.G. (2000), Organizational citizen ship behaviors: A critical review of the theoretical and empirical literature and suggestions for future research, *Journal of Management* **26**(3), pp. 513-563

Pryce-Jones, J. (2010) *Happiness at Work, Maximising Your Psychological Capital for Success,* West Sussex: Wiley-Blackwell

Pryor, J., and Fitzgerald, L. (2003) Sexual harassment research in the United States. In Einarsen, S., Hoel, H., Zapt, D. & Cooper, C. (eds.), *Bullying and emotional abuse in the workplace.* London: Taylor and Francis. pp. 79-100

Rahim, A, (2002) Toward theory of managing organizational conflict. *The International Journal of Conflict Management,* **13** (3), pp. 206-235

Rahim, M. A. (1983) A measure of styles of handling interpersonal conflict. *Academy of Management Journal,* **26**, pp. 368-376

Rajah, R., Song, Z., & Arvey, R. D. (2011) Emotionality and Leadership: Taking stock of the past decade of research. *Leadership Quarterly* **22**(6), pp. 1107-1119

Randall, P. (1997) *Adult bullying: Perpetrators and victims.* London: Routledge

Rayner, C., Hoel, H., & Cooper, C., L. (2002) *Workplace bullying: What we know, who is to blame and what can we do?* London: Taylor and Francis

Rentzenbrink, C., (2015) *The last act of love.* London, UK: Pan Macmillan

Resch, M., and Schubinski, M. (1996) Mobbing-prevention, management in organizations. *European Journal of Work and Organisational Psychology*, **5**(2), pp. 295-307

Robinson, S., & Bennett, R. (1995) A typology of deviant workplace behaviors: A multi-dimensional scaling study. *Academy of Management Journal*, **38**, pp. 555-572

Romain, T. (1997) *Bullies are a pain in the brain*. Minneapolis:
Free Spirit Publishing Co.

Roseman, I. J., Smith, C. A. (2001) Appraisal Theory. In: K. Scherer, A. Schorr, T. Johnstone (eds.) *Appraisal processes in emotion: Theory, methods, research*. Oxford: Oxford University Press, pp. 173-186

Rosen, C., Chang, C., Johnson, R., & Levy, P. (2009) Perceptions of the organizational context and psychological contract breach: Assessing competing perspectives. *Behaviour and Human Decision Processes*, **108**(2), pp. 202-217

Rosh, L., & Offermann, L. R. (2013) Be yourself, but carefully: How to be authentic without oversharing. *Harvard Business Review*, **91**(10), pp. 135-139.
doi: 10.2469/dig.v43.n4.88

Rosiek, J. (2003) Emotional scaffolding an exploration of the teacher knowledge at the intersection of student emotion and the subject matter. *Journal of Teacher Education*, **54**(5), pp. 399-412

Ross, J. A. (1994) The impact of an in-service to promote cooperative learning on the stability of teacher efficacy. *Teaching and Teacher Education*, **10** (4), pp. 381-394

Rousseau, D.M. (1989) Psychological and implied contracts in organizations. *Employee Responsibilities and Rights Journal*, **2**(2), pp. 121-139

Ruderman, M.N., Hannum, K., Leslie, J.B., & Steed, J. (2001) Making the connection: Leadership skills and emotional intelligence. *Leadership in Action*, **21**(5), pp. 3-7

Runde, C. E. (2014) Conflict competence in the workplace. *Employment Relations Today*, **40**: pp. 25-31. doi:10.1002/ert.21430

Runde, C., & Flanagan, T. (2012) *Becoming a conflict competent leader*. 2nd ed.
San Francisco, CA: Jossey-Bass

Runde, C., & Flanagan, T. (2013) *Becoming a conflict competent leader: How you and your organisation can manage conflict effectively*. 2nd ed. San Francisco, CA: Jossey-Bass

Ryan, K., and Oestreich, D. (1991) *Driving fear out of the workplace: How to overcome the invisible barriers to quality, production and innovation*. San Francisco, CA: Jossey-Bass

Ryan, R. M. (1995) Psychological needs and the facilitation of integrative processes. *Journal of Personality*, **63**(3), pp. 397-427. doi: 10.1111/j.1467-6494.1995.tb00501.x

Sackney, L., Noonan, B., & Miller, C.M. (2000) Leadership for educator wellness: an exploratory study. *International Journal of Leadership in Education*, **3**(1), pp. 41-56

Salovey, P., & Mayer, J. D. (1990) Emotional intelligence. *Imagination, Cognition, and Personality*, **9**, pp.185-211

Schon, D. A. (1983) *The reflective practitioner: How professionals think in action*. New York: Basic Books

Schwarzer, R. (Ed.) (1998) *Advances in Health Psychology Research*. CD ROM Volume. Berlin: Freie Universität.

Scott, S. (2009) Take responsibility for your emotional wake. *Journal of Staff Development*, **30**(4), pp. 63-64

Seligman, M.E.P. (1991) *Learned optimism: How to change your mind and your life*. New York, NY: Pocket Books

Seligman, M.E.P. (2004) Can happiness be taught? *Dædalus*, **133**(2), pp. 80-87

Senge, P. M. (1999) *The dance of change: The challenges of sustaining momentum in learning organizations*. New York: Currency/Doubleday

Sergiovanni, T. J. (1994) *Building community in schools*. San Francisco: Jossey-Bass.

Shade, P. (2001) *Habits of hope: A pragmatic theory*. Nashville: Vanderbilt University Press

Shade, P. (2011) Time and Ordered Richness. *Southwest Philosophy Review* **27**(2), pp. 103-106

Sheppard, B., Lewicki, R. & Minton, J. (1992) *Organisational justice: The search for fairness in the workplace*. New York: Lexington Books

Silverman, S. B., Johnson, R. E., McConnel, N., & Carr, A. (2012) Arrogance: A formula for leadership failure. *The Industrial-Organizational Psychologist*, **50**(1), pp. 21-28

Silverman, S.L. & Casazza, M.E. (2000) *Learning and development: making connections to enhance teaching*, San Francisco: Jossey-Bass

Sinaceur, M., & Tiedens, L. Z. (2006) Get mad and get more than even: When and why anger expression is effective in negotiations. *Journal of Experimental Social Psychology*, **42**, pp. 314-322

Sky, M. (2002) *The power of emotion: Using your emotional energy to transform your life*. Rochester, VT: Bear & Company

Solomon, S., Greenberg, J., & Pyszczynski, T. (1991) A terror management theory of social behavior: The psychological functions of self-esteem and cultural worldviews. In M. E. P. Zanna (ed.), *Advances in experimental social-psychology*. San Diego, CA: Academic Press, pp. 261-302

Sousa, D.A. (2009) Brain-friendly learning for teachers. *Educational Leadership online*, **66**, pp.1–6. Retrieved from http://www.ascd.org/publications/educational_l eadership/summer09/vol66/num09/Brain-Friendly_Learning_for_Teachers.aspx

Staw, B. M., Sutton, R. I., & Pelled, L. H. (1994) Employee positive emotion and favorable outcomes at the workplace. *Organization Science*, **5**(1), pp. 51-71

Steinmeyer, B. (2012) *What's Good About Sleepless Nights?* Bernadette Steinmeyer. Retrieved from https://bernadettesteinmeyer. wordpress.com on 24 Sept. 2016

Swearer , S. and Doll, B. (2001) Bullying in schools: An ecological framework. In Geffner, R., Loring, M., and Young, C. (eds.), *Bullying behaviour: Current issues, research, and interventions*. New York: The Haworth Press, Inc

Tehrani, N. (2001) Building a culture of respect: Issues for further consideration. In Tehrani, N. (ed.), *Building a culture of respect: Managing bullying at work*. London: Taylor and Francis

Tehrani, N. (2003) Counselling and rehabilitating employees involved with bullying. In Einarsen, S., Hoel, H., Zapt, D. & Cooper, C. (eds.), *Bullying and emotional abuse in the workplace*. London: Taylor and Francis, pp. 270-284

Thomas, K. W., & Kilmann, R. H. (1974) *Thomas-Kilmann Conflict Mode Instrument*. Mountain View, CA: Xicom, a subsidiary of CPP, Inc.

Thompson, L., & Loewenstein, G. (1992) Egocentric interpretations of fairness and interpersonal conflict. *Organizational Behavior and Human Decision Processes*, **51**, pp.176-197

Thorndike, E. (1920) *Intelligence and its Uses* Harper's Magazine, 140. pp. 227-235.

Tice, D., (1993) The social motivations of people with low self-esteem. In Baumeister, R. (ed.), *Self-esteem: The puzzle of low self-regard*. New York: Plenum Press

Tice, D. M., & Baumeister, R. F. (1993) Controlling anger: Self-induced emotion change. In D. M. Wegner & J. W Pennebaker (eds.), *Handbook of mental control* Englewood Cliffs, NJ: Prentice Hall, pp. 393-409

Tice, D. M., & Bratslavsky, E. (2000) Giving in to feel good: The place of emotional regulation in the context of general self-control. *Psychological Inquiry*, **11**(3), pp. 149-159

Trudel, J., & Reio, T. G., Jr. (2011) Managing workplace incivility: The role of conflict management styles – antecedent or antidote? *Human Resource Development Quarterly*, **22**, pp. 395-423

Tschannen-Moran, M. & Woolfolk Hoy, A. (2001) Teacher efficacy: Capturing and elusive construct. *Teaching and Teacher Education*, **17**, pp. 783-805

Turney, L. (2003) Mental health and workplace bullying: The role of power, professions and 'on the job' training. *Journal for the Advancement of Mental Health,* **2**(2) Retrieved from http://www.tandfonline.com/ doi/abs/10.5172/jamh.2.2.99

Van Kleef, G. A. (2009) How emotions regulate social life: The emotions as social information (EASI) model. *Current Directions in Psychological Science*, **18**, pp. 184-188. doi:10.1111/j.1467-8721.2009.01633.x

Vartia, M. (1996) The Sources of bullying: Psychological work environment and organizational climate. *European Journal of Work and Organizational Psychology*, **5**(2), pp. 203-214

Watson, C. (1991) *Managing with Integrity, Insights from America's CEOs.* NY: Praeger Publishers

Wilkie, W. (1996) Understanding the behaviour of victimized people. In McCarthy, P., Sheehan, M. & Wilkie, W. (eds.), *Bullying, from backyard to boardroom.* New South Wales: Millennium Books

Wright, L. & Smye, M. (1997) *Corporate abuse: How lean and mean robs people and profit.* London: Simon & Schuster

Yukl, G. & Mahsud, R. (2010) Why flexible and adaptive leadership is essential. Consulting Psychology Journal: Practice and *Research*, **62**(2), pp. 81-93

Zapf, D., & Einarsen, S. (2003) Individual antecedents of bullying: Victims and perpetrators. In Einarsen, S., Hoel, H., Zapf, D. & Cooper, C. (eds.), *Bullying and emotional abuse in the workplace*. London: Taylor and Francis

Zapf, D., & Einarsen, S. (2005) . Mobbing at work: Escalated conflicts in organizations. In S. Fox & P. E. Spector (eds.), *Counterproductive work behaviour.* Washington, DC: American Psychological Association, pp. 237-270

Zapf, D., Knorz, C., Kulla, M. (1996) On the relationship between mobbing factors and job content, social work environment and health outcomes. *European Journal of Work and Organisational Psychology*, **5**(2), pp. 215-237